The Early Roxburghe Club 1812–1835

The Early Roxburghe Club 1812–1835

Book Club Pioneers and the Advancement of English Literature

Shayne Husbands

ANTHEM PRESS

Anthem Press
An imprint of Wimbledon Publishing Company
www.anthempress.com

This edition first published in UK and USA 2020
by ANTHEM PRESS
75–76 Blackfriars Road, London SE1 8HA, UK
or PO Box 9779, London SW19 7ZG, UK
and
244 Madison Ave #116, New York, NY 10016, USA

First published in the UK and USA by Anthem Press 2017

Copyright © Shayne Husbands 2020

The moral right of the authors has been asserted.

All rights reserved. Without limiting the rights under copyright reserved above,
no part of this publication may be reproduced, stored or introduced into
a retrieval system, or transmitted, in any form or by any means
(electronic, mechanical, photocopying, recording or otherwise),
without the prior written permission of both the copyright
owner and the above publisher of this book.

British Library Cataloguing-in-Publication Data
A catalogue record for this book is available from the British Library.

Library of Congress Cataloging-in-Publication Data
Library of Congress Control Number: 2019953379

ISBN-13: 978-1-78527-250-9 (Pbk)
ISBN-10: 1-78527-250-0 (Pbk)

This title is also available as an e-book.

CONTENTS

List of Figures vii

Acknowledgements ix

Introduction 1

1. The Persistence of Myth 5
2. Scandal, Libel and Satire 15
3. The Roxburghe Club and the Politics of Class 35
4. Politics, Religion, Money 47
5. Club Members and Their Book Collections 65
6. The Passion for Print 87
7. The Literary Works of the Roxburghe Club Members 101
8. The Club Editions 125
9. The Legacies of the Club 149

Conclusion 173

Appendix 1: The Club Membership 1812–1835 177

Appendix 2: Roxburghe Club Editions 1812–1835 191

Bibliography 199

Index 211

FIGURES

0.1 Thomas Frognall Dibdin by Henry Meyer after
Henry Edridge. © National Portrait Gallery, London ... 2
1.1 Sir William Bolland by James Lonsdale. © National Portrait
Gallery, London ... 10
6.1 The dedication pages from Volume I of Johnson's *Typographia* ... 93
7.1 The Society of Antiquarians by Cruikshank. Reproduced by
kind permission of the Society of Antiquaries of London ... 103
8.1 *Caltha Poetarum*. Reproduced by kind permission of the Bodleian
Libraries, the University of Oxford, Roxburghe
Club 2, 3rd Title Page ... 140
8.2 *A Roxburghe Garland*, 'L'Envoy'. Reproduced by kind
permission of the Bodleian Libraries, the University of Oxford,
Roxburghe Club 12, p. 17 ... 148

ACKNOWLEDGEMENTS

My sincere gratitude is owed to Professor Helen Phillips for her unfailingly erudite guidance and support over what has proved to be a very long haul. I am indebted to her for her immense kindness and encouragement. Many thanks are also due to many other members of the School of English, Communication and Philosophy (ENCAP) at Cardiff University including Dr Rob Gossedge and Professor Ann Heilmann. I am grateful for the financial assistance offered by ENCAP which has contributed to research trips to Oxford, Cambridge and London.

Foremost among the many people outside of Cardiff University to whom I owe thanks are the Roxburghe Club for their generosity in allowing me access to their archive, and with especial thanks to Nicolas Barker and Dr John Martin Robinson for their patience in answering my queries. Thanks are also due to the many archivists and librarians who have assisted me, with especial mention owed to those of the Society of Antiquaries, John Rylands Library and Chatsworth House archives.

INTRODUCTION

The Roxburghe Club, a name well known to book collectors but often unfamiliar outside of their circles, was founded in 1812 and has enjoyed an unbroken record of private publishing to the present day. It was formed against the backdrop of bibliomania, that delirious period during which book prices soared beyond all expectations, creating a financial bubble that would eventually dissolve, taking with it more than one patrician fortune. Antiquarians, a group who were already often ridiculed for their perverse taste in old and forgotten works of literature, now suddenly gained far more ostentatious and objectionable facets to their dusty character by a display of conspicuous wealth and social prominence that confused the comfortable stereotypes. The Roxburghe Club was founded by a group of wealthy bibliophiles, led by the flamboyant bibliophile and bibliographer, Thomas Frognall Dibdin (see Figure 0.1). Sharing as they did an interest in the earliest printed books, the group wished to distribute among themselves reproductions of rare volumes published at their own expense. The print runs were normally small, and the volumes were usually made available only to members and occasionally to close friends. The membership is still small, but today the club publishes volumes for its members with an additional limited number for sale to the public. The modern incarnation of the Roxburghe Club is that of a respected printing society publishing highly collectable modern editions and facsimiles of rare and important texts from the fifteenth to the early nineteenth century, with high standards of scholarly editing and luxurious presentation. Posterity has tended, however, to view the early years of the Roxburghe Club and its founder members in a distinctly dismissive manner, sometimes with ridicule, often with belligerence, but seldom with open-minded serious enquiry. If one wishes to examine the Roxburghe Club and its long and complex connection with, and contributions to, the world of literature and the histories of editing and literary studies in Britain, it appears to be necessary to look almost anywhere *but* in British literary history for answers. The history of the club has been up to now almost entirely played out in the footnotes of books on other topics, which is a testament to the importance of many of the Roxburghe

Figure 0.1 Thomas Frognall Dibdin by Henry Meyer after Henry Edridge. © National Portrait Gallery, London.

volumes, and yet explicit references to the club's early years tend to be with an eye to its denigration as a group of gourmandizing, dilettante bibliomaniacs who published unscholarly editions of trivial works, only of value to other collectors as a consequence of their manufactured rarity. The result of what can be seen as this belittling yet surprisingly tenacious creation myth about the club has been to minimize and almost render invisible its serious and significant contributions in the early nineteenth century to the development of English literary studies, the formation of the history and canon of English literature, and also to the evolving practice and theory of editing and facsimile making in this period.

Given the pioneering character of the Roxburghe editions during the club's first decades and the importance of the debates and discussions undertaken under the club's aegis at a period of crucial importance for European attitudes towards literature in the vernacular traditions, it may seem surprising that there has not to date been a thorough examination of this period of the club's history. Perhaps that partly reflects a process of almost self-conscious disassociation between the academic study of the book and its antiquarian past with its taint of emotional rather than analytical response. This prejudice against the world of book collectors, enthusiasts and scholars of the early nineteenth century, perceived as still embedded in an age of romanticism, of antiquarianism, of amateurism and of unscientific approaches to editing by a later nineteenth-century, increasingly institutionalized, academic establishment, is, in the case of the Roxburghe Club's activities exacerbated by the larger problem posed by the frequently repeated impression – the Roxburghe myth of origins – that the Roxburghe Club represented merely the hobby and extravagance of Regency aristocratic playboys, rather than a significant contribution to literary study and scholarly editing in early nineteenth-century Britain.

This book therefore looks at the period between 1812, when the club was founded, and 1835, when Viscount Clive became its second president, at which time the club began to change its methods and became more consistent and predictable in its organization. This foundational period was a rich and varied one which saw the club change and develop in important ways. It ends in what is in many ways a natural break in the club's history, not least because thereafter a set of written rules was established rather than a loose set of what were essentially gentleman's agreements. At this point too, an annual subscription of five guineas was introduced, with the intention of printing club editions as a jointly funded venture rather than as individually financed publications. Hitherto the books had been presented to the club by individual members at their own expense, and also without any interference from a club policy regarding the editing or presentation of the volumes. Consequent upon this creation of club funds it became necessary for the club to be answerable for those monies, and so for the first time a bank account was opened in the club name and a treasurer elected.

The period from 1833 onwards also signals the end of what Seymour de Ricci calls the 'Dibdinian age', which he considered culminated with the sale of Richard Heber's vast collection.[1] Following the massive auctions of Heber's books the market was saturated and prices were low. The great collectors who had followed Dibdin's lead were already dead or had ceased in their headlong

---

1 Seymour de Ricci, *English Collectors of Books 1530–1930* (Bloomington: Indiana University Press, 1960), p. 102.

accumulation of books as a result of infirmity, diminished interest or lack of funds. The Roxburghe entered a new phase, as an editing and literary society, at a point where many new societies dedicated to fostering interest and studies in English texts came into being. Publishing and scholarship were changing and, like the post-1830s Roxburghe, were becoming more institutional and even professionalized. The world of books, and of discussion and study of books, had been a strongly social and associational one during the eighteenth and early nineteenth centuries, whether in coffee houses, salons or clubs. Though societies for the promotion of literary knowledge, and their publication of research and editions, were a major force in Victorian academic developments, they represented a more institutional, less collegial, forum for these. As the founder Roxburghe members were swiftly dying away or becoming too infirm to continue to meet, it was natural that the club, under the direction of its new president, should strike out on new paths, more suited to the emergent new age and very different to the hedonistic Regency Age that had inspired its foundation.

These two decades provide a particularly rich narrative that not only covers an important period in book history but also spans an exciting and volatile era in British history during which huge changes were taking place on every front. Society was witnessing the growth of the Industrial Revolution, huge political and social changes including the fight to abolish slavery and Catholic emancipation were dividing opinion, and devastating outbreaks of cholera towards the end of the period created a climate of fear and increased social isolation. On the international stage politics were fraught, with war and revolution creating an anxious context to matters closer to home. The story of the early Roxburghe Club is, in many ways, the story of Regency England and its cultural transformation into Victorian Britain, and many of the changes taking place in the wider society can be seen reflected in the activities and attitudes of its members. Foundations were laid during this period that would bear fruit decades later under the more solemn gaze of their successors, but this foundational period supplied the imaginative spark, and in many cases the groundbreaking initiative that enabled later achievements and which, as will be seen, are well worth examining in their own right.

Chapter 1

THE PERSISTENCE OF MYTH

> The scholler lookes upon his bookes,
> And pores upon a paper.
> The gentle bloud likes hunting,
> Where dogs doe trace by smelling.
> And some like hawks, some groves and walks,
> And some a handsome dwelling.
> Yet all these without sack, old sack, boyes,
> Makes no man kindly merry.
> The life of mirth, and the joy of the earth
> Is a cup of good old sherry.[1]

The Roxburghe Club, although destined within two years to find its vocation as the prototypical book club, at first started with a far more humble intention. According to Thomas Frognall Dibdin's later reminiscences, it was originally intended merely to commemorate, on a yearly basis, a particularly enjoyable gathering of book lovers at a dinner held to celebrate a red-letter day during the sale of a library reputed to be 'one of the finest and most perfect ever got together'.[2] The collection that had come up for auction had previously belonged to John, Duke of Roxburghe, a renowned bibliophile who had died on 19 March 1804. The sale took place over a period of 42 days and was carried out by the auctioneer R. H. Evans at 13 St. James's Square, the late Duke's residence. One of the most eagerly anticipated lots of the auction was the Valdarfer Boccaccio of 1471, believed at that time to be a unique copy, and which finally went under the hammer on 17 June 1812. Dibdin, in his extensive accounts of the day, trumpeted that 'it has been said that the amount of that *one day's* sale equalled what had been given for the ENTIRE COLLECTION'. He goes on to say that on the evening of 16 June a number of 'enthusiastic and resolute bibliomaniacs'

---

1 Pasquil, 'Palinodia', in *A Roxburghe Garland* (London: Bensley, 1817), p. 9.
2 William Roberts, *The Book-Hunter in London* (Chicago: A. C. McClurg, 1895), p. 52.

met for dinner at the home of Mr William Bolland in Adelphi Terrace, an agreement was made to meet for dinner at the St. Albans Tavern on the evening of the seventeenth after the sale and that the choice of venue was made 'from an affectionate respect to the memory of the St. Albans' Press', a strong indication that the group were already meeting in a spirit of commemoration of the early printers and in celebration of their shared interests. Though Dibdin states that the dinner took place on this date, an invitation for the event still held in the Roxburghe Club archives shows the date of printing as 12 June 1812. This obviously signifies that it would have been impossible for the decision to dine to have been made at the last minute on 16 June, casting doubt on Dibdin's account of events. Even at this early stage the gathering is described on the invitation as the 'Roxburghe Dinner', implying an intention of continuation and a beady eye cocked towards posterity, although Dibdin laid the responsibility for the actual wording of the invitation (the 'pleonasm' at least of 'to dine with the Roxburghe dinner') on the proprietor of the hotel.[3]

That the meeting had been agreed some time before the eve of the sale is borne out by Dibdin's friend and fellow club member Joseph Haslewood in his journal the 'Roxburghe Revels'. He writes that 'upon Wednesday the 17th day of June "Il Decamerone di Boccaccio" was to be sold and that for being considered the rarest article in the whole of the Duke's library [...] the Rev. T. F. Dibdin, who therefore justly claims the title of Founder of the Club, suggested some few days before the sale, the holding of a convivial meeting at the St. Albans Tavern after the sale of that day.'[4] It is possible that Dibdin, writing many years after the event, had become confused over the particulars or he may have intended to imply that the dinner was already arranged at an earlier date and that on the eve of the sale he merely convinced the group with whom he was dining to accompany him the next evening. It is, however, also possible that Dibdin, who over the course of his life wrote about and amended the 'lore' of the Roxburghe Club many times, considered the shorter time frame more romantically dramatic for the purposes of myth-making, carrying as it does, an implication of a passionate, spur-of-the-moment decision which led to the founding of the illustrious club. Dibdin was genuine in his bibliographic pursuits and aims, but in any of his more romantic, mythologizing writing about the club, it pays to treat him as a somewhat unreliable narrator. In the modern world he would have made an excellent public relations man. Returning to the dinner party, apart from Dibdin and the host, Bolland, the

---

3 Dibdin, *Reminiscences*, pp. 378–79.
4 Joseph Haslewood, 'Roxburghe Revels', Roxburghe Club Archives.

friends and fellow book enthusiasts present on the evening of the sixteenth included another soon-to-be-Roxburgher, Mr George Isted, a barrister and prominent member of Boodle's club, who later amiably contested with Dibdin for the honour of having been the instigator of the club's founding. Neither man was an aristocrat, so whichever of the contenders actually founded the club, the impulse was not aristocratic in its origin, a point of which the significance will later become apparent.

The club was born from friendship and a shared love for antiquarian books; most of the people who made up the original membership already knew each other, and its initial impetus had its roots and inspiration in the collecting of early printed books. Dibdin had for many years acted as an instigator, focus and hub for a network of collectors, and, rather than viewing the dinner as an impulsive act and the chance beginning of a new venture, it is tempting to see the foundation of the Roxburghe Club as the crystallization of this group's bookish enthusiasms and, in particular, Dibdin's ambitions for bibliography and early English literature. It seems likely that the decision to form a club had been discussed among the group for some time previously, with the significant (in book-collecting terms) date of the sale of the Valdarfer being chosen as an auspicious day for the founding of such a venture. Fate, in the form of an unusually high sales price (one that the members could have possibly guessed at, knowing as they must that several of their number would be bidding and willing to pursue the matter to extravagant heights) gave the day an added piquancy that ensured that posterity would remember the day as a central event of the bibliomania.

During the course of the following day's auction more avid book collectors were added to the invitation, bringing the party up to 18. These 18 original diners were Earl Spencer, George Granville Leveson-Gower, Mark Masterman Sykes, Samuel Egerton Brydges, William Bentham, Bolland, John Dent, Dibdin, Francis Freeling, George Henry Freeling, Haslewood, Richard Heber and his brother Thomas Cuthbert Heber, George Isted, Robert Lang, John Delafield Phelps and Roger Wilbraham, an interesting range of class and wealth which represented a cross section of the cream of antiquarian book buyers. The auction had been the triumphant scene of the notorious bidding war between Earl Spencer and Lord Blandford, later portrayed in such breathlessly romantic terms by Dibdin in the *Bibliographical Decameron*. The famous Valdarfer Boccaccio was eventually won by Lord Blandford for £2,260, which was an unprecedented amount of money to pay for a book and a sum that remained unequalled until the sale of the Syston Park 1459 Psalter in 1884. A mere five years earlier than the Roxburghe sale, William Beloe, recently the keeper of printed books at the British Museum, had estimated the future selling price of the Valdarfer at 'not much less than five hundred pounds', a misjudgement which indicates how quickly book prices were rising during this period, taking even the collectors by surprise.[5]

The group of collectors who met that evening were in understandably high spirits and ready to celebrate the fortunes of book collecting after such a spectacle of unrivalled bidding. Dibdin later maintained that the purpose of the dinner was 'not so much for convivial, as for belles-lettres, or if the reader pleases, for bibliomanical, purposes', but critics had their doubts.[6] The club weathered heavy disapproval regarding the lavish nature of the early dinners, but the social aspect did not undermine or negate the more serious purpose of those early Roxburghe meetings. Even today it is difficult to find any society or association, however learned or austere, which does not include dining or drinking as some part of its activities, even if it is only the annual Christmas or conference conviviality. Famously, at the first Roxburghe dinner a number of toasts were proposed that were thereafter used at all later meetings. These were

1. the immortal memory of Christopher Valdarfer, printer of the Boccaccio of 1471;
2. the immortal memory of John Duke of Roxburghe;
3. the same of Gutenberg, Fust and Schoiffher, fathers of the art of printing;
4. the same of William Caxton, father of the British Press;
5. of Dame Juliana Barnes and the St. Albans Press;
6. of Messrs Wynkyn De Worde, Pynson and Notary, the successors of Caxton;
7. the Aldine family at Venice;
8. the Giunti family at Florence;
9. the Society of the Bibliophiles Français at Paris;
10. the prosperity of the Roxburghe Club; and in all cases as the last toast, the cause of Bibliomania all over the world.

This series of toasts, with their (one assumes) slightly tongue-in-cheek emphasis on the names of the early practitioners of printing, could be viewed as acting as a sort of catechism, the repetition at each dinner ensuring that the raison d'être of the club has not been forgotten or sidelined.[7] Although the

---

5 William Beloe, *Anecdotes of Literature and Scarce Books*, 2 vols (London: F. C. and J. Rivington, 1807), vol. 2, p. 235.
6 T. F. Dibdin, *Reminiscences of a Literary Life* (London: Bloomsbury, 1836), p. 375.
7 Glanmor Williams describes a similar set of toasts given in the 1820s at the annual St David's Day dinner of the Cymreigyddion (Welsh Patriotic Society), where the celebrants enjoyed 'as lavish a dinner as they could rise to. At the dinner the usual order

toast may well have arisen from a lighthearted situation during the first dinner, its preservation displayed a dedication to those early printed books and their printers which had brought the members together and neatly encapsulated what was dear to the founders' hearts. If the club were to be established today, the toasts would undoubtedly form the framework of its mission statement.

The evening proved to be such a roaring success (Haslewood wrote up his exultant account of the dinner at 1 a.m. on the morning of 18 June, if that can be taken as an indication of how long the dinner lasted from its 6:30 p.m. start) that it was agreed that it should be repeated as a yearly anniversary, and so the club was duly formed. The number of members, it had been agreed, should be increased, and by the next meeting in June 1813 the membership stood at 24, with the addition of the Duke of Devonshire, the Marquis of Blandford, Lord Morpeth, Thomas Ponton, Peregrine Towneley and James Heywood Markland. By the third dinner the membership had reached 31, with the inclusion of Viscount Althorp, Mr Justice Littledale, Edward Littledale, Rev. William Holwell Carr, James Boswell and James William Dodd. It is interesting that although the first dinner had been held to allegedly celebrate the sale of the Valdarfer, Blandford, the winning bidder was not included in the group until the first anniversary and had little to do with the club afterwards, perhaps being a collector of a different stripe. The membership remained at this number, although Dibdin cryptically says that 'there have been many attempts to enlarge it, but unsuccessfully'.[8] This is not overly surprising given the club's well-known and strictly exclusive approach to membership: the presentation of even one black ball sufficient to debar a postulant from inclusion. According to one source, 'it used to be remarked, that it was easier to get into the Peerage or the Privy Council, than into "The Roxburghe"'.[9] This method of election was not, of course, unique to the Roxburghe and was the same process used by Johnson's Club to which Earl Spencer already belonged, and indeed Spencer may have been instrumental in carrying over this stringent means of preventing the acceptance of uncongenial nominees.

The idea of reprinting items for distribution among the membership is attributed to Bolland, who had volunteered at the first anniversary dinner to present the first edition himself the following year. Haslewood, in his journal

---

of the toasts was: "The King and the Church"; "the principality of Wales", and the "Immortal memory of Saint David", followed by a bewildering, not to say, intoxicating, miscellany of other toasts', 'Language, Literacy and Nationality in Wales', in *Religion, Language and Nationality in Wales: Historical Essays* (Cardiff: University of Wales Press, 1979), pp. 127–47 (p. 121).

8 Dibdin, *Reminiscences*, pp. 376–78.
9 John Hill Burton, *The Book-Hunter* (Edinburgh: Blackwood, 1862), p. 267.

Figure 1.1 Sir William Bolland by James Lonsdale. © National Portrait Gallery, London.

entry for the 1814 dinner, hints at unexplained difficulties which delayed the production of the promised volume ('NB Mr Bolland's reprint was not ready'), but such problems notwithstanding, the volume carries the date of 1814; so presumably Bolland went on to present the company with the first Roxburghe volume at some point during the remainder of the year or at the following year's dinner.[10] Bolland (see Figure 1.1) is also credited with formulating the idea of printing the alphabetical list of members' names in the front of the volume with the intended recipient's name in red, a custom adopted thereafter

---

10 Haslewood, 'Roxburghe Revels'.

in Roxburghe Club volumes. Although relatively unknown to history, certainly in the terms of the club's mythology, Bolland was instrumental in the formation of the club and its activities, not least because in printing the first volume he set a pattern for others to follow. From here onwards, the men (the club did not gain its first female member until 1985 when Mary Crapo, Viscountess Eccles, took that honour), theoretically working in alphabetical order of surname, took their turn to print a rare item for distribution among the other members. Some of these offerings were reprints of items in their own collections, others of texts that resided in the collections of museums and other libraries. There were no hard or fast rules about this process; in some years a number of editions were presented to the club simultaneously. In 1818, for instance, nine volumes by separate editors were presented at the dinner, but occasionally there would be a year such as 1823 or 1826 when nothing new was distributed. A few members, including Thomas Heber and Alexander Boswell, did not live long enough to present their copies, and several men produced more than one edition.

This activity was not going unnoticed and in 1816, in the liberal literary and philosophical periodical the *Monthly Magazine*, 'bibliomaniacs' were criticized for neglecting the memories of men of literary genius in favour of the early printers. A contributor, Mr E. Evans, asserted that bibliomaniacs had failed to subscribe to a proposed memorial to John Locke, which had resulted in the abandonment of the project, but that should it be proposed to erect a memorial to Caxton they would be at the front of the queue to hand over their money.[11] The Roxburghe Club appeared to respond in a typically insouciant fashion when in 1820 it attempted to erect a stone tablet in Westminster Abbey to the memory of Caxton. Dibdin describes this initial choice of venue as proceeding 'from the fact of Caxton having erected the FIRST PRESS IN ENGLAND within those walls'.[12] Haslewood recorded the choice as at first falling between Westminster Abbey, where Caxton had installed his printing press in workshops belonging to the Abbey and St. Margaret's Church, where Caxton was buried in 1479. A committee comprising Earl Spencer, Heber, Bolland, Utterson, Hibbert and Dibdin was elected to organize the project, and Dibdin, Markland and another unnamed member chose a suitable spot for the memorial in the Abbey and sought permission from the clerk of the Chapter. Unfortunately the fees demanded to site the memorial in the Abbey proved to be unacceptable, and the club decided to install the monument in St. Margaret's Church instead as this site, apart from its equal claim to Caxton's memory, carried the added benefit

---

11 'Mr Evans on the Pretensions of the Bibliomaniacs', *Monthly Magazine* (1816), 42, pp. 115–18.
12 Dibdin, *Reminiscences*, pp. 386–87.

of being free.[13] Even this story may not be as straightforward as it might first appear. The sum demanded by the clerk of the Chapter of Westminster Abbey was £120, which would not appear to be an excessive sum to a group predominantly formed by extremely wealthy men, but perhaps the point was more one of principle than economics. Dibdin portrayed it in this light, announcing rather huffily that 'all that I choose further to say upon this subject is, that if *any* monument might have been allowed a *gratuitous* entrance within the walls of the Abbey, it was surely that of the FATHER OF THE BRITISH PRESS – who first exercised his art *there*'.[14] Although it is perhaps tempting for critics to view this as a transparent attempt to disguise parsimony on the part of the club under a high-minded pretext, Dibdin's angle on the matter is somewhat borne out by the letter received by the club in reply to their application to the dean and the Chapter of Westminster Abbey. The clerk writes that neither of the prominent sites proposed by the club for the memorial have been approved and that instead a position in St. Edmund's Chapel is offered for its location. The reaction of the club members is expressed by Haslewood, who, writing in his journal at the time of the event, indicates that the club had already agreed to the amount to be paid but objected to the proposed site, saying that 'this day reversed all gone before [...] the Goths that guide there, can have no other God than gold: for they gave such a choice of situations that to have followed their sinister wishes wo^d have been not to bury the body, but to bury the monument'.[15] Haslewood was not a particularly wealthy man and would, perhaps of all the members, have been most justified in resenting the demands of the Chapter for a high fee to be paid but instead objects most forcibly to the proposed site of the memorial. That the Chapter did not deem Caxton's monument worthy of a more prominent position is in itself telling of the generally held opinions of the time towards the reputations of the early printers. A memorial to Caxton was eventually installed in Westminster Abbey in 1954.

Such excitement aside, the club continued to meet yearly, although the fortunes of book prices and the popularity of book collecting had begun to wane. The continued interest of the members is perhaps the strongest argument against accusations (both contemporary and modern) of mere bibliomania levelled against the club as such a superficial adherence to fashion would

---

13 Ibid.
　The inscription on the stone reads, 'To the memory of WILLIAM CAXTON, who first introduced into Great Britain the art of printing, and who, A.D. 1477, or earlier, exercised that art in the Abbey of Westminster, this tablet in remembrance of one to whom the literature of his country is so largely indebted was raised Anno Domini MDCCCXX, by the Roxburghe Club. Earl Spencer, K. G. President.'
14 Ibid., p. 387; italics in original.
15 Haslewood, 'Roxburghe Revels'.

surely have resulted in the club closing when fashion quickly moved on. In fact, in 1825 club meetings were made a more frequent occurrence rather than the once-yearly dinner previously held. Although possibly coincidental, it is interesting to consider whether the coming of the railways in any way affected this decision, allowing as it did, for quicker, safer travel to London from the outlying regions where members lived. Francis Wrangham mentions, in a letter to Egerton Brydges, his long and no doubt arduous journey to attend the Roxburghe Dinner, saying, 'five hundred miles travelling will, I trust, be a pledge to the club of my gratitude for their kindness and my sense of their importance'.[16] Many of the members who were perhaps not in London for the summer must have had equally long journeys to make, and there were significant risks to travelling by road.

In 1828, in a significant departure from its usual protocol, the club produced a club edition at the members' joint expense and employed the young scholar Frederic Madden to edit the volume. This was the *Ancient English Romance of Havelok the Dane*, and the high quality of the edition and the ambitious scope of the notes, introduction and appendices accompanying the edition make it a major contribution to the study of English literature and of editing in Britain. The change of direction was rumoured to have not been unanimously popular within the club, however, with more senior members, including Haslewood and Dibdin, reputedly regretting the introduction of an editor from outside the ranks of the club, gossip that is not entirely borne out by Dibdin's own comments on the matter, which are covered in more detail in Chapter 3. What is more certain is that the face of the Roxburghe Club was changing both figuratively and literally. One member, Blandford, who was by now Duke of Marlborough, had unsurprisingly become bankrupt in 1819 and, although he remained a member, was in a poor financial position to collect antiquarian books; however, he did fulfil his club obligation by presenting an interesting volume in 1822. The older members of the original group had naturally been dying over the first two decades, and even some of the younger members such as the Boswells had met untimely deaths, leaving room for new book devotees to take their places at the table. In 1833 Heber and Haslewood died, both of whom were, arguably as much as Dibdin, driving forces behind the ethos of the fledgling Roxburghe Club. Haslewood's death and the subsequent careless dispersal of his estate in particular, inadvertently caused a series of relatively minor but far-reaching problems for the club which adversely affected its public reputation. Sir Walter Scott, the most successful author of this period, had

---

16 Extract from a letter between Archdeacon Wrangham and Samuel Egerton Brydges, dated 19 January 1825, Michael Sadleir, 'Archdeacon Wrangham: A Supplement', *Library* 4 (1939), 422–61 (p. 439).

died in the previous year, and although never a regular attendee at the dinners (in fact only attending once), he was certainly the club's most famous member. He was also one of the period's most committed proponents, and successful popularizers, for the cause of book collecting and antiquarianism in general and a steadfast supporter of the Roxburghe Club in particular.

The literary world, as much as the political and public world, was changing fast. Earl Spencer headed the club until his death in 1834, and by the time Viscount Clive (later Earl of Powis) took the chair as President in 1835 the club was transforming from its exuberant Regency foundations to a more solemn and orderly incarnation, more befitting of the Victorian Age that Britain was already entering in outlook if not in name. This earlier, more vibrant, period of the club, with its eccentric members who belonged to a more individualistic, less organized and earnest age, has tended to be ignored or deplored by critics and academics who have favoured the club's later, standardized and more obviously scholarly presentation. These formative years of the club are often overlooked or viewed as the poor and indeed embarrassing foundation from which later and greater things grew, almost despite the worst efforts of the founding members. My intention in the remainder of this book is to examine in detail these wild formative and fascinating times, between the club's foundation and Earl Spencer's death, in the hope of forming a clearer picture of the activities of these early years, and of demonstrating that the club was already a positive and far-reaching influence on the development of literature, literary studies and national culture.

Chapter 2

SCANDAL, LIBEL AND SATIRE

> What wild desires, what restless torments seize
> The hapless man, who feels the book-disease.[1]

As might be expected, such high-profile bibliophilic pursuits did not go unnoticed in the media of the day hungry for titbits of recyclable society gossip. Aristocratic activities represented a large percentage of the celebrity culture of the period, and unconventional, not to mention expensive, pastimes were certainly always going to be given plenty of column inches. In fact, bibliomania could be argued to have been, to some extent, a media construct. The high prices, obsessive collecting and identification (and often self-identification) of collectors as bibliomaniacs was defined, discussed and promoted by the newspapers, books and periodicals of the day, and the fiery debates that it aroused in the letters pages provided welcome fillips to sales figures. As so often when a previously private and solitary avocation gains sudden and visible popularity, it also becomes the cause of much public ridicule, criticism and hand-wringing. The Roxburghe Club, possibly as a result of its highly publicized aristocratic membership and a certain taste for self-promotion, provided a useful focus for this anxiety and opprobrium. There was no shortage of opinionated correspondents ready to blame bibliomania for every possible shortcoming in the contemporary literary (and in some cases moral) world.

In the satirical poem *Bibliomania* by John Ferriar, written in 1809 and dedicated to his friend the soon-to-be Roxburghe Club member Richard Heber, 'bibliomania' is delineated as the collecting or hoarding of books to a point where social relations or health are damaged – this obsessive-compulsive disorder gradually expanding in the public mind to include book collectors in general. Ferriar, a collector himself, was making a wry joke, a point often missed both then and now, perhaps in part because Ferriar's day job was that of a physician and pioneer researcher into psychiatric disorders.

---

1 John Ferriar, *The Bibliomania, an Epistle to Richard Heber, Esq.* (London: T. Cadell and W. Davies, 1809), lines 1–2.

Dibdin, while grasping the joke, readily acknowledged the dim view taken of bibliophiles, and their conflation with bibliomaniacs in the minds of the public, in his answering work, *Bibliomania*, which is part satire, part warning and part celebration of the obsessive collecting of books. It was first published in 1809 as a relatively brief essay, but later it was extended and the format altered to become a series of discourses between a group of friends who participate in a rambling discussion on various aspects of book collecting and collectors. This later version contains an exchange between the collector Lysander (an alias for Dibdin) and the more scholarly Philemon in which Lysander asserts that he is 'an arrant bibliomaniac' who loves books 'dearly – that the very sight, touch, and more the perusal', at which point his friend cuts in and says, 'hold, my friend, you have renounced your profession – you talk of *reading* books – do Bibliomaniacs ever *read* books?'[2] This witticism acknowledges a criticism often levelled against antiquarian book collectors and against the Roxburghe Club: that is, that they cared more for the appearance and rarity of the books that they collected than for the literary contents. Paradoxically, given such a low public opinion for the literary worth of the books they produced, the club was simultaneously criticized for not making copies available for purchase by the general public. A blustering letter from the *Gentleman's Magazine* of September 1813 complained that 'the honourable members of the Roxburghe Club have no doubt, persuaded themselves that they are aiding the diffusion of useful knowledge, and promoting the interests of literature. But, instead of diffusing knowledge they selfishly cut off the springs which should feed it; and, instead of promoting the interests of literature they materially injure them'.[3] The judgement seems somewhat premature as the club was just over 12 months old and had not yet printed anything by which they could be judged for good or ill – all that was known for certain at this point were the *type* of books that the members favoured and perhaps a degree of hearsay. Another ten months would pass before William Bolland presented the club with its first volume. It remains open to doubt to what degree the 'springs of literature' would have been welcomed by the reading public should the club have chosen to publish more extensively.

The club helped nurture a taste for early books that was not at this period widely developed outside of antiquarian circles. The Scottish Bannatyne Club, while inspired by and emulating the Roxburghe example in most matters of organization, attempted to avoid the accusation of withholding literature from

2 Ibid., p. 4; italics in original.
3 J. M., *Gentleman's Magazine*, September 1813, pp. 211–12.

the reading public by making its volumes available for sale to the public. The club secretary later admitted that it 'always proved a complete failure'.[4]

Apparently the public wanted the option to purchase the books without the burden of actually buying them. What was perhaps desired was a sense of opportunity, equality and inclusion in the pursuits of the wealthy, not to own the actual volumes of early English (or in the case of the Bannatyne Club, Scottish) literature themselves. In a reply to the above complainant, 'A. C.' argued that the club may provide services to literature other than those of directly supplying books to the masses. Even the uncommonly high prices being commanded by books at auction could be seen as a benefit if it inspired, through dreams of avarice, the ordinary person to preserve old books that might otherwise be allowed to perish. The writer points out that 'within my recollection, and that of many others, Old Books, out of the common course of reading, found their way in large quantities to the cheesemongers', going on to say that 'hence it is that copies of some works have become so rare, and that others are supposed to be extinct, because references to them occur in different works while the books themselves are nowhere to be found'.[5] Another interesting point raised during the debate is the usefulness of celebrity, insofar as it could make fashionable any pursuits that it chose to follow and that if the latest hobby of the aristocracy happened to be literature, then that could only be a good thing if it were to encourage the love of books in the lower ranks of society. These arguments imply that the Roxburghe members might assist the cause of literature despite themselves rather than by design: faint praise, grudging even, but praise nonetheless. This was a point raised by yet another letter in the same issue (this was a hot topic), written by an author who signs himself 'A lover of reason and good sense, yet, a staunch Bibliomaniac', presumably because the two characteristics were generally considered to be mutually exclusive: 'To contend merely for the harmlessness of the Institution in question would be, in my mind, a culpable humiliation; yet who can deny that it is at least inoffensive?'[6] A letter written in reply to 'AC' in the *Gentleman's Magazine* of December 1813 countered his point regarding old books being sold as waste paper, saying with a complacent rejection of any notion that literature not readily admired by modern society could be worth digging out or reprinting that 'if an old work is truly valuable, it will not be necessary to search monasteries, dive into vaults, pore over bookstalls, or grub up all the

---

4 David Lang, Appendix 'Testimonial to the Secretary', in *Adversaria: Notices Illustrative of Some of the Earlier Works Printed for the Bannatyne Club* (Edinburgh: Bannatyne, 1867), p. 6.
5 A. C., letter, *Gentleman's Magazine*, October 1813, pp. 338–39.
6 'A Staunch Bibliomaniac', *Gentleman's Magazine*, October 1813, p. 339.

trash which has been consigned to the silence of centuries, and which, but for their officious zeal, would have been of much more service in the shops of cheesemongers'. It is sobering to consider how many early books may have been lost to posterity as a result of such complacency.

Samuel Egerton Brydges, an indefatigable proponent of the resurrection of early literature, later addressed this exact point in the *Theatrical Inquisitor, and Monthly Mirror* of August 1819, arguing that if modern works of 'great intrinsic beauty or sublimity' sometimes failed to gain popularity with the reading public, then it was equally likely that valuable and rewarding works from the past may have sunk into obscurity.[7] In a letter, written a year earlier to a soon-to-be fellow Roxburgher, Archdeacon Wrangham, he had addressed the same issue, writing,

> I know there is a very general impression, that what has once fallen into oblivion is not worth reviving: – that it is bigotry, & whim, & fanciful & factitious curiosity, which finds charms in these rusty treasures dug from the grave! As if the present age monopolized all knowledge, all wisdom; & all genius!!! A mere collector is, to be sure, a mighty dull & contemptible sort of animal – but when a man of talents & literature extends his inquiries into the productions of past ages, he greatly increases his intellectual stores, & can scarcely fail to ameliorate & enlarge his heart – In such a mind a selfish pride, & narrow & undue estimate of living eminence can scarcely continue to find food & encouragement.[8]

We can see here within the Roxburghe membership already a recognition of the cultural and historical construction of taste, long before this became an essential perspective in the study of literature. Long domination by the Latin and Greek classics in the education and literary tastes of middle- and upper-class men led all too readily to an assumption that literary quality was a fixed, easily recognizable and indeed universal value. Interestingly, in the *Theatrical Inquirer* article, Brydges uses the word 'bibliomaniac' in a precise and positive way, writing that 'there is a strong opinion among those who are not infected with the Bibliomania that no books or at least no works claiming the praise of genius have sunk into oblivion but such as have deserved to be forgotten'.[9] In this context bibliomaniac is used to refer simply to a collector of early printed books, without any reference to the collection of rarities, oddities or

---

7 Samuel Egerton Brydges, 'On Bibliomania', *Theatrical Inquisitor, and Monthly Mirror*, April 1819, 277–79 (p. 277).
8 Sadleir, 'Archdeacon Francis Wrangham: a supplement', p. 450.
9 Brydges, 'On Bibliomania', p. 277.

rich bindings at high prices that loomed so large in the public's imagination. Both sides in the argument were using the term but seemingly each with their own definition of what it meant, although there was obviously some degree of overlap.

Be that as it may, once the club had been judged a priori to be a group of dilettante bibliomaniacs and its members as being in possession of a faulty or frivolous taste for worthless curiosities, then this obviously signified that anything printed by the club must be without intrinsic literary value. And this was not their only sin as another criticism, reappearing at intervals, maintained that the collecting, and especially reprinting, of old, neglected works channelled money away from the development of modern books. One example, a letter in the *Monthly Meteor* of August 1812, asserted that

> the sums expended upon the Valdarfer Boccaccio, or upon Caxton's earliest printed works [...] would reward and stimulate to future labours authors whose productions, filled with learning and ability, are calculated to delight and instruct mankind. The price of a worm-eaten pamphlet, if properly directed, might relieve the distresses of the Chattertons and Burns of our day, nourish the opening buds of genius, now nipped by poverty and want.[10]

There seem to be two overt and possibly erroneous assumptions being made here: firstly that the customer base for modern works in that period represented the same readership as those purchasing and reprinting early English works, and, secondly, that even if this were true, reducing spending on one area of literature would naturally increase the spending in another area deemed more deserving of attention. It is not, however, evident that the bibliomaniacs of the early nineteenth century were underwriting their collections of rare books by reducing their expenditure on contemporary publications or, conversely, that all those who collected early printed texts were also significant purchasers of contemporary books, although some undoubtedly were as their names appear in the subscription lists of various new works.

When they had first gathered to celebrate book collecting, it is unlikely that the club could have had any real notion of the degree of contempt, disapproval and criticism that their actions were soon to attract. Over the succeeding two centuries the activities of the early days of the club have often been dismissed as producing books of no value and the members as lacking the discernment or literary taste necessary to be considered as anything other than an amusing footnote of bibliophilic history. One high-profile, contemporary detractor,

---

10 'The Bibliomania', *Satirist or Monthly Meteor*, 11 (August 1812), p. 125.

John Payne Collier, was scathingly critical about the black-letter enthusiasms of the club. He was particularly vitriolic in his views on Dibdin, presumably because as the most visible, flamboyant and, if one were to suspect Payne Collier of cowardice or obsequiousness, non-aristocratic personality of the club, he made an easy target. Reviewing Dibdin's *Typographical Antiquities of Great Britain* he writes that 'while all investigations of the origin and progress of printing must almost necessarily be productive of some useful information [...] this excuse [...] will not apply to the mere divers into the depths of black-letter darkness, who exhaust those lives that might have been devoted to valuable acquisitions, in employments to which they blindly attach an imaginary and factitious importance'.[11] Allowing that Dibdin was 'a man of profound learning in the science of bibliography', he immediately attributes this learning (with possibly just the slightest trace of envy) to Dibdin's access to 'all the collections of curious and rare books in the three kingdoms' and goes on to describe his learning as 'a very inapplicable and comparatively useless kind'.[12] Collier, employed as the Duke of Devonshire's librarian, must have been more than aware of the club's activities and how central Dibdin was to its ethos. Collier shared an interest in the books that concerned the club, making his spleen all the more inexplicable, or perhaps utterly understandable if one takes the obvious view that he was simply envious and wounded at not being included in the club. In his review Collier particularly singles out for criticism Dibdin's habit of pointing out 'insignificant peculiarities', and it is tempting to suggest that Dibdin's annoying attention to details of typography may have been of particular concern to a man later exposed as a forger of literary antiquities. Whatever the case, Collier appears slightly more appreciative of the activities of some other club members. He was happy, for example, to receive copies of the rare items (even those reproduced in black letter) printed at the Beldornie press by E. V. Utterson, and in 1844 Collier edited the club edition of *Household Books of John Duke of Norfolk and Thomas Earl of Surrey*.

Individual antipathy aside, underlying much of the criticism appears to have been a degree of hostility towards the Georgian forms of sociability of which the Roxburghe were an obvious and high-profile example lasting into the opening of the Victorian period. In the more staid and serious era, there appeared to be a perceived impropriety in the use of dining and drinking as a forum for scholarly pursuits, a distaste made evident in articles such as one that appeared in the *Retrospective Review* of 1827, which, while it accepted that

---

11 John Payne Collier, 'Review of Typographical Antiquities of Great Britain', *The Critical Review: or Annals of Literature* 4 (London: W. Simpkin & R. Marshall, 1816), 245–54 (p. 246).
12 Ibid., p. 245.

'few objects would be more worthy of praise than a body of literary men joining their purses and talents for the dissemination of valuable neglected literature, by printing impressions accessible to those who are interested in the subject' went on to claim that 'the very reverse has hitherto been the conduct of this society of bibliomaniacs' – strong words which display an overt disapproval of the items being reproduced and of the moral standing or character of men who would carry out the seemingly reprehensible act of printing limited editions. The club, however, was apparently not entirely beyond salvation as the author writes that 'opportunities are, however, given them of redeeming their characters as literary men, by acting in a manner consistent with common sense and the age in which we live', which presumably included acts of duly sanctioned literary philanthropy.[13]

While the club attracted negative reactions for many reasons and from many sources, the most damaging attack occurred in the *Athenaeum* in 1834. This unpleasant episode concerning a manuscript titled the 'Roxburghe Revels', heaped ridicule and accusations on the club, which dogged its reputation for many years and is still occasionally uncritically quoted in present-day articles about the Roxburghe. This virulent attack was made following the death of one of the club's founding members, Joseph Haslewood, and the subsequent discovery of notebooks among his papers which among other matters related the proceedings at a number of early club meetings. The notebook, given the title by Haslewood of the 'Roxburghe Revels', was a vibrant private journal rather than an official club minute book, and included copies of the menus from their dinners, rough minutes of the business transacted at the meetings, personal letters sent between the members and other related ephemera. Haslewood's description of the journal, inscribed at the front of the book, is of 'an account of the annual display, culinary and festivous interspersed incidentally with matters of memento merriment, also brief notices of the press proceedings by a few lions of literature combined as the Roxburghe Club founded 17th June 1812'.[14] His jocular tone indicates that it was undoubtedly intended for Haslewood's personal amusement and included occasional observations regarding the other club members that, while not particularly offensive, were obviously not meant for publication (e.g., his observation that 'after Lord Gower left the chair it was filled by Mr Dent and Dent and dullness are synonymous').[15] Haslewood at the time of his death had left detailed instruction in his will for the disposal of his library and personal papers. He had requested that his books be sold by Samuel

---

13 Sir Thomas Croft, 'Early English Poetry', *Retrospective Review* 2, p. 156.
14 'Roxburghe Revels' journal held in the Roxburghe Club Archive, deposited with the Society of Antiquaries, London.
15 Ibid.

Sotheby, with the proceeds going to his brother and nephew; he specifically requested that his personal papers should not be sold. At a later date Haslewood had (apparently under the misapprehension that a recent legal alteration would mean that Sotheby's would be considered a legatee because of the wording of his will, and thus render the auction proceeds liable to legacy duties) changed his will to request that a friend should choose the auction house, adding that he expected that his friend would 'probably adopt my original wish', a clear indication of his intentions that was disregarded by his executors along with his wish that the auction be held at the Easter following his death.[16] His brother declined to act as executor, and the friend who dealt with his estate must have held strong doubts about the propriety of selling the 'Roxburghe Revels' manuscript because he sent it to various individuals, some of whom excised passages from the journal before it went to be auctioned by Mr Evans in December 1833. An article in *Gentleman's Magazine*, sympathetic to the memory of Haslewood, related that 'there was a general outcry at the "Roxburghe Revels" being brought to sale' and adding the perceptive observation that 'if only forty shillings had been bidden for the book, it might have been bought in; but as it was run up to forty pounds, that sum so far outweighed any scruples of respect which might have been entertained for the character of the deceased, that the temptation could no longer be resisted'. The author concluded, with understandable distaste, that 'this is the palpable and barely disguised truth'.[17]

The manuscript was bought by a bookseller named Thorpe, who immediately offered it to Haslewood's closest friend, T. F. Dibdin, effectively giving him the opportunity to suppress its publication. Dibdin, with admirable moral conviction but perhaps a degree of naivety or lack of foresight, declined to buy it, viewing it as tantamount to blackmail and later explaining that 'of course no gentleman would think of putting his hand into his pocket with a view as it might have been said of hushing up any strictures advanced upon such an association. The characters and rank in life of the members placed them far above it'.[18] Shades perhaps of the Duke of Wellington's famous retort of 1824 'publish and be damned'? Eventually, through a series of sales, the notebook came into the possession of the proprietor and editor of the *Athenaeum* magazine, Charles Wentworth Dilke, who declared that he had 'resolved therefore to purchase it at any price, that we might gratify curiosity, and give our readers its principal contents'.[19] Shortly after, a series of vitriolic

16 An excerpt from Haslewood's will in 'Sale of the library of Joseph Haslewood, Esq. F.S.A.', *Gentleman's Magazine* 1 (London: 1834), 286–88 (p. 287).
17 Ibid., p. 287.
18 Dibdin, *Reminiscences*, p. 426.
19 'The Roxburghe Revels', *Athenaeum* (4 January 1834), 1–6 (p. 1).

articles appeared, in which Haslewood's memory was thoroughly desecrated and he was erroneously and maliciously held to be an illiterate, vulgar and dishonest fool, who had fraudulently insinuated his way into the club. The article was published anonymously, and although the article's author is generally considered to be James Silk Buckingham, the *Athenaeum*'s founding editor, it seems just as likely that it was written by Dilke himself as he had bought the manuscript at great personal expense and with obvious intent to publish the contents. The *Athenaeum* during his editorship established itself as a widely read, highly influential periodical, and any article appearing in its pages, especially of such a scurrilous nature, would have found a large readership. While there was clearly an element of spite, envy or possibly moral disapproval against the Roxburghe Club as a whole, there must also, presumably, have been a concrete reason for carrying out such a vicious posthumous attack on an individual such as Haslewood, and Dilke, as will be seen, had the personal motive necessary for an act that otherwise displays inexplicable malice towards a man so recently deceased. If Dilke was not the sole author, then the article was almost certainly a joint endeavour between Dilke and Silk Buckingham, with Dilke making (or rather purchasing) the arrows for Silk Buckingham to fire.

While Haslewood appears to have been a quiet, religious man who avoided literary quarrels, it would appear that there had, at an earlier date, occurred a brief and not particularly cordial correspondence between Haslewood and Dilke. There exists an undated and unsigned letter, apparently in Haslewood's handwriting, and now in the Roxburghe Club archives, in which Haslewood recounts to an unidentified recipient, how he had previously encountered Dilke:

> The edition of old plays announced in the preceding prospectus as edited by a gentleman of the name of "C. W. Dilke" who resided at "No. 10 Stanhope Street, Newcastle Street," i.e. Stanhope Clare market. I take this from a letter addressed to myself. Before the first number appeared for the plays were published periodically the first of every month, I considered it necessary to have an interview with Mr. Martin the publisher, communicated to him as much as appeared necessary that such a work was in contemplation on an enlarged scale and to form a very complete and valuable collection of early dramatic pieces. Fortunately Mr. Martin informed me the said Mr. Dilke had formed his own selection and plan and same could not be in any manner altered. I say fortunately for could a co-operative plan have been formed it would have been the means of attaching to a respectable work an impotent coadjutor in Mr. Dilke whose plays form a tasteless selection and whose notes prove him an [undecipherable word] for such an undertaking.

He has stuck my name at the head of those from whom he derived assistance, having answered a letter of his on the subject of Marston and which answer, had he duly considered, he might have discovered was a most palpable sneer at his work, by telling him the volume he enquired about was "neither of sufficient rarity to keep as a curiosity, or of any value to an editor.

The escape from this coalition was unquestionably fortunate: – but it was unfortunate for the public this imperfect project was ever attempted as it made those who had contemplated a work reputable to all parties, to consider the market forestalled [...].[20]

The volume referred to is undoubtedly the anthology *Old English Plays*, published in 1814. Dilke's edition does indeed include the acknowledgement mentioned above, saying that 'to Mr. Haslewood he is indebted for some information respecting the prefixture to the octavo edition of Marston's plays', but it also seems likely that he did indeed 'duly consider' the insult offered towards his edition and his own talents and chose to take his rather cowardly but effective revenge anonymously after Haslewood's death through public character assassination.[21] This conjecture seems confirmed by a letter from Alexander Dyce to Samuel Egerton Brydges in which Dyce attributes Dilke's act to 'revenge' for Haslewood's review of the edition (although Haslewood's letter makes it clear that the argument had originated earlier in its production) and further comments that Dilke's publication 'might have annihilated the Roxburghe Club', an apprehensive, but eventually groundless, judgement of the situation from a contemporary.[22]

Paradoxically, given the presumable intention of damaging Haslewood's personal and professional reputation, this episode actually instead confirms that Haslewood, far from being the uneducated amateur that the *Athenaeum* would have liked to paint him, was of sufficient standing as an editor and expert on early literature to have been approached by other editors working in similar areas looking for advice and soliciting collaboration. Haslewood was of sufficient professional standing to have been approached by Dilke himself, who clearly did not consider him either ignorant or without influence in their

---

20 Letter from Joseph Haslewood to an unknown recipient contained in a scrapbook which forms part of the Roxburghe Club Archive, deposited with the Society of Antiquaries, London.
21 *Old English Plays: Being a Selection from the Early Dramatic Writers*, ed. by Charles Wentworth Dilke (London: Whittingham and Rowland, 1814), p. xxiii.
22 'in private hands', but extracts appear in the 2011 Bonhams catalogue of auction 19386 (The Roy Davids Collection) at which it was sold.

field of shared interest. Dibdin confirms this in his defence of Haslewood and indicates that he understands who is behind the article and why they have written it, when he writes that 'if the deceased had been the weak, harmless, ignorant and puzzle-headed creature described by this anonymous libeller, why take so much pains to 'draw his frailties from their drear abode?' And why, on dramatic points, betray such unusual sensitiveness and acrimony of feeling and expression? There seems throughout the whole to be something like an undercurrent of rivalry in the histrionic department'.[23]

The accusations made against Haslewood, spiteful and wide ranging, formed a formidable destruction of both his character and professional competence. The original 'Roxburghe Revels' manuscript was quoted lavishly throughout the article but usually taken out of context, purposely misconstrued or slanted to show both Haslewood and the club in the worst possible light. This wilful attempt to misrepresent Haslewood's meaning can be illustrated by taking just one example from the article, which quotes a passage relating a small gathering of the club in which Haslewood writes, 'we were friendly without argument, jocose, lively, and consistent. There was no seeming hero of the table and therefore no one injudiciously loquacious: A complaint perhaps less to be advanced as against the R. Club, than any collective party I was ever in'.[24] This is a straightforward description of a dinner party at which no one person takes the limelight or is overly garrulous, but to the *Athenaeum* writer it appears that 'these few lines contain, as it were, the essence of Haslewood: the allusion to the "seeming hero of the table," was a hit at Sir Walter Scott, and shows the paltry envy of our Roxburgher's character.'[25]

Throughout the piece Haslewood's class forms the subject of many of the jibes, and the author asserts that 'we think it extraordinary, as we have over and over again said, that such a man should for a single hour have been tolerated as a member of such a body'.[26] As evidence of Haslewood's unacceptability in such company he writes that he was 'sprung from the very humblest class – we happen to know that he was born in Brownlow Street Lying-in Hospital – he never had any regular education, and he never remedied this original misfortune by subsequent exertion; yet, by strange accidents, he was brought in contact with some of the most scholar-like, best informed, and most accomplished men of the age'.[27] Early in the article, the author, rather

---

23 Dibdin, 'Observations on the Attack on the Late Joseph Haslewood Esq., F.S.A.', in *Roxburghe Revels and Other Relative Papers* (p. 80).
24 'The Roxburghe Revels, MS.', *Athenaeum* (25 January 1834), 60–64 (p. 63).
25 Ibid., p. 63.
26 Ibid., p. 64.
27 'The Roxburghe Revels, MS.', *Athenaeum* (4 January 1834), 1–6 (p. 1).

perversely and in direct contradiction of many of his later accusations, comments that 'while living Mr. Haslewood was a very cautious and polite man, and, had he extended this feeling to his death few would have had reason to complain'.[28] This admission does not prevent the author from proceeding to accuse Haslewood of various crimes against propriety, sensationally spread over three weekly instalments of the magazine. Dibdin later asked, 'Is a man to be pointed at, or hooted at, because later in life he has associated with gentlemen – when his evil stars, at an earlier period, had driven him in an opposite direction?'[29] The *Athenaeum* author thought that, yes, he *should* be ridiculed for moving out of his own class and socializing with men on the basis of a shared interest rather than shared class or equal wealth. In this way he displays a degree of snobbery that was, on his side, considerably beyond that of the 'elite' Roxburghe Club itself. If it was Silk Buckingham, this attitude is difficult to understand as he himself was a self-made man, who had risen in society from his origins as a farmer's son and should therefore have had a degree of empathy for another man who had overcome an unpromising background. Dilke, in his turn, was a liberal known for his radical political commentary, who should therefore have (theoretically at least) welcomed such overt evidence of social mobility as that displayed by Haslewood's alleged rise in social position during his lifetime. This line of attack on the basis of inferior class appears to be a hypocritical line for this pair to take, and presumably shows just how desperate they were to score points against Haslewood and the club. It is, of course, possible that during its procession from person to person, both prior to and following the auction, the contents of the journal had been exaggerated and that, after paying such a high sum for the manuscript in the hope of finding salacious details he could use against Haslewood and other club members, Dilke was disappointed to find little that could be held against them. It may also be the fact of the matter that anything truly scandalous had been removed by those parties lucky enough to have been allowed prior access to the journal in order to eradicate mention of themselves. Whatever the case, left with source material that carried little real leverage, Dilke may have felt obliged to stoop to a more desperate level of ridicule than originally anticipated in order to find his mark and justify his purchase.

Returning to the article itself, the author has much amusement at the expense of Haslewood's unorthodox use of English, although the faults in the journal are far less prevalent or significant than he claims and almost every example to be found in the original is quoted and ridiculed, suggesting that such is the standard found throughout the document which is far from the case. He criticizes

28 Ibid.
29 Dibdin, *Reminiscences*, p. 428.

Haslewood's speech and education and accuses him of displaying 'vulgarity and ignorance'.[30] The author claims that 'though he could scarcely open his mouth without committing an offence of some kind or other against his mother-tongue, he was prudent enough not to open it often in company where his blunders were likely to be detected', although how this might be achieved at a Roxburghe dinner is not explained.[31] Presumably the writer does not imagine that he did achieve this feat as he ponders 'how the waiters could have kept their countenances, while attending upon the Roxburghers, when Haslewood opened his mouth, we cannot imagine'.[32] An article in response to the *Athenaeum* appeared in the *Gentleman's Magazine*, a journal to which Haslewood had been a regular contributor. Its author points out that 'with respect to his personal manners, he was perfectly quiet and unobtrusive in society; and therefore the gentlemen of rank and education who have composed the Roxburghe Club had no cogent reason (as his slanderer has pretended) to dismiss from their society a man possessed of very extensive information on subjects connected with their favourite pursuits'.[33] Dibdin, defending his late friend, argues that 'throughout the whole of this writer's strictures he boldly affirms, although necessarily he was never present, that the Members of the Roxburghe Club were shocked and disgusted with the conversation of the deceased. The assertion is CONTRARY TO TRUTH. Never was speech more harmless than that which fell from his lips. As above observed, it was only Haslewoodian'.[34] It can also be pointed out that as the writer of the article was under the erroneous impression that the Roxburghe Club was no longer in existence, he could not have based his accusations on any conversation with a contemporary member or even a close associate of a member.

Another, rather deceitfully ingenuous, line of attack in the 'Roxburghe Revels' was that of holding the alliterative titles of the many manuscripts that Haslewood left behind him up to ridicule, presenting them as examples of his ridiculous lack of taste. The author writes that 'if [Haslewood] had termed himself "a lion of literature and alliteration," he would have been nearer the mark; for his only forte seems to have been "affecting the letter." He had a sort of knack of this kind, and much of the rubbish he collected, and which was recently sold by Mr. Evans, was recommended to purchaser about as sagacious as Haslewood himself, not by comical, but by coxcombical, titles'.[35] Dilke, as an editor working in the same literary fields as Haslewood, must have recognized that such titles

---

30 'The Roxburghe Revels, MS' (11 January 1834), 28–30 (p. 29).
31 'The Roxburghe Revels, MS' (4 January 1834), p. 1.
32 'The Roxburghe Revels, MS' (25 January 1834), p. 64.
33 'Sale of the Library of Joseph Haslewood, Esq. F.S.A.' (p. 287).
34 Dibdin, *Reminiscences*, pp. 428–29.
35 'The Roxburghe Revels, MS', *Athenaeum* (4 January 1834), p. 1.

(*Garlands of Gravity, Poverty's Pot Pourri, Wallet of Wit*), while not appealing perhaps to contemporary tastes unfamiliar with earlier literature and intolerant to works considered inelegant, were an erudite and witty nod to the alliterative titles of Elizabethan works such as the *Batchelars Banquet* (1603), the *Garland of Goodwill* (1579), *Paradise of Dainty Devices* (1579) or *A Caveat for Common Cursetors* written in 1566. This last work had been reprinted by T. Bensley in 1814, and actually carried a dedication to Haslewood, 'as a testimonial of esteem for his bibliographical talents and persevering research in the revival of ancient literature'.[36]

The Roxburghe Club itself received a share of criticism, but the jibes levelled at the club appear mild in comparison with those levelled at Haslewood, generally confined to spiteful comments regarding the quantities of eating and drinking carried out at the dinners, while managing obsequiously to avoid any direct criticism of the aristocratic members. Possibly the author was all too aware that living targets were in a position to take action against libellous attacks or even perhaps to demand satisfaction in the manner that had resulted in Alexander Boswell's premature demise. Whatever the reason, the titled members are somewhat bizarrely treated as victims, innocent bystanders forced to endure Haslewood's continuing presence in the club – a viewpoint which strangely and conveniently overlooks the power and influence wielded by the aristocracy in social situations, which would have made any question of them tolerating Haslewood's company under protest unthinkable. The author does discuss in detail, and disapproves of, the high cost of the dinners. This topic is one that has been raised repeatedly in subsequent discussions of the early club and is therefore a subject worth looking at in more detail. The Roxburghe dinners of this period were of course extravagant by most modern standards, and the amount of alcohol consumed, or at least purchased, impressive. The most expensive dinner quoted in the article is that of 1818, at which 15 members incurred a bill of £87 9s. 6d. or £5. 14s. per head. This was, however, exceptional even for the club. The amount per head was more usually around £2 10s.[37] The amounts are exorbitant but not unusual when

---

36 Thomas Harman, *A Caveat or Warning for Common Cursetors Vulgarly Called Vagabonds* (London: 1814).
37 More representative amounts given for other years are the following:
   1813 – £50 among 21 members
   1814 – £2 5s. per person
   1815 – £57 or £2 17s. per person
   1816 – £62 13s. 6d among 23 members
   1817 – £49 among 22 members
   1819 – £55 13s. among 21 members

the venues at which they dined are taken into account. One hotel at which they ate on a number of occasions was the Clarendon Hotel, described as 'the only place in England where a French dinner was served that was worthy of mention in the same breath with those obtainable in Paris at the Maison Doré or Recher de Cancalle's'.[38] Obviously, such quality and reputation did not come cheaply.

Be that as it may, compared with the dinners held by similar specialist-interest dining clubs, the sums involved would not appear to be too unusual and neither would this form of meeting. It was common practice for many of even the most scholarly of societies to hold meetings in social settings. For example, the Geological Society, when first founded in 1807, as a dining club, met once a month, later twice a month, from November to June, and the cost of their dinner was initially set at 15 shillings per person.[39] While less than half the cost of an average Roxburghe dinner, given the frequency of congregation, this represents a far higher expenditure per year per member, and meeting twice a month would ensure that only the wealthy could have afforded to attend. In other words, the Roxburghe Club had an exceptional capacity for expensive partying once a year, but over the long haul it was a relatively affordable and abstemious club. Membership of many clubs at the end of the eighteenth and beginning of the nineteenth century could be prohibitively expensive, not only involving the cost of the dinner but also incurring any number of extraneous costs. An article, probably written by Dibdin, which appeared in the *Gentleman's Magazine* in March 1834, addresses this point, and makes a telling reference to charitable organizations of the time:

> The alleged extravagance of the Roxburghe Club Dinners would equally apply, we conceive, to every party patronizing the same expensive houses; and should rather be regarded as the tax paid for the fancied advantage of being entertained at an aristocratic tavern, with foreign cookery, and rare foreign wines (though perhaps scarcely tasted), than as the particular profusion of the Roxburghe Club. A retired literary student might say, and we should agree with him, that the cost would have been far more profitably spent on intellectual instead of sensual gratifications; but does not this argument apply to every tavern dinner, so many of which divide the money expended, not on the mere researches of a private literary club, but on the objects of public charitable institutions?

---

38 Lewis Melville [pseud], *Some Eccentrics and a Woman* (London: M. Secker, 1911), p. 80.
39 M. J. S. Rudwick (1963). 'The Foundation of the Geological Society of London: Its Scheme for Co-operative Research and its Struggle for Independence', *The British Journal for the History of Science* 1 (1963), 325–55 (p. 329).

And yet such dinners are considered advantageous to those institutions, and promoted with that view.[40]

The *Athenaeum* article's repeated criticisms of the club's drinking habits and insistence on reprinting the menu and alcohol bill from each dinner might be partly explained if Silk Buckingham were involved in its composition. A committed temperance campaigner, he would presumably have taken a dim view of the Roxburghe's, or any other club's, excesses. Furthermore, while direct criticism of the significance of the club's literary activities may have been difficult to prove and open to intelligent debate, holding the club up to ridicule for its dining habits was an easy target in any attempt to undermine their claims to being taken seriously. The author's disapproval of the alleged frivolity also resonates with developing evangelical sobriety and its increasing influence on social mores at this period. The piece was perhaps carefully calculated to invoke an easily aroused public censure. This motif of expensive, gluttonous dining has become one that is used often even in modern discussions around the subject of the early club, with the ubiquitous turtle from the menu of 1818, which was quoted in the *Athenaeum* article, seemingly used as shorthand for frivolous, gourmandizing aristocratic ineffectuality.

Haslewood's friends of course did not take the slander lying down. The article was eventually reprinted privately alongside a spirited rebuttal of its claims under the title *Roxburghe Revels and other relative papers; including answers to the attack on the memory of the late Joseph Haslewood, Esq. F.S.A. with specimens of his literary productions*, edited by James Maidment, a friend of Haslewood, and with contributions by Dibdin.[41] Dibdin also revisited the subject in *Reminiscences of a Literary Life*, but however strongly Haslewood's friends voiced their dismay and rebutted the accusations, the damage was done and the reputations of both Haslewood and the Roxburghe Club were injured with lasting effect. A gossip column in the *Athenaeum* in 1848 returned to the subject, saying that 'our readers will agree with us in thinking that the club *was* "shewen up" "finely larded" with sauce of its own preparing; and it is only proper to add that the resolute purchaser of Piccadilly subsequently sold the volume for 50l. to the editor of this paper at the risk of its being so. It would have been a pity to disappoint the prophecy'.[42] It is difficult to speculate why the magazine thought it necessary to revive the subject after such a long interval, and considering that the original members were mostly already deceased by that time, who the *Athenaeum* thought might be interested in such old, reheated slander.

---

40 'Sale of the library of Joseph Haslewood', p. 287.
41 *Roxburghe Revels and Other Relative Papers*, ed. by James Maidment (Edinburgh: 1837).
42 'Our Weekly Gossip', *Athenaeum* 1073 (20 May 1848), p. 509; italics in original.

Over the intervening period commentator's views regarding this episode have divided largely into two groups: those who, however spirited the defence by Haslewood's friends, have chosen to take the slanderous version of Haslewood's character as truth, and, ignoring the views of the people who knew him, have seen his acceptance into the club as an aberration by an otherwise elite and judicious membership during their wayward early years. The other group comprises those who consider the attack on Haslewood to have merely been a way of hitting out at the club itself, with Haslewood as an individual largely irrelevant. Neither approach presents an adequate picture of the events or their lasting damage to the reputations of the club and to Haslewood. Moreover, they seemingly ignore that Haslewood *had* a reputation to lose, rather than being merely the uneducated nonentity or fool that he was painted by the *Athenaeum*. Looking at the first group, a number of critics have been content to simply repeat, without debate, the points of the *Athenaeum* article itself. The most well-known exponent of this viewpoint is the Victorian book collector and historian John Hill Burton in the *Book-Hunter*. In 1861 an article appeared in *Blackwood's Magazine* titled 'The Book-hunter's Club', which, although unattributed, is obviously the material that Hill Burton would later publish as his work *The Book-Hunter* and which includes a vitriolic passage referring to the *Roxburghe Revels* and Haslewood's membership of the club:

> It is singular that so small and exclusive a club as the Roxburghe should have proved an exception to the rule of secrecy [which controlled the public images of other clubs] and that the world has been favoured with revelations of its doings which have made it the object of more amusement than reverence. In fact, through failure of proper use of the black ball, it got possession of a black sheep, in the person of a certain Joseph Haslewood. He had achieved a sort of reputation in the book-hunting community by discovering the hidden author of *Drunken Barnaby's Journal*. In reality, however, he was a sort of literary Jack Brag. As that amusing creation of Theodore Hook's imagination mustered himself with sporting gentlemen through his command over the technicalities or slang of the kennel or the turf, so did Haslewood sit at the board with scholars and aristocratic book-collectors through a free use of their technical phraseology.[43]

This article and the book that evolved from it became, directly and indirectly, a major conduit through which the malicious and slanted *Athenaeum* claims

---

43 'The Book-Hunter's Club', *Blackwoods Edinburgh Magazine* 90 (October 1861), 440–62 (pp. 446–47).

were repeated in later articles and commentaries which referred to the early Roxburghe Club. Although writing only 30 years after Haslewood's death, Hill Burton appears to have accepted Dilke's evaluation of Haslewood's character and abilities without making any attempt to check the veracity of the accusations. He is in fact so immoderate in his class-based attacks on Haslewood and Dibdin that Richard Grant White, the editor of the 1862 American edition of the *Book-Hunter*, felt compelled to distance himself from the opinions expressed and in a footnote explains that the author had relied too heavily on the opinions of the 'Roxburghe Revels' *Athenaeum* article, which he goes on to describe as 'an exceedingly dishonorable [sic] and malicious performance'.[44] There is no such note of caution in the British edition of Burton's book, and inevitably works thereafter that rely to any extent on Hill-Burton's views are problematic in terms of their veracity. The judicious comments made by Grant White have failed to prevent later authors from freely quoting Hill Burton's repetition of the original article in a literary echo chamber of misrepresentation.

Thirty years after the publication of *The Book-Hunter*, Haslewood's alleged character was still being raked over, with the library historian Edward Edwards in his, for the most part well-measured and perceptive *Libraries and Founders of Libraries*, saying of Dibdin and his Roxburghe friendships that 'when you read his *Reminiscences* of the men with whom he had mixed in life, you are left in considerable doubt whether or not he quite understood the difference between two men, both of whom were "Roxburghians" and editors of black-letter rarities – Walter Scott and Joseph Haslewood'.[45] Edwards does not make clear what he himself considers to be the prime difference between the two men, especially in view of the fact that beyond the obvious disparity in fame, both came from relatively humble backgrounds and raised themselves through the medium of literature and bibliophilic pursuits. W. Powell Jones in his work *Three Unpublished Letters of Scott to Dibdin* also draws an arbitrary line between Scott and the rest of the club, writing that 'there were numerous disciples, some of them erudite with futile eagerness like Samuel Egerton Brydges, some learned and profound like Richard Heber, and a few sane gentlemen–scholars like Walter Scott'.[46] Again, it is interesting to consider what the difference between a 'learned and profound' man and a 'sane gentleman–scholar' might be and also to note the wild differences in opinion that occur when critics attempt to put relative values on the individual club members. However

---

44 John Hill Burton, *The Book-Hunter etc.*, ed. by Richard Grant White (New York: Sheldon, 1863), p. 271.
45 Edward Edwards, *Libraries and Founders of Libraries* (London: Trübner, 1864), p. 419.
46 W. Powell Jones, 'Three Unpublished Letters of Scott to Dibdin', *Huntington Library Quarterly* 4 (July 1940), 477–84 (p. 477).

that may be, Scott clearly had no objections to sharing a dinner table with Haslewood: he did so at the one Roxburghe dinner that he attended during his membership, although the *Athenaeum* article of course implied that Scott must have found his company insufferable. The article attempted to attribute Scott's failure to dine with the club again to Haslewood's presence, saying that 'he had quite enough of it: One day perfectly satisfied him; for, although he met on that occasion Earl Spencer, the Duke of Devonshire, Lord Althorp, Lord Clive, Mr. Phelps, Mr. Markland, Mr. Towneley and other accomplished gentlemen, Haslewood seems to have been a sort of "frog in the fire" or a wet blanket, which cast a damp over the whole company: his uninformed dullness was like a cloud that overshadowed and oppressed'.[47] In fact, Scott himself had commented on the dinner in his journal, saying that 'Lord Spencer presided, but had a cold which limited his exertions. Lord Clive, beside whom I sat, was deaf, though intelligent and good-humoured. The Duke of Devonshire was still deafer. There were many little chirruping men who might have talked but went into committee. There was little general conversation'.[48] If Scott was disappointed, it was over the relative boredom from sitting with the two leading aristocrats that night, whereas he perceived the busily chatting lesser men – the committee members – as likely to have included some he regretted not conversing with. There is neither any mention of Haslewood nor of the wild carousing for which the club was criticized. Moreover, Scott appeared to value Haslewood's abilities as an editor and critic and mentions him in a letter written to another Roxburghe member, Sir Francis Freeling, saying, 'I was much pleased with the two plays printed by Mr Haslewood which threw the most curious & valuable light upon various disputed points of dramatic history. I sincerely hope Mr Haslewood will print the rest which cannot fail to give the highest interest whether restricted to the club or published in the proper sense'.[49]

Unfortunately, Joseph Haslewood's once robust literary reputation never recovered from the blow dealt to it by the *Athenaeum* attack and the significance of both the early Roxburghe and Haslewood in the formation of the history and canon of English literature has subsequently been largely ignored. Other factors have, of course, contributed to this neglect, significantly adverse opinions that have proceeded from perceptions of the club's 'aristocratic' nature, but the role of the 'Roxburghe Revels' in this process and its strength as an entertaining and therefore easily transmissible historical meme should not be

---

47 'The Roxburghe Revels, MS.', *Athenaeum* (11 January 1834), p. 61.
48 Walter Scott, *The Journal of Sir Walter Scott* (New York: Burt Franklin, 1890), p. 181.
49 *The Letters of Sir Walter Scott*, ed. by Herbert Grierson, 12 vols (London: Constable, 1932–37), vol. 10, p. 285.

overlooked. Perhaps, before moving on to look at the issue of class politics and its influence on the reputation of the club, it is best to leave the subject of slander with the *Athenaeum's* author, who apparently without irony lamented that 'people may talk as they will of the envy of actors and artists, but it is nothing compared with the envy of authors of an inferior grade: your low literati form the most grudging, carping, fretting, and in some respects most mischief-making and malignant class of the community'.[50]

---

50 'The Roxburghe Revels, MS', *Athenaeum* (25 January 1834), p. 63.

Chapter 3

THE ROXBURGHE CLUB AND THE POLITICS OF CLASS

The Roxburghe Club, its publications and its place in the world of literature is a subject whose outlines frequently become hazy and unreliable because, as indicated in the previous chapter, it is almost invariably viewed through the lens of class politics or at the very least what could be described as a heightened class awareness. It is, for instance, difficult to find any reference to the club that does not, at least in passing, refer to its perceived aristocratic membership, even in contexts in which the make-up of its membership is entirely irrelevant to the subject under discussion. The idea of British class division, with its connotations of among other things breeding, education, land ownership, heritage and established bloodline, does not simply mark out a social or financial demographic but also creates a preconception, or ideal, of aristocracy and its imagined relationship with and responsibilities towards society, other social classes and especially activities that relate to culture and intellect.

There was, in actuality, a vast range of affluence, political persuasion and religious belief represented within the ranks of the club, all of which factors may have had a greater influence on the pursuit of cultural objectives than class alone, but none of which (with the possible and partial exception of money) have been so uniformly referenced in discussions on the club's activities. It is interesting to note that comments referring to a perceived class disparity between the founding members of the club came entirely from outside its ranks, except on those occasions when Dibdin felt stung into remonstration. It is difficult to ascertain what feelings the other members may have held on the matter, as published sources have little to say on the topic, and in private there may have been as many opinions as there were members. If that is the case, it did not provoke any reaction that reached print, and it did not apparently result in members resigning their place in the club or forcing the resignation of others. Through its early history there were few resignations, and those occurred due to ill health, advanced age and the difficulties of travel in the early nineteenth century. It also bears repeating that if any single man had objected to the election of another, his opposition would have been sufficient to prevent it occurring through the use of the 'black ball' without any need on his behalf to convince the other members of the reasonableness of his position. In the very specific case of Haslewood, who was a founding member and therefore not subject to the judgement of the black ball, if the aristocratic members had objected to his presence in the club they simply would not have agreed to return, year after year, to dine in his company.

The messages about class discernible in discussions regarding the club are complex and often contradictory. Initially among contemporary commentators there can often be seen a tacit approval of the anticipated aristocratic sophistication, education and breeding of the club members, which serves to make the foundation and activities of the club extremely newsworthy. Letters to the *Gentleman's Magazine* discuss the activities of the club, using phrases that are full of instinctive assumptions that class delineations form an important context to their actions, whether in a positive or, very occasionally, a negative sense. In one such letter the writer asserts that 'the example of men of such distinction as the Roxburghe Club, certainly affords a precedent of no little weight'.[1] In a reply to his letter, his correspondent refers to 'the revival of a literary taste amongst those who have spacious palaces in which to deposit such ornamental entertaining and intellectual furniture', and later the same writer refers to 'the introduction of Literature amongst the amusements of the higher ranks of Society', and yet more precisely 'the revenues of Noblemen and Gentlemen of liberal mind and literary taste'.[2] If we view the aristocracy and gentry of the early nineteenth century as the primary focus of early nineteenth-century celebrity culture, then the founding of a book club by a number of high-profile bibliophiles fits easily into the context of coverage of the fashionable activities of famous people. Bibliomania is at the height of its notoriety; the high prices paid at the Roxburghe Sale, not just for the Valdarfer Boccaccio but for many of the other books as well, are a talking point; and the formation of the club provides more column inches of domestic news, or arts and society news, for the periodicals to recycle. It did not take long, however, before disapproval started to appear in letters submitted to the periodicals complaining that the club was failing to promote literature in ways that were considered to be appropriate, implying that the members carried the weight of 'noblesse oblige', equally in the realm of books as in other activities, where their social status must necessarily incur heavy responsibility. It was not morally sufficient to merely follow their own interests; they must set an example to those below them (primarily those immediately below them in social terms and therefore all the more anxious to emulate them), and preferably provide

1 J. M., Letter, *Gentleman's Magazine* (September 1813), p. 212.
2 A. C., Letter, *Gentleman's Magazine* (October 1813), pp. 338–39.

the means by which those less financially and socially privileged might be enabled to aspire to the same pastimes and interests. The extent to which the upper classes could be expected to act for the good of all, rather than merely personal satisfaction, became a matter of anxious debate, with the club's supporters often falling back on moral argument as much as its detractors, as can be seen from one correspondent's assertion that 'the noble members of the Roxburghe Club are setting a most meritorious example to the world; they have done, and are doing, all that can be wished of them'.[3]

Another letter printed in 1816 raises a note of middle-class alarm at the notion that the upper classes, in the guise of the Roxburghe Club – the writer obviously unaware of or ignoring its middle-class membership – might be using limited edition printing as a way of excluding the middle class from their sphere, complaining that 'this mode of printing and publishing will gradually throw a monopoly of the means of instruction into the hands of the wealthy, depriving the middling class of society of their proportion of knowledge by the difficulty of procuring it'.[4]

Among the comments which quickly started to appear questioning the propriety of the club and its activities was a slightly puritanical letter written to the *Morning Herald* in 1818 criticizing Dibdin for his attendance at a dinner in Paris. Of course, it was not just aristocrats who were expected to fulfil a moral role: clergymen, with perhaps more justification, were also expected to set an example, and the correspondent writes that 'it may be thought that a Clergyman might employ himself better in his own country, than in promoting a convivial festival in the most licentious capital of Europe. This by the way. This Clergyman, as might be expected, acted as the President of the feast [...] an honour, if an honour, which he certainly deserved, as it was at his own expense. Of course, he cannot be a poor curate'.[5] The writer goes on to criticize the toasts given at the dinner (these being the usual toasts given at the Roxburghe Club dinners), saying,

> Let me, then, ask all friends of morality and religion, whether it was commonly decent, not to say unsuitable, to use the mildest term, to the character of an English Clergyman, to toast the memory of a man [Valdarfer] because he was the first printer of a work that, instead of being held valuable, ought never to have seen the light, because its

---

3 'A Staunch Bibliomaniac', Letter, *Gentleman's Magazine* (1813), p. 339.
4 E. Evans, 'To the Editor of the Monthly Magazine', *Monthly Magazine, or British Register* 42 (September 1816), pp. 115–18.
5 John Bull, Letter printed in the *Morning Herald* (25 September 1818), excerpt contained in 'The Roxburghe Revels' MS. in the Roxburghe Club Archives.

obscenity far over-balances any humour which it may contain? [...] I respect the character of Earl Spencer too much, not to sympathise with him in the regret which he must feel, in standing next, in a silly revel, to a licentious Printer [...] There is no necessity to say, common sense sufficiently points out the laudable purposes to which [the Club] might have been directed, if instead of being devoted to antiquated obscenity, it had been employed in patronizing genius.[6]

This letter betrays a number of assumptions regarding the social positions of the club members: firstly, the immediately overt assumption that a clergyman's position must be incompatible with his attendance at a social occasion in Paris, and that his being there automatically means that he is 'no poor curate'. Dibdin was far from being in the position of the wealthy cleric and was in fact often in financial difficulties, in large part it must be allowed due to his expensive book-collecting and printing habits. A second assumption is that Earl Spencer, being a man of such generally accepted moral standing, must of course object to his name being associated with an early printer whose name is connected with such an immoral work, although the writer does not indicate what he supposes Earl Spencer might be doing at the 'silly revels' if he feels such regret. The writer was also, presumably, unaware of how many clergymen were members of the club besides Dibdin and may have been shocked to find out how many clerics were perfectly willing to belong to a group who collected and reproduced such works.

Criticisms of this kind, questioning the moral probity of the club's activities and pointing towards notions of noblesse oblige, eventually gave way, as we have seen, to the overt snobbery presented in the publication of the defamatory *Roxburghe Revels* article. This act of petty revenge, among its many angles of attack, contained the horrified suggestion that Haslewood was attempting to bring other perceived undesirables of his own class into the club, such as 'Mr. Bliss, the son of a bookseller at Oxford'.[7] This carries the suggestion that Haslewood's lower-class (or possibly middle-class by this point as he was a partner in his uncle's legal practice) background might lead him to further seek to infect the club, his class propagating itself like a virus through the healthy body of aristocratic club life. It is left as usual to Dibdin to point out that 'the application was made to the Rev. Philip Bliss of St. John's College, and now Dr. Bliss, Registrar of the University of Oxford. The father of Dr. Bliss was a Clergyman, and not a bookseller. But what if he had been? The late Rev. Peter Elmsly, Principle of St. Alban's Hall, was the nephew of a bookseller of

6 Ibid.
7 'The Roxburghe Revels', MS, *Athenaeum* (4 January 1834), p. 5.

that name in the Strand: and when did Oxford boast a more perfect ATTIC-GREEK SCHOLAR than that excellent man?'[8] Dibdin answers the accusers by meeting the snobbery head-on, pointing out that social standing (and that apparently dangerous proximity to commercial life) is no indication of knowledge or enthusiasm, and while it is impossible to say whether this would have been a unanimous opinion, it is probably as close as it is possible to get to the views of the members on the question of class and its significance within the world of the club's activities, that is, that class was of secondary concern to the love and knowledge of books. This may be a point that Dibdin felt personally. He himself possessed the perceived correct minimum grade of social class, being solidly middle class, but in his flamboyance and excitability he lacked the expected characteristics of understated reticence that marked a gentleman. Without the shared arena of books he would have been unlikely to move so easily in the aristocratic circles he obviously enjoyed, so he was both damned and simultaneously saved socially by his love of bibliography. This issue of professional or scholarly knowledge and its value in social terms also leads into another, more modern and strangely contradictory, facet of the class issue. Today, in discussions on the early Roxburghe, there is often betrayed an implicit belief that, because the club is perceived as containing a high percentage of aristocrats among its membership, it must therefore follow that it was comprised of men who were also probably superficial, lacking in taste, bereft of learning and by nature dilettantes. There often appears to be an unspoken assumption that wealth and learning, or even a genuine enthusiasm for intellectual matters, must have been incompatible.

The Roxburghe Club at this time was certainly and unashamedly elitist. Another correspondent to the *Gentleman's Magazine* jokingly describes the difficulty of obtaining entry as such that 'a Directorship of the India Board, or of the Bank of England, will henceforth be a position of comparative insignificance'.[9] This exclusivity obviously did not adhere to typical class boundaries as closely as would perhaps be supposed, and it would be a mistake in this case to conflate 'elitist' with 'aristocratic'. The elitist nature of the club was primarily about book collecting of a particular type, not class. While undoubtedly a small but significant percentage of the club were members of the aristocracy, a far larger number adhered to the more stereotypical picture of a bibliophile: lawyers, schoolmasters and clergymen, in other words, those men who would have developed a love of books during their university education and continued to come into daily contact with books in the course of their career. It appears that the aristocratic members exerted a weight upon the popular

---

8 Dibdin, *Roxburghe Revels and Related Papers*, p. 82.
9 A Letter by 'Templarius', *Gentleman's Magazine* (July 1813), pp. 3–4.

imagination (and possibly on their own club mythology as well) that was not reflected by their actual numbers in the club.

Out of the 18 men present at the original dinner (those who could therefore be considered to be the founding members) only two were peers and a further two baronets. A baronet is technically classed as a commoner and therefore not strictly a member of the aristocracy. At that dinner they appointed a further six members, of whom three were peers. By the first anniversary dinner, when the club was increased to number 31 members, it contained seven hereditary titles if Egerton Brydges is counted, an eccentric whose right to any title at all was a matter of dispute.[10] Only five of these titled men were nobles. Aristocratic members were a definite minority, equalled in the club by clergymen and far outnumbered by the practitioners of law and Members of Parliament (MPs). This tendency to give extra weight to the number of club members who can be classed as aristocratic has perhaps led to a greater percentage of titled members joining since the early days, a fact already noted in 1929 by Harold Williams who pointed out that '[the club's] membership list is still narrowly closed, and is more definitely aristocratic in personnel to-day than in its earlier years'.[11]

It is not difficult to understand why the issues of class carried such importance in the early nineteenth century when some romantics (including, of course, Walter Scott) considered the feudal past to be recent enough to be considered both possible and desirable as a political pattern for the future. More prosaically, wealth, authority, education and class had been intrinsically entwined until the Industrial Revolution, and society would take some time to accept the changing face of affluence and increasing social mobility. The idea that a commoner, even one with the considerable financial means and expert knowledge required to amass a collection of expensive rare books, should be able to fraternize with members of the aristocracy and gentry on equal terms, merely on the basis of a shared passion for books, must have seemed daring. Kristian Jenson has noted this social unease between the custodians of hereditary collections and active book collectors, and relates that the Earl of Pembroke was reluctant to lend Earl Spencer a book, demanding that 'Spencer kept the book well away from the disreputable company which

---

10 He had attempted to claim the Barony of Chandos, although it appears that he had little or no connection to the family that had previously held the title, but in fact descended from an entirely different family of the same name but less social standing. Eventually, after a long period of humiliating failure, he was created a baronet in his own right in 1814.

11 Harold Williams, *Book Clubs and Printing Societies* (London: The First Edition Club, 1929), p. 27.

he kept: "your fraternity of book collectors or their associates"'.[12] Such blurring of class boundaries must have appeared deliberately perverse, coming as it did on the heels of the French Revolution and at a time when the British were already uneasy and distrustful of social change and the potential for civil disruption. The overtly elitist nature of the club must have made this oddity appear even more striking as inevitably many men, who no doubt considered themselves to be eminently socially suited to belong to the club, may have been blackballed or simply overlooked in favour of a socially inferior but bibliophilically more committed postulant. Ironically, what would, from a modern perspective, appear to be a bastion of the existing social hierarchy, might to contemporaries of its early years, have appeared to be a frighteningly radical and egalitarian group. The club's political make-up, covered in detail in the next chapter, may have only added to this unease. To the members it may have seemed unremarkable that a commoner with the right sort of bibliophilic obsession and knowledge should take precedence over one who possessed all the social prerequisites but lacked the necessary depth of passion for their shared vocation. To the layman the Roxburghe Club appeared to be the literary equivalent of the 'Four-in-Hand Club', those wild young aristocrats who gathered to use the working-class vernacular, dress in stable uniform and who delighted in bribing public coachmen into letting them drive the coaches. A correspondent in 1816 makes a direct comparison between the Roxburghe Club and the Four-in-Hand or Whip Club, saying, 'that these thirty-one noblemen and gentlemen have an undoubted right so to employ themselves, can be no question: that their eccentric companions, the members of the Whip Club, have an equal right to spend their money in horses and equipage, is equally indisputable'.[13] In the case of the Roxburghe Club, here we have aristocrats descending to the level of book dealers and penurious scholars.

A review of Dibdin's *Library Companion* in the *Quarterly Review* of June 1825 is critical of his use of 'booksellers' slang' and contemptuous of what is described as his willingness to 'lower himself into a walking puff for booksellers and book-collectors, engravers and auctioneers'.[14] He was regarded as associating too closely with the perceived sordidness of mercantile life at a time when, interestingly, some spheres of the publishing world itself were also attempting to distance themselves from association with other forms of

---

12 Kristian Jensen, *Revolution and the Antiquarian Book* (Cambridge: Cambridge University Press, 2011), p. 123.
13 E. Evans, 'To the Editor of the Monthly Magazine', *Monthly Magazine, or British Register* 42, 288 (September 1816), pp. 115–18.
14 'The Library Companion; or, the Young Man's Guide, and the Old Man's Comfort, in the Choice of a Library', *Quarterly Review* 32, no. 63 (June 1825), p. 152.

selling. Dr. Thomas Rees, looking back at the literary scene at the turn of the nineteenth century, recalls the founding of two journals, the *British Press* and the *Globe* in 1803, to represent the interests of publishing booksellers. It was not simply a matter of the necessity for a specialist trade magazine but rather a financially sound solution to the high prices charged for advertising in newspapers and more especially their injured professional pride in the face of the 'heedless manner in which notices of fine and expensive literary publications were associated with vile and disgusting quack puffs'.[15] Here we see the desire to distinguish books from other types of merchandise, preferring perhaps to emphasize their connection with learning and the arts, and to escape from any association with the interests of other, less elevated, tradesmen. Obviously, from the perspective of the upper classes, trade was trade and no such distinctions were being made, and Dibdin was seen by many of his contemporaries as displaying a dangerous propensity for ignoring the boundaries between gentlemen and tradesmen. He certainly was not wealthy enough to support his book-collecting habit without financial strain, which may have also led him to be open to suspicion, perceived as not wealthy enough for the company he kept and the interests he followed and therefore almost certainly as having financial interests in book dealing himself. It would also be a mistake to discount the possibility of simple social envy, inhabiting as he did, a high-profile circle of well-connected men, many of whom appeared to actively encourage the book-dealing exploits that formed the unspoken basis of so many of his works even if they did not all approve of his mode of expression.

These class-based judgements could only later become more pronounced as the people who had actually known the early members gave way to the later Victorian critics, who wrote from a position of strong morals and sometimes social conscience but who had little or no personal experience of the early club or its activities. Society had arguably become more rigidly conformist and less forgiving of eccentricity, leading to a number of censorious pronouncements in this later period against the club's prime movers. A common theme running through many of these opinions is that of the early days of the club, seen as a disastrously adolescent stage out of which it eventually matured, once the dangerously louche founders were no longer in a position to lead it astray, into the valuable publisher it later became. The Roxburghe appears in this later period as a club which would guard its social boundaries more carefully, less ready perhaps to accept as members people such as Haslewood or Dibdin (or at least the flawed picture of those two men's characters as penned

---

15 Dr. Thomas Rees and John Britton, *Reminiscences of Literary London, from 1779 to 1853* (London: Suckling & Galloway, 1896) Rep. (New York and London: Garland Publishing, 1974), p. 135.

by the *Athenaeum*). A writer such as John Hill Burton does all the early members of the club a disservice when he describes the two men as 'these, who in some measure fed on the crumbs that fell from the master's table, were in a position rather too closely resembling the professionals in a hunt or cricket club'.[16] This willingness to believe that the relationship between the wealthy members and those with less secure finances could only have been that of master and servant rather than one of fellow enthusiasts is not only demeaning towards Dibdin and Haslewood but also simultaneously towards the aristocratic collectors in its assumption that they could not function in the world of collecting without the assistance of professionals to guide them. Dibdin, in his *Reminiscences* of 1836, had already been stung enough by similar accusations, in the *Roxburghe Revels* article and its aftermath, to declare that his accuser 'may as well be informed that I am not the Secretary – that I receive no emolument – that the office of Vice-president is one of no trouble and no indignity'.[17] In the specific case of the relationship between Lord Spencer and Dibdin, the latter did act as an agent for the Earl, but it is unclear to what extent he was employed to do so or whether it was a more complex matter of direct payment, common interests, friendship and some degree of patronage of a less immediately monetary type. There is also, of course, an often fine line between payment and reimbursement of expenses incurred. Dibdin certainly gained in both social and career terms from the personal connection and later occupied a living at St. Mary, Bryanstone Square obtained for him by Spencer in 1823. The other supposedly professional agent, Haslewood, as previously mentioned, was a partner in his uncle's legal firm, a business which he later inherited. He was not reliant on the income made from his literary pursuits, though it no doubt helped to finance his book-collecting habit. He carried out paid literary services such as editing for people both within the club and without, but that would not appear to be the basis for his membership. Rather, his friendships with Dibdin and Egerton Brydges, his acquaintance with a number of the other founder members and his reputation as an editor of antiquarian literature appear to have led to his inclusion at the initial dinner. There is little indication that any other members carried out any paid services for peers within the club, and services carried out as a result of friendship would be too commonplace to require comment.

Nonetheless, other Victorian writers appear to have taken their cue from Hill Burton's book and more directly from the *Athenaeum*, and William Roberts echoes the casual snobbery of many critics of the time when he writes of the club that it 'might have sustained its raison d'être, if it

---

16 Burton, *The Book Hunter, etc*, p. 245.
17 Dibdin, *Reminiscences*, p. 429.

had drawn the line at such men as Thomas Frognall Dibdin and Joseph Hazlewood [sic]'.[18] Probably the most viciously prejudiced and class-based essay about the club published during this period is one written by Francis Hitchman in 1881, which is also, incidentally, the most blithely inaccurate of the accounts written at this time. Among its numerous errors it states that Earl Spencer was the winning bidder for the *Decameron* at the Roxburghe sale and confidently assures the reader that the Roxburghe Club ceased to exist in 1831.[19] The essay's greater part is expended on a far from unbiased biography of Dibdin (yet again the unfortunate focus for other authors' spleen) and makes no attempt to disguise the writer's feelings on Dibdin's style, saying that 'Dibdin is one of the worst of writers. He cannot even spell correctly – unless, indeed, his printers were more stupid than printers generally are – and his style is painfully pompous, stilted, and lumbering. His jokes are incessant, and remind the reader of nothing so much as of the gambols of an infantile elephant'.[20] The essay continues in this strain, implying that Dibdin's literary and social success rested primarily on a willingness to flatter, taking as its proof Dibdin's account of reading to one of his friends a passage about them from one of his books. Hitchman frames this account as one in which 'a cynic might find a malicious pleasure in the spectacle of an elderly gentleman purring with self-satisfaction, whilst the "illustrious bibliographer" read to him four pages of egregious flattery'.[21] For Hitchman this provides all the answer he requires to the question of Dibdin's unfathomable popularity, and he considers him to have been 'the head and chief of a great mutual admiration society' and to have gained his position solely on the basis of his willingness to fawn and flatter the aristocracy.[22] Continuing on its theme of social inequality inevitably leading to literary inadequacy, the essay predictably (taking its cue from the *Athenaeum* article) moves on to another attack on the memory of Haslewood, describing him as being admitted into the Roxburghe Club by accident and as 'one of the most ignorant men in existence'.[23] These themes are familiar from the 'Roxburghe Revels' article, but Hitchman goes on to give them a new twist, presenting the other members as being somehow held to ransom by the terrible machinations of Dibdin and Haslewood, writing that 'it was not until Dibdin

18 Roberts, *The Book-Hunter in London*, p. 63.
19 Francis Hitchman, 'Mr. Dibdin and the Roxburghe Club', *Eighteenth Century Studies: Essays* (London: S Low, Marston, Searle & Rivington, 1881), pp. 273–303.
20 Ibid., p. 273.
21 Ibid., p. 274.
22 Ibid.
23 Ibid., p. 288.

ceased to be its principal member, and Haslewood its editor, that a better state of things came about. Remonstrance, mockery, and severe criticism, however, at last did their work, and, in 1827, the Roxburghe Club, much to their credit, emancipated themselves from the absurd tyranny under which they had until that time existed'.[24] Hitchman makes no pretence of seeing Dibdin and Haslewood as equal members of the Roxburghe, but rather views them as aberrations, commoners who should not have been admitted and who prevented the club from exhibiting the taste and judgement that could have otherwise been expected from men of social standing, although throughout the piece he indicates that his view of the other club members is far from admiring. Fairly certainly the founder members of the Roxburghe Club, having known them for some time previous to the inaugural dinner, did not view Dibdin or Haslewood in that light, but the club appears to have later been swayed to some extent by the negative received opinions of commentators. A club history, published in 1928, dismisses Haslewood as 'an interesting but mysterious character, a friend of Dibdin's and not unlike him in his affection for birth, books and banquets and in his lack of scholarship. He had been the club's earliest chronicler and the loss of his papers deprived it of some interesting records'.[25] There is overall an interesting tendency to overlook that it was the invitation of Dibdin (and probably by extension his close friend Haslewood) which brought together the founder members at that initial dinner. It was an invitation that they would have declined no doubt if they had held any misgiving as to the desirability of either man's company.

Generally critics have in the past, and in many cases continue to, view the Roxburghe Club during its Regency years primarily through the prism of the particular class stereotype they expect to find, without any investigation of its actual make-up. It is so often viewed (with the exceptions of Dibdin and Haslewood, those perfidious infiltrators of class) as a homogenous group, one that is predominantly aristocratic in demographic, and characterized by the wealth, political bias and social or moral conscience (or lack of) that are held to be typical in some way of such an obvious example of the establishment. In the next chapter I consider the actual make-up of the early club in some detail with a view to evaluating to what extent the early club has been misrepresented and whether the expected biases can indeed be discerned in its early composition.

---

24 Ibid., p. 296.
25 Clive Bigham, *The Roxburghe Club: Its history and Its Members 1812–1927* (Oxford: Printed for the Roxburghe Club at the OUP, 1928), p. 8.

Chapter 4

POLITICS, RELIGION, MONEY

Having looked at some of the commonly held opinions and assumptions made about the demographics of the early Roxburghe Club and how these views have influenced appraisals of their literary activities, it is now time to examine the actual membership and how it measures up against those claims. It is probably not spoiling any potential surprise to say that, far from being the homogenous group assumed by many commentators, the men who made up the early Roxburghe Club represented a wide spectrum, with a bewilderingly complex range of belief and opinion. It may be true to say, for instance, that all the members were comparatively wealthy. They obviously had to be to collect rare books during the high tide of auction prices, but the differences in wealth between the richest among them such as the Duke of Devonshire and the least wealthy such as Dibdin or Haslewood was vast. One might state too that they were largely establishment figures, but they ranged from the ultraconservative, almost rabidly antiradical, political activist such as George Watson Taylor or Alexander Boswell to the somewhat surprisingly radical Archdeacon Wrangham. In terms of religion many were clerics, some were High Church, some evangelical, one Catholic, but in character with the time, none were publicly atheist.

Of the first 31 members, 10 were at some point in their life an MP. The majority of the aristocratic members were MPs in the Commons until the subsequent succession to their title pushed them into the Lords, and a number of the landed gentry held a seat at some time. Of the 21 men not formally involved in Parliamentary politics, most were either clergymen or practised law, although of course not being officially parliamentarian does not imply an absence of political opinion, activity or influence. A number of the members held positions that could be interpreted as politically active outside of Parliament, such as Francis Freeling, who, while secretary of the post office, was accused by William Cobbett of acting to suppress the circulation of Cobbett's series of radical political pamphlets the *Porcupine*.[1] Freeling denied the accusations but was also speculated to have been instrumental in founding

---

1 This 'suppression' perhaps had financial causes too: the socialist historian G. D. H. Cole writes, 'The Porcupine was not a financial success. Cobbett had looked to secure a

or overseeing a government financed newspaper, the *Sun*, published with the intention of counteracting public subversion. Freeling used his position to make very effective inroads into the political controversies of the day and their promotion in publications, but in this he was far from unique among contemporary civil servants. In religious terms he was equally active in publishing and circulating anti-Catholic propaganda, a political position that makes him relatively unusual in the club and which must have been a tricky position to diplomatically negotiate with his fellow (Catholic) Roxburgher, Peregrine Towneley, and this would be far from the only potential point of friction between club members.

The founding of the Roxburghe Club was set against a backdrop of national change. The early nineteenth century was a politically volatile period, and gathered around the table at the annual dinner were staunch representatives of both the Whigs and the Tories; pro and anti-abolitionists; the most conservative of traditionalists; and those who were verging-on-radical social reformers. Although a general view of the parties of the time would be of the Tories supporting the status quo and generally standing in defence of establishment institutions including the church and the existing hierarchy, and the Whigs as promoting reform and supporting changes that would bring more freedom and equality overall, in reality personal rank, political party adherence and attitudes on the key controversies of the day were far from clear cut. The Roxburghe members illustrate not only a wide spectrum of political affiliations and causes but also the tendency in individuals, including politically engaged figures, to a greater extent in the early nineteenth century than even now, to espouse a multiplicity of viewpoints, not necessarily corresponding to simple 'left-wing' or 'right-wing' allegiances.

Many of the wealthiest families were traditionally Whig, with their political allegiance forming a part of their aristocratic credentials with so-called revolutionary principles and party affiliations that could be traced directly back

---

considerable circulation in America; but he found that a Mr. Freeling, Secretary of the Post Office, had secured a monopoly of the right of forwarding periodicals to America by the King's packet-boats, then, in time of war, the only safe means of conveyance. Freeling wanted five guineas a year for each copy sent. He subsequently offered to take three guineas, provided that Cobbett kept the transaction quiet, but Cobbett refused this bargain, and appealed to the Postmaster-General, Lord Auckland, from whom he got no redress. This severely injured his American sales, and also got him the enmity of the Post Office, which withdrew its advertisements from his paper. He also alleged that his deliveries of The Porcupine in Great Britain were constantly hampered by the postal authorities, orders for other newspapers being maliciously substituted by the Clerks of the Roads, who took most of the orders in the country districts.' G. D. H. Cole, *The Life of William Cobbett* (Abingdon: Routledge, 1924), p. 49.

to the 'Glorious Revolution' of 1688 and the ousting of the Catholic James II. Even within this broad picture there were many factions, and it would be completely wrong to denote the party as a uniform set of ideals and opinion. For one thing, factions existed within the Whig Party which were often based in blood ties such as those between the Cavendish and Althorp families. Moreover, the so-called revolutionary principles mentioned above and the political changes that came with the change of regime in 1688 were not the same as the radical principles held by many political activists and propagandists in the period from the French Revolution to the 1848 revolutions in Europe. Many Whigs distanced themselves from radicalism and egalitarianism. Individual differences and opposition to extreme contemporary radicalism notwithstanding, the overall Whig ideals have been neatly encapsulated as a 'philosophy of disinterestedness and support for public opinion as long as it took a constitutional form'.[2] The founding members of the Roxburghe Club included a substantial number of leading Whig politicians from the traditionally aristocratic Whig families, notably the Cavendish, Howard and Althorp families. Among the club members representing these families were the Duke of Devonshire (Cavendish), Earl Spencer (Althorp), Viscount Morpeth, later Earl Carlisle (Howard) and the Earl of Cawdor (Campbell).

Earl Spencer, by the time the club was founded, was of course the head of the Althorp family, but during his earlier career he had entered Parliament in 1780 as MP for Northampton, then returned for Surrey in 1882 serving as part of the Rockingham administration. He declined to serve under Shelburne but later supported the Fox–North coalition. In 1783 he succeeded to his title and thereafter held a number of posts, including that of Lord Privy Seal under William Pitt; First Lord of the Admiralty (in which post he remained between December 1784 and February 1801) and later secretary of state for the Home Department in the Grenville-Fox ministry. After retiring from office he continued to attend the Lords until his death in 1834. Earl Spencer regarded his work in these posts to be his public duty, and by all accounts it was a duty that he carried out diligently and with intelligence. Unsurprisingly his son, John Charles Spencer, Viscount Althorp (a member of the Roxburghe Club as well), was also a loyal Whig supporter and similarly had a lengthy and illustrious, if somewhat reluctant, political career. He acted as leader of the Whig Party in the Commons despite his reluctance to take public office and was another example of the aristocratic sense of civic obligation which overrode his preference for a quiet country life. He was a strongly religious man who said that 'there is only one object ... worthy of the ambition of a man of sense,

---

2 Rohan McWilliam, *Popular Politics in Nineteenth Century England* (London: Routledge, 1998), p. 49.

and that is, to obtain the favour of God. Political pursuits and political rivalships are not the means to conduce to this end ... The occupations and the compliances which necessarily belong to a political man must ... have a tendency to diminish religious feelings'.[3] Despite, or perhaps because of, this lack of personal ambition, Althorp became a respected and popular politician, leading Sir Edward Littleton, a fellow MP, to write to his wife that

> I sat next to Althorp, whom I like more and more daily. He has more simplicity and honesty about him than any man I ever knew. He laughed at the badgerings he has had in Parliament and said he cared less about them than he could have imagined, talked about his farms and his calves ... and his not having a minute night or day to himself ... He spoke most satisfactorily on the cordiality and union of the cabinet. Reform is to be brought on by Lord John Russell ... The government have thought it due to him not to take the question out of his hands, Althorp said he had always considered himself a pretty good radical before, but that he was ten times more so now, since he had been in office and had a peep behind the curtain.[4]

The Duke of Devonshire was another highly political man with a strong sense of the duty that accompanied privilege. He made regular attendance in the Lords and strongly supported reform in a variety of political areas. The duke had no opportunity to sit in the Commons because he succeeded to his title (and all the associated responsibilities) at age 21 and therefore went almost straight to the Lords. Later in life the duke acted as Lord Chamberlain to George IV (between 1827 and 1828 and 1830 and 1834), albeit sometimes against his better judgement. Until 1924 this role was considered to be a political one, and up until 1782 had been of Cabinet rank. It was certainly a role that gave the duke a great deal of influence with the king and the royal household, although he had at times been in opposition to the king, most notably in his disapproval of the king's treatment of Queen Caroline in 1820.

George Howard, styled Viscount Morpeth and later the Sixth Earl of Carlisle, was yet another member of an illustrious Whig family, who supported Pitt's government. He was an MP in the family's interest for Morpeth, Northumberland and later for the County of Cumberland. He contributed a number of political items to the *Anti Jacobin* in the late 1790s, and spoke against

---

3 Le Marchant, pp. xv–xvi, in 'John Charles Spencer, Visct. Althorp', *History of Parliament* (*HP*), www.historyofparliamentonline.org.
4 Hatherton MS., Littleton to wife, 3 February 1831, in *HP*, www.historyofparliamentonline.org.

Fox's motion for the repeal of the Treason and Sedition Acts. These are clear examples of the fears present among otherwise liberal Whigs of the dangers of extreme radicalism in a revolutionary age. Morpeth married the Duke of Devonshire's sister Georgiana in 1801, and through that Cavendish connection became associated with Fox. He was in favour of Catholic emancipation and made a speech in 1812 advocating sincere and cordial conciliation with the Catholics. Also a pro-Catholic supporter and another liberal peer among the Roxburghe membership was John Frederick Campbell, Earl of Cawdor, who was instrumental in seeking reforms to the criminal laws and of a number of judicial traditions.

Among the non-aristocratic club members who were Whig MPs were Roger Wilbraham, Richard Heber and Samuel Egerton Brydges. Wilbraham was MP for Bodmin and Helston, and an amusing anecdote involving Wilbraham illustrates the forthright nature of political sparring in the period and his own reformist viewpoint, both on the abuses evident in contemporary party politics and on the use of political bribery:

> Play was taken very seriously, for the stakes were always heavy, and conversation was resented. Sir Philip Francis came to Brook's wearing for the first time the ribbon of the order of the Bath, for which Fox had recommended him. "So this is the way they have rewarded you at last", remarked Roger Wilbraham, coming up to the whist-table. "They have given you a little bit of red ribbon for your services, Sir Philip, have they? A pretty bit of red ribbon to hang about your neck; and that satisfies you, does it? Now I wonder what I shall have? What do you think they will give me, Sir Philip?" "A halter, I trust and hope!" roared the infuriated player.[5]

Richard Heber, although mostly concerned with his scholarly pursuits and book collection, had an interest in politics. He stood unsuccessfully as the candidate for the representation of Oxford University in 1806 but was later successful in being elected to the same seat in 1821. His political career ended prematurely when the Tory periodical *John Bull* printed an article which hinted that he was homosexual, an allegation that led to his temporary exile abroad and the destruction of his reputation. Samuel Egerton Brydges also had a political career of limited success, which is summed up, somewhat despondently, by this extract from his autobiography:

> I regret that I ever had any ambition, literary or political; but, unfortunately, one of my early desires was to obtain a seat in Parliament, and

---

5 Melville, *Some Eccentrics and a Woman*, p. 87.

I never succeeded till I was on the verge of fifty – viz. Oct. 1812. Then I was successful in a contested election for Maidstone, and sat six busy years, till the dissolution in June, 1818. But I was not altogether unhappy during the discharge of that function, though I had innumerable sorrows and wrongs to distract me, which enfeebled and bound in chains any small faculties I might otherwise have displayed. I took an active part in the poor laws and the copyright bill.[6]

Brydges, perhaps too easily seen as merely an eccentric absorbed with self-induced woes and imagined slights, shows here at least the satisfaction he found during his career as an MP in two liberal causes.

While many aristocrats, for historical reasons, identified with the Whigs, the landed gentry overall tended towards being Tory (Conservatism, developing at this period within Toryism, had formed as a reaction to the French Revolution and was strongly associated with the landed gentry and with the Anglican Church). Among the Roxburghe members who were Tory supporters was George Grenville Leveson-Gower, who started out as a relatively rare example (at least among the Roxburghe membership) of an aristocratic Tory, although his family were traditionally Whig, and later in life he himself became a Whig. His political career started with his election as MP for Newcastle-under-Lyme and later for Staffordshire. After 1807 he took little part in active politics although he did support Catholic emancipation. Also a member of the Tory aristocracy, Edward Herbert, Viscount Clive became MP for Ludlow and took the opposite side in the matter of Catholic emancipation. He was described by the *Spectator*, in 1832 as a 'sagacious, clear-headed man of business, with perhaps the most insinuating address and plausible exterior of any Tory leader in the kingdom; and although no debater, [he] is a formidable parliamentary tactician'.[7] In 1837, Viscount Clive's brother, the Hon. R. H. Clive, although not himself a Roxburghe member, presented a text to the club which provides a striking example of how the choice of a presentation can display a marked link to individual political inclinations. The text is called *The Love of Wales to their Soveraigne Prince expressed in a true Relation of the Solemnity held at Ludlow, in the Countie of Salop, upon the fourth of November last past, Anno Domini 1616, being the day of the Creation of the high and mighty Charles, Prince of Wales, and Earle of Chester, in his Maiesties Palace of White-Hall* and is an extravagantly worded encomium of the British royal family, celebrating the installation of

---

6 Samuel Egerton Brydges, *The Autobiography, Times, Opinions and Contemporaries of Sir Egerton Brydges* (London: Cochrane & McCrone, 1834), vol. 1, pp. 104–5.

7 *Spectator*, 27 October; *Salopian Journal*, 2 November 1832, in Margaret Escott, 'Edward Herbert, Viscount. Clive', *HP*, www.historyofparliamentonline.org.

an English Prince of Wales (later King Charles I) in 1616. The Clive family were landowners who possessed large areas of land in Wales, including 3,127 acres in the area of Merthyr Tydfil. Recently, in 1831 Merthyr had been the scene of political upheaval, with a working-class uprising against low wages and unemployment which ended in a brutal suppression of the protesters and the execution, imprisonment or transportation of many of those involved. Against this background of unrest and suppression of rebellion, the reprinting of a tract celebrating the subjugation of the Welsh by the English nobility can be seen as a pointed, if not inflammatory, political act. It is interesting that it was contributed by the president's brother, perhaps indicating a desire on the part of Viscount Clive himself to retain some degree of personal distance between himself and the act of publishing and presenting such a politically significant text.

Alexander Boswell and Mark Masterman Sykes were both Tory but displayed very differing degrees of political passion. Cliché as it may be, Boswell can only be described as a staunch Tory and an unfortunately hot-headed politician. An opponent of parliamentary reform, in 1816 he had bought the Plympton Erle seat in Devon, using his inheritance to do so. Boswell's voting history shows a strong support of the government and a tendency to vote with proposed suspensions of personal freedoms and rights in the name of national security.

Boswell was also a man of action, renowned for his vigour and fine stature, and in 1820 he acted as head of the yeomanry and was highly active in suppressing dissent in Ayrshire or taking, as Paterson described it 'an active part in opposing the democratical spirit which pervaded the country'.[8] Boswell was voted into the Roxburghe Club in 1819, six years after his brother James. It is interesting to consider that in such a fiery political age, political affiliation seemed to play so little part when it came to choosing club members. The high-profile Whigs in the Roxburghe at that time must have unanimously voted for his inclusion, but it must have offered a curious proposition to mix socially with someone who considered one to be a treacherous force for anarchy and destruction. It was perhaps even a dangerous choice of dining partner in an age where duels, although illegal, still occasionally took place. Indeed, Alexander Boswell's untimely death was the result of a duel related to his political views and hot-headed approach to political disagreement. Perhaps the lens of time has magnified at least some of these issues? Alternatively, perhaps in most cases (with the notable exception of the Scottish politician James Stuart who challenged Boswell to the duel), the

---

8 *The Contemporaries of Burns*, ed. by James Patterson (Edinburgh: Hugh Paton, 1840), p. 322.

urbane manners and respect for debate, typical at least in theory, of gentlemen of the time, allowed the owners of such polemical opinions to mix easily and exchange insults without taking such views as a personal slight? Possibly Boswell's undoubted intelligence, passion for books and entertaining nature were more important to the club than political agreement, and Alexander Boswell was far from being the only passionate, opinionated political animal at the table. There was certainly plenty of choice when it came to contentious topics, and perhaps it came as a much-needed buffer that some members, ostensibly political, were far more laissez-faire in their opinions: Sir Mark Masterman Sykes acted as the Tory MP for York for 13 years following his election in 1807, throughout which time he apparently did not give a speech on any subject and only rarely voted. His political reticence must have made a pleasant change.

It must be emphasised that the political divisions between individual members was a complex, far from clear-cut area. Even in cases where it appears obvious to us that an individual falls within the boundaries of party politics, even when he might self-identify with a particular flavour of political opinion, there is still a very real possibility that many views held and expressed by that person might often conflict with their professed alignment as we would understand it. An example of such conflict appears in the political beliefs of Sir Walter Scott, a Tory, but one who also desired to see social reform. He feared radicalism and unrest but rather than advocating the legal repression of dissent, as a romantic he yearned for a modernized, idealized form of feudalism in which a modern, enlightened aristocracy would produce charismatic, popular leaders, men of principle and ability who could lead the populace to a state of civil harmony under a wise and fair leadership. This vision appears in many Scott fictions, including 'The Lady of the Lake' (1810) and *The Abbott* (1820).

Considerably less romantic in outlook was John Dent, overall a political independent, who in 1790 became MP for Lancaster in a change to the social and professional make-up of Parliament, in which the fast increase in the importance of the banking sector, necessitated by the Industrial Revolution, was reflected by the growing influence of bankers both socially and politically. In 1790, 16 bankers, all from non-elite backgrounds and therefore unlikely in traditional terms to be in Parliament, were elected as MPs.[9] Dent was one of these 16 men, and was a partner in a city bank, Child & Co. Although by and large an independent MP, he gave general support to Pitt's first administration. He is perhaps best remembered for attempting to introduce legislation in

---

9 Ian R. Christie, *British 'Non-Elite' MPS, 1715–1820* (Oxford: Oxford University Press, 1995), p. 77.

1796 for the taxation of the ownership of certain dogs, a subject which caused hilarity among his colleagues and the press alike and led to his nickname of 'dog' Dent. Thomas Moore, in his memoirs, repeats an anecdote regarding Dent that reflects this amusement, writing that 'S[heridan] came early to the house, and saw no one but Dent sitting in a contemplative posture in one corner. S. stole round to him unobserved, and putting his hand under the seat to Dent's legs, mimicked the barking of a dog, at which Dent started up alarmed, as if his conscience really dreaded some attack from the race he was plotting against'.[10] The proposed tax on dogs was not a purely anti-canine or frivolous matter as the proceeds of the tax were intended to be 'appropriated solely to the relief of the poor'. As a final note on the dog tax, it received a passing reference in *Waverley*:

> Another part in this concert was sustained by the incessant yelping of a score of idle useless curs, which followed, snarling, barking, howling, and snapping at the horses' heels; a nuisance at that time so common in Scotland, that a French tourist, who, like other travellers, longed to find a good and rational reason for every thing he saw, has recorded, as one of the memorabilia of Caledonia, that the state maintained in each village a relay of curs, called *collies,* whose duty it was to chase the *chevaux de poste* (too starved and exhausted to move without such a stimulus) from one hamlet to another, till their annoying convoy drove them to the end of their stage. The evil and remedy (such as it is) still exist: But this is remote from our present purpose, and is only thrown out for consideration of the collectors under Mr Dent's dog-bill.[11]

More seriously Dent was a vociferous anti-abolitionist as might be expected of the MP for Lancaster, a city that relied on slavery for much of its wealth. Furthermore, he was married to the sister-in-law of Isaac Gascoyne, the MP for Liverpool, another slaving port, and Gascoyne unsurprisingly was also an outspoken opponent of abolition. In 1793 Dent argued in Parliament that abolitionist principles, 'however they might be suited to England, were destructive of the property of the planters' and that 'people should be prepared for liberty before they could enjoy it'.[12] Later, in 1799, he put forward the argument that 'the grievances of the slaves no longer existed as the Liverpool merchants

---

10 Thomas Moore, *Memoirs, Journal and Correspondence of Thomas Moore,* ed. John Russell (London: Longman, Brown, Green, and Longmans, 1853), pp. 179–80.
11 Walter Scott, *Waverley* (1829), reprint, ed. by Susan Kubica Howard (Peterborough, ON: Broadview Press, 2010), p. 93; italics in original.
12 R. Thorne, 'John Dent', *HP*, www.historyofparliamentonline.org.

had done everything possible to improve conditions on the middle passage'.[13] Although the contemporary argument raged between the abolitionists and the anti-abolitionists, such views, however repugnant to the modern mind, were not considered to be particularly extreme at this period.

George Watson Taylor was another extremely political figure and, again, not a particularly sympathetic one to the modern outlook. During his lifetime he produced a number of highly political works including the play *England Preserved*, set during the minority of Henry III and apparently staged 'at the request of George III, at the Theatre Royal, Covent Garden in February 1795 [where it] was applauded for its anti Gallic Spirit'.[14] Early in his career Watson Taylor had been employed as secretary to Lord Camden, the Lord Lieutenant of Ireland, whose term of office had culminated in the Irish Rebellion of 1798. Sharing Camden's opposition to Catholic emancipation Watson Taylor wrote the lyrics to 'Croppies Lie Down', a loyalist, anti-Catholic, anti-French, highly inflammatory folk song. It was composed during the Irish Rebellion of 1798 amid fears of a French invasion in support of the Catholic rebels. Presumably his beliefs had calmed somewhat with the passing of time as, after a subsequent meeting with Watson Taylor in June 1828, Thomas Moore, the Irish Catholic songwriter and poet, reflected in his memoirs on how they 'felt, both of us, how strange it was that he and I who, thirty years ago, were placed in a position where either might have been called upon to hang or shoot the other, were now chatting over the whole matter amicably in his barouche'.[15] Moore goes on to describe 'Croppies Lie Down' as a 'song to the tune of which more blood has been shed than often falls to the lot of more lyrical productions'.[16] As well as being anti-Catholic, Watson Taylor was anti-abolitionist in contemporary politics. He was the son of a West India plantation owner, and in 1816, as MP for Newport in the Isle of Wight, he acted as the seconder on Palmer's amendment to the motion put forward by Wilberforce against slavery. In addition to making use of the usual defence of slave labour – that of treating his slaves well – he appears to have defended his anti-abolitionist stance through a particularly unpleasant and whining self-justification, complaining to Parliament in 1824 that 'it was not his fault' that he had inherited his plantations.[17] However disagreeable his politics appear to the modern eye, his electorate must have found him more congenial; after standing as the

---

13 Ibid.
14 *The Times*, 23 February 1795; H. Bull and J. Waylen, *Hist. Devizes*, 527, in 'George Watson Taylor', *HP*, www.historyofparliamentonline.org.
15 Moore, *Memoirs, Journal and Correspondence of Thomas Moore* 5, p. 314.
16 Ibid.
17 R. Thorne, 'George Watson Taylor', *HP*, www.historyofparliamentonline.org.

member for Newport from 1816 to 1818, he was later the member for Seaford from 1818 to 1820, for East Looe from 1820 to 1826 and for Devizes from 1826 until 1832.

A curious subset of political career was that of the Parliamentary agents for the plantation owners and merchants of the West Indies. The agents were usually solicitors who worked within the political system to represent the interests of this influential group. Watson Taylor has already been mentioned as the son of a plantation owner but among the club membership were a number of men whose livelihoods were dependent to some degree on this arrangement. George Hibbert was an example of this subset, acting specifically as an agent for Jamaican planters, and Robert Lang was a West India merchant. Incidentally, Lang's daughter married Francis Freelings's son George in 1816, highlighting the interesting point that a degree of intermarriage occurred between the families of the Roxburghe members, and these familial ties hint at another possible reason for the amicable nature of relations between the participants.

Another member who worked as a Parliamentary agent for the West Indian planters was James Heywood Markland, but although he followed a superficial parliamentary career his driving force became religious rather than political. He was a steadfast High Churchman who strongly supported church societies, and by the time of his club membership had already anonymously published short essays on theological subjects, including *A Few Plain Reasons for Adhering to the Church*, 1807. He was later entrusted with the administration of a number of religious charitable trusts including overseeing the distribution of £14,000 in private donations to various colonial missions. Presumably his experience as an agent for the West Indies recommended him for the task of liaising with colonial charitable concerns. He appears to have been a genuinely pious man, and from a present-day perspective it is difficult to reconcile his religious activities with his work as a lobbyist for the slave-owning plantation owners. Certainly, looking at the combined effects of these vested interests and the pressures on individual political and mercantile careers, one can gain an impression of how formidable a task it must have been to turn the tide of public opinion on slavery.

Those members of the Roxburghe Club who were lawyers tended to be notably less politically active, perhaps because of the professional necessity of being perceived as unbiased. This is probably best summed up by Sir Joseph Littledale, a judge, who when questioned about his political viewpoint was renowned for having answered, 'my politics are the politics of a special pleader'.[18] Of course, away from the public eye they were as likely to hold

---

18 Edward Foss, *Biographia Juridica* (London: John Murray, 1870, p. 410.

strong political views as anyone else. For instance, Edward Vernon Utterson, another lawyer, did not have a political career but was a Tory by persuasion, and in fact was described by his son in his biography of his father as an 'uncompromising old tory', a tendency that he did not attempt to disguise.[19]

The other group of Roxburghers who generally avoided any form of political reputation were the clerical members with one notable (and to some extent unintentional) exception, the Venerable Archdeacon Francis Wrangham. He appears to have been a sincere and cheerfully religious man who held strongly practical political views in support of what he saw as his Christian duty. He was radical in outlook but took no part in public politics, a point that he underlined in a letter to Egerton Brydges, saying, 'from politics, like you, I abstain – not only on the ground upon which you do it of the unfair surveillance of foreign post offices – but also because I understand them far less as a science – as matter of party, hold them in equal disesteem – and in every respect think them the least suitable exercise of declassement for a clergyman'.[20] Although Wrangham may have abstained from party politics, politics showed no inclination to avoid him, and excerpts from his letters show him to have felt himself to be hampered materially by his views on social justice and the upholding of the rights of the underprivileged. As he wrote to Samuel Egerton Brydges, it was 'not that my life has not upon the whole been a very happy one, for my disposition is naturally a buoyant one and my fortunes have been gradually and slowly mounting. That they would have risen more rapidly I can well believe if my opinions had been more in unison – actually or ostensibly – with those of the governing powers in the country. But I was bred a Whig. The lessons of Greece and Rome have no tendency to correct this propensity'.[21] Wrangham appears to have been unlucky, insofar as his diocese fell within the boundaries of an administrative district that was unsympathetic overall to his liberal politics and religious tolerance, and this variance of outlook appears to have led to him being in some conflict with his fellow deacons. At least one of the ways in which he seems to have marked his card with his superiors, and indeed the media of the time, was in his support for Catholic emancipation. As he again explains to Egerton Brydges, 'against the anti-Catholicism of my Cleveland Archdeaconry I have ventured to oppose myself, and at a meeting of about 30 had ten hands in favour of toleration […] I trust your continental experience of Catholic toleration will lead you to think me justified in meditating this retribution to an oppressed portion of our fellow Christians'.[22]

---

19 *Letters of a Literary Antiquary*, ed. by A. T. Utterson (n.p.: Privately printed, 1938), p. 12.
20 Michael Sadleir, 'Archdeacon Francis Wrangham: A Supplement', *Library* 4 (1939), p. 437.
21 Ibid., p. 438.
22 Sadleir, 'Archdeacon Francis Wrangham: A Supplement', p. 437.

Wrangham's political views went beyond Catholic emancipation, and his quiet radicalism largely presented itself as a propensity for social programmes, which included starting a saving scheme for his parishioners, a free dispensary, a lending library and the lending of a sum of money to allow the purchase of a village cow. This was not simply a series of charitable acts but well-thought-out programmes designed to improve education, alleviate poverty and promote self-sufficiency among the disadvantaged of his diocese. He was not content to merely carry out these acts in his own diocese either but also attempted to promulgate the ideas among other clergy and was forthright in support for those whom he considered to be fighting the same fight. The most conspicuous example of this is his support for Leigh and John Hunt even through their prosecution for libel, by subscribing to *The Examiner* and encouraging others to do the same, which was a brave and unusual act for a cleric of the period. The courage he displayed in supporting his ideal of social justice is especially striking because in his letters and other writings Wrangham appears to be a mild-mannered and humble man, certainly not an obvious candidate as a fiery social campaigner. His mixture of politics and religion also highlights the fact that many of the Roxburghe Club, whether overtly political or not, were clergymen, which, of course, was a vocation which often carried with it implicit notions of social duty for those who were sincere in their calling. Then, as now, there was often a wide crossover between social conscience and political activity.

Not all clerics were, of course, so committed, and seemingly less sincere in his vocation was the Hon. and Rev. George Neville Grenville, who was a successful clergyman, at least in monetary terms, and who, at least from the distance of time, appears to have been more interested in the career aspect of his calling than the religious element. Certainly, if the obituaries of the time are anything to go by, he was considered by his contemporaries to be a man who had made unfair use of his family's connections in the cause of his own advancement. One obituary describes how he was first nominated (by his father Lord Braybrooke) to be the master of Magdalene College, Cambridge, at the age of 24 and despite the objections of the fellows who primarily objected to his youth but also, possibly, to the overt nepotism of the appointment. He went on to be appointed to the lucrative livings of Butleigh in Somerset and Ellingham in Norfolk before finally being appointed as dean of Windsor. 'He was', as the article icily phrased it, 'a singular instance of family preferment.'[23]

---

23 'Obituary of the Year', *The Church of England Quarterly Review* 36 (London: Sampson Low, 1854), p. 525.

However, in his defence it should also be noted that after his death he was praised for his great generosity towards the poor. His fellow Roxburgher, the Rev. William Holwell Carr, was another man of the cloth with no obvious religious calling; his only interests appear to have been collecting, and he is described as being 'an assertive man, obsessed with prices and provenance' and as a person incapable of small talk or inconsequential pleasantries.[24] He had hurriedly acquired a degree in divinity in order to gain a valuable living at Menheniot in Cornwall, and on gaining the desired post he immediately employed a curate at £100 per year, retained the remaining £1034 income and never visited the living, preferring to spend his time collecting books and artwork.

Surprisingly perhaps, the Reverend T. F. Dibdin, having at first trained for law and finding himself dissatisfied with his career choice deciding to take a divinity degree, was a considerably more sincere cleric. Although he could not be said to have lived the life of an ascetic, he did appear to be genuine and well meaning in his duties as vicar of the valuable living of Exning in Suffolk and later additionally as the Rector of the newly built St. Mary's in Bryanstone Square and as Chaplain in Ordinary to her Majesty.[25] A High Church Protestant, he published sermons which are straightforward, realistic, tolerant and kind in tone. While it is easy to imagine that, because he dedicated so much time to the pursuit of books his clerical duties may have suffered accordingly, he certainly was not an absentee cleric and appears to have had a genuine vocation to the church.

One extremely important group of early Roxburghe Club members and clerics who have, so far, been omitted from this list are the schoolmasters. While this group lacks the obvious glamour of the aristocratic members or the high profile of many of the MPs, they should not be dismissed as dull, chalk-dusted and ink-stained background characters. These men were powerful within their own sphere, and in literary terms their influence within the public school system (and therefore in society) offers a credible mechanism through which the study of literature and, in particular, early English texts gained a popularity and acceptance previously unknown. An excellent example of such a man is the Rev. Edward Craven Hawtrey, who was the son of a vicar and educated at Eton, becoming in turn assistant master, headmaster and later provost of the school. Hawtrey is discussed at some length, and with affection, in the memoire *Eton in the Forties*, written by Arthur Duke Coleridge, great-nephew of the poet. This work gives an interesting insight into Hawtrey's

---

24 Judy Egerton, 'William Holwell Carr', *Oxford Dictionary of National Biography* (Oxford: Oxford University Press, 2004), www.oxforddnb.com/view/article/4757.
25 'Rev. T. F. Dibdin, D.D.', *Gentleman's Magazine* 29 (1848), 87–92 (p. 87).

religious views, especially concerning Anglo-Catholicism, and explains that, while he was no theologian and had no understanding of the 'controversies of the age in which men were swayed by Newman or by Arnold', this offered no obstacle to him forming closing working relationships with those of his staff who were themselves Anglo-Catholic.[26] Coleridge states that had Hawtrey been 'suspicious, narrow-minded, or cold-hearted, he would certainly have quarrelled with three or four of the best of his assistants in the first ten years of his government'.[27] This was not simply a matter of overlooking his colleagues' religious views but rather an active stance on his part that necessitated his support of teachers who might otherwise have been driven from their posts by religious intolerance, a point overtly referenced by Coleridge, who writes that 'had he even let them be thwarted, more than they were thwarted, by the alarmed Protestantism of Eton College, he would have lost the services of men who could not be replaced'.[28] As well as underlining Hawtrey's personal religious tolerance, this account serves to demonstrate how he approached his administrative duties within the school and how his methods differed enough from those of other headmasters as to make them memorable. In a more general sense it illustrates the degree to which the personal views of clerical masters within the public schools could and did impact upon the careers of their subordinates and, by extension, the day-to-day teaching of pupils and the knowledge and opinions to which they were exposed within the school environment.

In a more straightforward sense, Hawtrey's personality, his love of learning and his desire to encourage academic ability in his charges, even though his own abilities were sometimes outshone by his pupils, were viewed by his former pupils as formative in their later careers. Coleridge writes that 'year after year Hawtrey's beloved young men went to the Universities, better read and better trained than their predecessors, even if not so well read or well trained as many representatives of less fashionable schools [...] whole tribes of Eton men seasoned with the accurate philology which he had never himself acquired – men who knew his defects, and were, notwithstanding, indebted to him, and consciously grateful to him for their better schooling'.[29] What Hawtrey lacked as a teacher in terms of specialization, he made up for in breadth of interest and enthusiastic pursuit of knowledge from a wide range of sources, many of which one might presume proceeded from his own

---

26 Arthur Duke Coleridge, *Eton in the Forties by an Old Colleger* (London: Richard Bentley, 1896), p. 288.
27 Ibid.
28 Ibid., p. 289.
29 Ibid., pp. 284–85.

extensive library, as Coleridge writes 'of this Headmaster's teaching and influence over his division I have always thought highly. The willing and intelligent boys gained much, learnt to take wider views of things, heard illustrations from many a language and literature'.[30] Here we see the truest public value of a Roxburghe Collector's library.

Similarly, another Roxburghe member, the Venerable Archdeacon Butler, Lord Bishop of Lichfield, was headmaster of the Royal Free Grammar School at Shrewsbury and the grandfather of the author Samuel Butler, who wrote the Archdeacon's memoir, *Life and Letters of Dr Samuel Butler*, in 1896. Butler appears to have had a positive effect on education in the public schools of that period, and a letter written to him by Henry Drury (of Harrow) states that 'the advance of learning among the young has decidedly, at all English schools of any note, generally taken its impulse from you, and where it has not, as at Westminster, the decadence has been doleful. Whatever Eton and Harrow may be, I can safely say they would not have reached even any moderate excellence if you had not been the agitator'.[31] Butler appears to have shared the sympathy towards Catholic emancipation expressed by many other Roxburghe members, and this topic formed the greater part of a controversial sermon preached by him at St. Mary's, Cambridge, in 1811. The sermon was delivered in front of the Duke of Gloucester to mark the occasion of the Duke becoming the Chancellor of St. Mary's, and was later published as an article under the title 'Christian Liberty'. Butler, like Hawtrey and Wrangham, was obviously not afraid to follow his conscience in supporting an unpopular cause against the tide of opinion favoured by his fellow clerics.

There were of course other, less celebrated, schoolmaster clerics among the club members, including the aforementioned Rev. Henry Drury, the son of Joseph Drury, the headmaster of Harrow. Drury became assistant master at Harrow from 1801, and master of the lower school from 1833 to 1841. He was a friend of Byron and conducted the funeral service for Byron's daughter Allegra. He was also a close friend of Dibdin's and apparently socially popular, but appears to have left little record of either his political or religious views. The Rev. James William Dodd, second usher at Westminster, again leaves little direct indication of his character or beliefs despite his being one of the Westminster staff blamed by Southey for his expulsion from the school and as a result mentioned several times in his poem 'To Ignorance':

Had I been ignorant I had been blest
Unmarkd by Vice by Calumny & Dodd —

30 Ibid., p. 388.
31 Ibid., p. 2.

[...]
Revenge & Infamy & Hell & Dodd
With ghastly smile await the Doctor's nod.
[...]
Revenge with ghastly pleasure smiles on Dodd
And Malice lurks beneath the sacred gown —[32]

To what extent Southey's obviously negative view of Dodd's character was a true portrayal is difficult to evaluate. Southey certainly bore a somewhat obsessive grudge against all the staff of Westminster for what he considered to be his unfair expulsion following his creation of a magazine called the *Flagellant*, which criticized the practise of corporal punishment in schools, but whether the conditions were worse at Westminster than at other public schools is open to debate (although Drury in his letter to Butler had certainly believed it to be a less progressive school). The purpose of including Dodd here is not to debate the rights or wrongs of the matter, but merely to illustrate the extent to which another Roxburghe member was an influential, if in this case contentious, figure in public schools of that period.

Overall, a picture begins to form of a group of men who are a long way from the frivolous, superficial dilettantes they have so often been painted. These are not empty-headed fops, playing at publishing and concerned only with the fashionable and superficial pursuits available to their rank; rather, it becomes clear that, whatever their faults and shortcomings, they were often deeply serious men who were profoundly involved in the most important and difficult events of their time. Many members were influential, hard-working political actors of the period who are striking for their obvious sense of social responsibility and conscientious in their duties as men of authority and power. It is thought-provoking to consider whether these widely disparate men who were brought together through a love of books, often to socialize with people whom they would have been unlikely to encounter under other circumstances, were creating a platform for an exchange of ideas – literary, political and religious – that could not have failed to form a unique club outlook on the books that they collected and reprinted.

The Roxburghe Club, in a world before methods of inexpensive mass communication such as the telephone or even cheap postage rates, acted, in the way of many such societies, as a forum for the exchange of ideas. Through the eighteenth century on to the period of the early Roxburghe, literary activities

---

32 Robert Southey, 'To Ignorance', *The Collected Letters of Robert Southey Part 1 1791–1797*, Romantic Circles, University of Maryland, http://www.rc.umd.edu/editions/southey_letters/Part_One/HTML/letterEEd.26.6.html [accessed 20 December 2013].

often took place in social settings, including coffee house groups, dining societies and taverns. The Roxburghe, formed by men whose own formative years often lay several decades earlier, unsurprisingly continued in this Georgian tradition. Not just a meeting place for wealthy high-status men, the Roxburghe created a social mix that brought together people with scholarship and people with money and power (and often considerable education, scholarship and intellect in their own right). The club allowed ideas to be exchanged but also to be disseminated back to members' country estates, parishes and constituencies and from there perhaps to their provincial friends and neighbours. Perhaps most importantly it allowed their ideas to be circulated within some of the most prestigious and influential public schools in Britain. The Roxburghe, and eventually other book societies and clubs like it, had the potential to be a vehicle for new ideas about publishing, the importance of protecting and promoting what had gone before and of looking forward towards the creation of a national literature. Many members, although perhaps not influential politically, were, as schoolmasters and clerics, responsible for the education of the new generation and instrumental in forming the shape of current education and future scholarship and attitudes. Many ideas raised at these dinners must thus have filtered into the processes that have created modern literary scholarship. The club provided an environment admirably suited to fruitful interaction between ideas of public duty, national heritage and nationalism and literary appreciation to create something that important nineteenth-century editors such as Madden, whose methods have seemed more acceptable to modern academic eyes, could build on when it came to reprinting and popularizing our older national literature.

Chapter 5

CLUB MEMBERS AND THEIR BOOK COLLECTIONS

Everybody knows that if a shabby tract may be lost or thrown away, a book once handsomely clothed in morocco is practically safe from destruction.[1]

This quotation from Seymour de Ricci highlights the immense importance of the act of placing a book into a collection, that is, the degree of safety imparted by the ennoblement of a text through its proximity to other equally beautifully preserved volumes. This is a frank admission of the truth that, however much scholars might stress the intrinsic value of a text over the aesthetic value placed on it by many book collectors, everyone in the end loves a beautiful book in a handsome binding. Such a binding will ensure that a text might last long enough to be appreciated for its intrinsic value. On this level alone it can be said that the Roxburghe founding members provided a solid service to literature by preserving between them a vast quantity of early printed books and manuscripts within their personal collections as well as helping create the wider appetite for and awareness of such items. That would be faint praise if they are viewed as mere bibliomaniacs, collecting indiscriminately and on purely aesthetic grounds.

Much information is available about the collections owned by these men because most of them were catalogued, if not for their own use and the convenience of their friends, then certainly when they came to auction. A look at the books contained within these collections reveals that their owners were not only collecting books that fell within the usual collector's remit such as rarities, first editions, large paper copies and so on but also that most of these bibliophiles were also constructing libraries that reflected their personal intellectual interests and expertise. It is easy to be dazzled by the expensive rarities that appeared in every big collection of the day, but often the greater interest lies in these more personal collections that

1 De Ricci, *English Collectors of Books 1530–1930*, p. 71.

coexist alongside the more famous works. In this chapter I attempt to give an, unavoidably brief, outline of the books collected by the Roxburghe Club members during this period in order to illustrate how diverse and specialized these collections really were.

One of the less well-known names amongst early Roxburghers was that of a friend of Sir Walter Scott, Robert Lang, whose library when auctioned in 1828, raised £2837 and contained volumes of sufficient interest and significance as to ensure that a number were bought for the Royal Library at Paris. His library reflected its owner's expertise in ancient French poetry, and his collection was described by Dibdin as 'not only one of the most curious and beautiful libraries in the kingdom – thoroughly *sui generis* – but he was intimately conversant with their contents'. He goes on to say that 'Mr. Lang's earlier French poetry was matchless in quality and condition; and it is no small commendation of their owner to say, that Mr. Douce affirmed he had a more intimate knowledge of early French literature than any individual (not even excepting himself) with whom he was acquainted'.[2] Although not one of the largest collections owned by a Roxburghe member, nor one of the most famous, it exemplifies the perfect combination of the collector's impulse with private avocation and specialist knowledge that characterizes so many of the libraries formed by the early club members. Similarly, Haslewood owned an interesting and significant collection that absolutely reflected his own personal interests. A partner in his uncle's legal firm, he inhabited 'two rooms (of the size of a housekeeper's china closet), on the second and third floors at the back of his house', where he lived among his collections of books, broadsheets and theatre memorabilia.[3] A quiet, very religious man, his enthusiasm and knowledge, on a wide range of literary subjects, led him to write and edit both books and a bewildering number and variety of articles. Producing such an output of work on such a range of subjects requires a great deal of reference material, especially in those days before easy access to specialist archives, and despite his relatively limited means (in contrast at least to many other members of the club), he accumulated several important collections, notably of ephemera, early poetry and books on hunting, hawking and fishing. These were not overall items that were hotly contested at auctions, but a private interest pursued with sufficient zeal and discrimination can prove to be a financially sound investment, and on his death his collection raised around £2,500 at auction for his beneficiaries. The auction catalogue describes his library as containing, among other items 'a very curious, extensive and extraordinary collection of

---

2 Dibdin, *Reminiscences*, p. 372.
3 Ibid., p. 418.

proclamations from the year 1590 to 1710, including that against Milton and many others of great rarity'.[4]

Another Roxburghe member who collected with an undeviating eye to his own intellectual interests was James Boswell, a talented poet and a writer with a strong sense of fun, described by Dibdin as being 'a happy vein of the broadest humour'.[5] His library was sold in 1825 following his untimely death, and it has been observed that the sale catalogue proved him to have had 'a knowledgeable interest in opera, music and continental literature, and to have been a capable Hispanist, and indicates the depth and range of his intellectual and collecting interests, as well as the breadth of his acquaintance with books, both old and current, and eminent literary people'.[6] His elder brother, Alexander, who inherited the Auchinleck Library, also possessed a personal, eclectic taste in literature, including a special interest in Scottish verse and ballads. His purchasing emphasizes an element that is easily overlooked for many of these collections, which is the sense of obligation often engendered in an inherited library. As a Victorian commentator wrote about Boswell's library, 'in its rich repositories he had gratified his strong literary tastes, and he was so unwearied in his efforts to repay the debt by increasing its treasures, that at *belles lettres* auctions he was the terror of every book-hunter'.[7] For many of the Roxburghe collectors there existed, alongside their impulse to gather books that interested them personally, an imperative to preserve and enhance the work of previous generations temporarily entrusted to their keeping.

Of course, most of the club members had no such burden to carry, needing only to please their own taste or, in the case of the more scholarly, creating a useful working reference library in a world without Google. Classical scholar Henry Drury, somewhat predictably, collected classical works in Greek and Latin. At his death, these constituted the greater part of his library, the rest being made up predominantly by Roxburghe volumes, editions printed by Alexander Boswell at the Auchinleck press and other works privately printed by friends and acquaintances. Drury also possessed more than 250 medieval manuscripts and his entire collection was sold in 1827 in 4,729 lots. His fellow bibliophile educator, Hawtrey, described by Dibdin as 'Priscian, the classical and the accomplished', also collected volumes that largely represented

---

4 *Catalogue of the Curious and Valuable Library of the late Joseph Haslewood, Esq, FSA* (W. Nicol, 1833).
5 Dibdin, *Reminiscences*, p. 388.
6 Gordon Turnbull, 'James Boswell', *Oxford Dictionary of National Biography*, www.oxforddnb.com.
7 *The Poetical Works of Sir Alexander Boswell.* ed. by Robert Howie Smith (Glasgow: Maurice Ogle, 1871), p. xxvii; italics in original.

his own working library and may perhaps fall under the description of what William Roberts classed as 'literary men, who aimed rather at getting together a useful library than one of rarities', adding sadly that 'the sale of all such libraries makes a very sorry show beside that of the more ostentatious collections'.[8] This description would certainly fit the disposal of Hawtrey's books, which sold for sums that Roberts, at least, considered to be 'far below their worth', and this is borne out by Dibdin, who considered Hawtrey's collection to have contained some significant rarities, writing in *Bibliophobia* that 'books are his "dear delight": and Bibles, among those books, the primary object of attraction. The owner has a rare set of them – such as, in a private collection, are eclipsed only by those at Kensington and Althorp'.[9] Praise indeed from Dibdin, and again in *Reminiscences* he writes, 'I know of few libraries which compete with that of our newly elected member. It is at once choice and copious, learned and resplendent'.[10] Hawtrey's library certainly mirrored his interest in linguistics, and Francis St. John Thackery, the author of his memoir, writing about his collections points out that 'comparative philology was only in its infancy in Hawtrey's time, but it was represented by such authors as Bopp and Benfey; and there was a host of Grammars: Arabic, Hindustani, Persian, Caribee, etc., a Basque Catechism printed at Bayonne, and monographs in all the different Italian dialects, Ferrarese, Milanese, Bolognese, the Maltese and Neapolitan, and the patois of Rome. Nothing of linguistic interest escaped his notice; recent issues were there from the continental presses of Dijon, Turin, Florence, Vienna, a Romaic-English Lexicon, and a collection of Sicilian poems printed respectively at Corfu and Palermo'.[11] Thackery also gives what is perhaps the simplest and truest explanation of why Hawtrey and many other Roxburghe members were not the superficial bibliomaniacs of the popular imagination, saying that

> it may be granted that he was not a profound scholar. To combine great erudition with the labour inseparable from the government of a large Public School is next to impossible, one of the two must give way. But neither was he a mere dilettante and amateur lover of books, and for every volume on his shelves he could give an excellent reason why it was there, and say something in connection with it of real interest and instruction, that was well worth listening to. He encouraged the love

---

8 Roberts, *The Book-Hunter in London*, p. 71.
9 T. F. Dibdin, *Bibliophobia* (London: Henry Bohn, 1832), p. 59.
10 Dibdin, *Reminiscences*, vol. 1, p. 411.
11 Francis St. John Thackery, *Memoir of Edward Craven Hawtrey* (London: George Bell, 1896), pp. 177–78.

of literature, not only by his munificent gifts, but by the very fact of his amassing literary treasures in a princely spirit, and imparting to others the pleasure they bestow.[12]

The study of linguistics is a common thread running through the club members' collections, and Roger Wilbraham, characterized as Sempronius in Dibdin's *Decameron*, focused much of his collection on early works printed in southern European languages. The books contained in his library were certainly rare, but that is of almost secondary importance to the range, which included 'many of the works of the Italian dramatic writers of the sixteenth and seventeenth centuries; facetiae, numerous volumes of old English poetry and plays; and most of the ancient and modern lexicographers'.[13] Despite this embarrassment of riches, Dibdin felt that the true stars of the collection were its volumes of travel and famous voyages, but both commentators could agree on Mr. Wilbraham's keen interest in lexicography, a subject in which Dibdin calls him 'as eminently rich as he was confessedly learned'.[14]

By way of a contrast, John Dent was almost certainly a collector whose primary interest lay in the rarity, beauty and financial value of books rather than in the intellectual importance of their texts. There is little proof of him possessing any specific literary interests beyond the normal pursuits of an educated man of the time but one area in which Dent's collection was particularly strong was that of illuminated manuscripts, which implies that he probably had a sophisticated awareness of the visual or historical aspects of some of his volumes, even if his literary interests may have been slighter than that of some other members. Dent's collection of printed and manuscript items was considered to be one of the most valuable libraries, for its size, of this period and was greatly augmented by his purchase of the Heathcote library, which Dent bought in its entirety in 1807, with the duplicates arising from this purchase being sold through two sales held in 1808. When Dent's collection was sold in 1827 at two auctions held on 29 March and 25 April, it raised only £15,040, and Dibdin noted the lowered prices commanded by choice items in this sale as the first indicator of the end of the golden period of bibliomania. He wrote that during the auction 'the GREAT GUN in the library was the first Livy of 1469, upon vellum [...] and when the hammer fell upon *that* book, how fell its *price* too! It had been obtained by Mr. Dent at the sale of Sir Mark's library for

---

12 Ibid., pp. 175–76.
13 William Clarke, *Repertorium Bibliographicum; or, Some Account of the Most Celebrated British Libraries*, 2 vols (London: William Clarke, 1819), II, p. 383.
14 Dibdin, *Reminiscences*, I, pp. 406–7.

about the half of its original cost to that Baronet – namely 903l.; and it was sold for little more than one *quarter*'.[15]

Dent's apparently somewhat unsympathetic personality led him to often be the butt of jokes, and occasionally these were targeted at his book collecting.[16] One such story recounts that 'Mr. Canning used to tell a story of Mr. Dent – a bibliomaniac of the true Dibdin type – whom he once caught with a book before him "upside down"'.[17] Whether this was true or not (it certainly sounds apocryphal), and whatever his own feelings were towards reading, his personal love of books did not extend to the desire for them to be generally available beyond the confines of his own library. Dent's stance in Parliament as an anti-abolitionist has already been mentioned, and during one debate Wilberforce argued that 'Africans must be considered to be civilised people as in some areas they were known to possess books'. Dent responded angrily, saying, 'Books! The blackamoors have books! and this the hon. mover gives as a reason for not exporting them as slaves! I think if the hon. gentleman had recollected all the mischief that books have done, especially of late years, in the world, he might have spared this argument at least. What produced the French revolution? Books! The house will not be induced to put a stop to the slave trade, in order that the inhabitants of Africa might stay at home to be corrupted by reading books'.[18]

In general the less individualistic collections such as Dent's, those that more closely followed the fashionable pattern of book collection, reveal themselves to be the largest collections, presumably because they often belonged to the richest club members, who could afford to compete for the rare or more sought-after items at auction. Book collectors without particular specialist tastes often acquired a large range of volumes, especially through buying entire libraries as Dent had done, but large collections did not always necessarily mean that the owner had any less intellectual interest in their collection. One of the foremost collections (in sheer numbers at least) was that belonging to Richard Heber, a classical scholar and an extremely wealthy man who owned at least eight houses throughout Europe, all at the time of his death apparently filled to capacity with his books. As his obituary described the situation,

---

15 Dibdin, *Reminiscences*, I, p. 409; italics in original.
16 His dour personality may be explained, at least in part, by the fact that he suffered from *tic douloureux*, or as we would now call it, trigeminal neuralgia. This disorder was painful enough to cause him to attempt suicide on at least one occasion.
17 Hitchman, p. 272. William Roberts, p. 69, also mentions this anecdote, without reference but possibly based on the account in Hitchman's essay.
18 Related by John Styles, *Memoirs of the Life of the Right Honourable George Canning* (London: T. Tegg, 1828), I, pp. 156–57.

Some years ago he built a new library at his house at Hodnet; which is said to be full. His residence in Pimlico, where he died, is filled like Magliabechi's at Florence, with books from the top to the bottom – every chair, every table, every passage, containing piles of erudition. He had another house in York-street, leading to St James-street, Westminster, laden from the ground floor to the garret, with curious books. He had a library in the High-street, Oxford, an immense library at Paris, another at Antwerp, another at Brussels, another at Ghent, and at other places in the Low Countries and in Germany.[19]

In retrospect, the vast quantities of books that he owned are unsurprising as he had been buying nearly every item of interest to himself that had come onto the market over the previous thirty years. Yet the obsessive scale of his collection only became apparent, even it seems to his friends, following his death, when the disposal of his estate became a vast undertaking. The sale of Heber's collection was described by Hill Burton as being 'the largest book-sale probably that ever was in the world', and he goes on to say that estimates of the collection containing 'books in six figures' may well have been correct as the sales catalogue filled 'five thick octavo volumes'.[20] This was confirmed by Percy Hetherington Fitzgerald, who on examining the copy of the sales catalogue held in the Athenaeum Library, wrote that 'it would seem that there were 119, 613 volumes sold! which it required no less than two hundred and two days, or nearly seven months, to sell; and the sum realised was £56, 774'.[21] Heber is famously reported to have often said, 'Well you see, Sir, no man can comfortably do without three copies of a book. One he must have for a show copy, and he will probably keep it at his country-house; another he will require for his own use and reference; and unless he is inclined to part with this, which is very inconvenient, or risk the injury of his best copy, he must needs have a third at the service of his friends'.[22] This may have been an 'after the fact' justification for what he must have eventually realized was an unhealthy approach to book collecting and one which saw him purchasing large quantities of duplicate volumes. He was, however, a generous lender of books and willing to allow scholars and authors the use of his library, so some duplicates may well have been required for that purpose.

19 'Richard Heber, Esq.', *Gentleman's Magazine* 155 (London: January 1834), p. 109.
20 Burton, *The Book Hunter*, p. 98, although Hetherington Fitzgerald states that it was six volumes in *The Book Fancier* (London: S. Low, Marston, Searle & Rivington, 1887), p. 231.
21 Fitzgerald, *The Book Fancier*, p. 231.
22 'Richard Heber, Esq.', *Gentleman's Magazine*, 155 (London: Jan 1834), p. 107.

Even this immense collection had originated with the perfectly reasonable desire to assemble a library of Latin poetry. That aspiration quickly turned into a passion for buying books of all types to the extent that even Dibdin, not usually at a loss for words, felt himself unable to say how Heber should be classified as a book collector. The Latin poetry collection led to an extensive collection of Greek and Latin classics, which he extended into Spanish (including a collection of Mexican books), French, Italian and Portuguese volumes. Thereafter Heber's collection expanded in limitless directions, although its strongest vein was that of early English literature of all types. He did not restrict himself to collecting printed books, and part four of the sale of his library consisted of 1,717 valuable manuscripts, many of which were bought to augment public collections such as those of the British Museum and the Bodleian.

Sadly Heber's later life was marred by scandal. In 1825 he had allegedly made sexual advances to two young men at the Athenaeum Club, one of whom had threatened to bring the matter to court. Heber made a partial confession to his friend Henry Hobhouse, who advised him to go into exile abroad where he would be safe from prosecution and public scandal. While Heber was still out of the country, an article appeared in the *John Bull* magazine alluding to his close attachment to Charles Henry Hartshorne and implying this was a homosexual relationship. This considerably more widely broadcast accusation added to Heber's difficulties and made his exile and the reason for it a far more public matter. Hartshorne, remaining in the country, prosecuted Edward Shackell, the editor, for libel and eventually, with financial aid from Heber, won the case. Heber, however, did not return to Britain until 1831 and thereafter lived the life of a recluse until his death in 1833, suffering social exclusion, ill health (physical and possibly mental) and the eventual dwindling of his wealth through his obsessive book collecting. Dibdin remained his friend to the end and was instrumental in finding Heber's will, which had been missing for several months after his death and which, inevitably, turned up on a bookshelf hidden between two volumes. Perhaps one of the best descriptions of Heber was by Leon H. Vincent, who wrote that 'the name of Heber suggests the thought that all men who buy books are not bibliophiles. He alone is worthy the title who acquires his volumes with something like passion. One may buy books like a gentleman, and that is very well. One may buy books like a gentleman and a scholar, which counts for something more. But to be truly of the elect one must resemble Richard Heber, and buy books like a gentleman, a scholar, and a madman'.[23]

---

23 Leon H. Vincent, *The Bibliotaph and Other People* (Boston and New York: Houghton and Mifflin, 1899), p. 2.

Earl Spencer, the club president, also bought books on a prodigious scale but in a purposeful and orderly process of acquisition, and he held a number of sales to dispose of duplicates when necessary and to recoup money to offset his debts.[24] This process of distillation was essential. As well as his constant ongoing purchasing, carried out with the intention of owning every volume in as perfect a condition as possible, Spencer also bought a number of complete library collections. These included Count Karoly Reviczky's library, bought in 1789 for £2,500; Stanesby Alchorne's library, purchased in 1813 for £3,400; and the Duke di Cassano Serra's collection, acquired in 1820. One sale, held by Spencer to dispose of, among other items, duplicates resulting from his purchase of the Alchorne library, raised £1,769. The Spencer Library has been catalogued, analysed and described in far greater detail than can be attempted here, but the barest outline serves to give an impression of the scale and importance of this famous collection.[25] Along with his title, Earl Spencer inherited an already extensive library, which he added to and improved throughout much of his life. He succeeded in gathering together an important collection of early and rare editions, which were later purchased from his grandson in 1892 by Enriqueta Rylands, the widow of John Rylands, a wealthy industrialist. She installed the collection at the public library she had endowed in Manchester in the memory of her husband. She paid £210,000 for the collection, at that time, the highest price ever paid for a private collection.

Principally Spencer collected early printed items, and his collection contained entire series of the works that had proceeded from the early presses, including, by 1864, 57 separate works by Caxton; this figure included three items believed to be sole surviving copies (out of 27 Caxton items existing in unique copies that were known of). This was at a time when the British Museum only owned 55 works by Caxton, although in its defence 11 of the Museum's volumes were considered unique copies. It is difficult to grasp the scale of Earl Spencer's collection or the financial and cultural value of the books it contained. De Ricci described Earl Spencer as 'one of the greatest book-collectors, not only in English history, but even in the history of the

---

24 For an interesting discussion of Earl Spencer's financial position, see Kristian Jensen, *Revolution and the Antiquarian Book*, p. 43.
25 Among works covering the contents of this massive library, see T. F. Dibdin, *Book Rarities, or a Descriptive Catalogue of Some of the most Curious Rare and Valuable Books of Early Date, Chiefly in the Collection of George John, Earl Spencer, K.G.* (n.p., 1811); T. F. Dibdin, *Bibliotheca Spenceriana* (1814–15); T. F. Dibdin, *Aedes Althorpianae* (1822); T. F. Dibdin, *Catalogue of the Books Printed in the Fifteenth Century Formerly in the Library of the Duke de Cassano Serra and Now in Earl Spencer's Collection* (1823); Samuel Timmins, *Lord Spencer's Library: A Sketch of a Visit to Althorp, Northamptonshire* (Northampton: Taylor, 1870).

world'.²⁶ That assertion seems reasonable given that by 1814 the collection contained 45,000 volumes, many of extraordinary intrinsic value. Dibdin, while attempting to convey the richness of the library, listed the Spencer collection's 23 Latin Bibles printed before 1500; a further 12 printed between 1500 and 1600;9 German Bibles printed before 1500; and 5 printed in the following century, besides numerous early Bibles printed in other languages and explains that 'there are also twenty-three more Bibles (and perhaps of late still more) in all the other languages of Europe. Be it remembered, too, that these Bibles have been selected, not with a view to number, but to critical importance and rarity'.²⁷ Edward Edwards neatly summarized the benefits to the wider literary world of such a collection, saying that 'Ebert [...] was once pleased to ask, "of what utility to literature is the Spencer library?" The question admits of very many and very conclusive answers. Many enduring works have drawn largely on its stores. Many pleasurable associations in literary biography connect themselves inseparably with its history'.²⁸ He goes on to list a few of the authors who accessed the Spencer library in the process of writing their own works, including Samuel Sotheby, who in the course of producing his *Principia Typographia* made extensive use of the rare volumes that could not be found elsewhere (and Edwards notes that Earl Spencer frequently sent the precious books from Althorp to London for Sotheby's convenience). Robert Southey also received access to the library, with Spencer generously allowing him to produce an edited edition of the 'Wygfair Caxton', which was published as the *Byrth, Lyfe, and Actes of Kyng Arthur*. Edwards also cites Edward Gibbon, the author of the *History of the Decline and Fall of the Roman Empire*, who visited Althorp to consult the 70 early editions of Cicero contained in the collection. This was a series of which Timmins later pointed out, 'nearly fifty [...] were printed before 1473, mostly representing different "texts," and thus practically as valuable as manuscripts now lost for ever'.²⁹

Some of Earl Spencer's methods of collecting may appear morally dubious to modern eyes (and raised a few contemporary eyebrows as well) and resulted in many early books passing from the ecclesiastic collections that had preserved them, to his own private collection. One specific example occurred in 1811 when Spencer, or rather Dibdin on his behalf, negotiated with the Chapter of Lincoln Cathedral for the purchase of several Caxtons bequeathed to the cathedral by Dean Michael Honywood in 1681. Hazlitt, not mincing words, describes it as 'the precious Honywood bequest, improperly sold to Dibdin for

---

26 De Ricci, *English Collectors of Books 1530–1930*, p. 76.
27 Dibdin, *Reminiscences*, I, pp. 579–80.
28 Edwards, *Libraries and Founders of Libraries*, pp. 409–10.
29 Timmins, *Lord Spencer's Library*, p. 9.

500 guineas'.[30] This type of transaction was far from rare in the early nineteenth century, and certainly not rare among the members of the Roxburghe Club. In another instance, Benjamin Wheatley, a bookseller and auctioneer, sold a bundle of 'poetical tracts' that he had purchased from the Chapter Library at Lincoln to William Bolland for 80 guineas. When the items later came to auction, one item from the collection, *The Rape of Lucrece*, raised 100 guineas on its own.[31] A justification of sorts can be found for the practice if, as has been said of Earl Spencer's purchases, those in charge of the ancient collections 'were of opinion that they better discharged their duty, as trustees, by parting with some extremely rare but, in their present habitation, unused books, and by applying the proceeds to the acquisition of common, but much wanted works of modern dates'.[32] Of course, in this capacity the Earl was more than happy to oblige and was apparently always prepared to pay the full market value of the works, thus supplying the libraries with their much needed funds. Whether or not this rosy picture was generally the case in such undertakings, it seems likely in the case of Earl Spencer that his public profile and wealth might have often brought more pressure to bear on trustees than the financial position regarding the collections they guarded. It could, of course, also be argued that the willingness of the trustees to part with the items supposedly in their care reflected a more general lack of regard towards such early works of literature, as already evidenced by the slighting remarks in the letters pages of journals referring to their suitability for use as waste paper. It is also a matter of conjecture as to what percentage of the funds raised in this fashion was actually applied to the supply of new books for those ecclesiastical libraries rather than making their way directly into the pockets of those guardians who were so eager to sell the volumes.

Although the Earl at the height of the bibliomania was one of the most prolific purchasers of that time, it would do him a grave disservice to call him a bibliomaniac. He spent vast sums but not indiscriminately, as demonstrated by his refusal to continue to bid for the famous Valdarfer at the Roxburghe sale after the Marquis of Blandford had raised his bid by the final £10. The Earl was content to let the volume go, and although he could not have foreseen it, to later purchase the same book for £900 after the auction of Blandford's library. As Leigh Hunt, a spectator at the Roxburghe Sale, later wrote, 'what satisfaction the Marquis got out of his victory I cannot say. The Earl, who

---

30 Quoted in W. Carew Hazlitt, *Book Collector* (London: John Grant, 1904), p. 34.
31 Roberts, *The Book-Hunter in London*, p. 69.
32 Edwards, *Libraries and Founders of Libraries*, p. 410.

I believe, was a genuine lover of books, could go home and reconcile himself to his defeat by reading the work in a cheaper edition'.[33]

Descending from the high-powered book-buying world of Earl Spencer, we come to Sir Mark Masterman Sykes, the possessor of another inherited library, although one of more modest dimensions. As with so many Roxburghe members, his library had been amassed over a long period of time and long predated the high tide of bibliomania. His father, Sir Christopher Sykes, had built the family library at Sledmere, and thereafter Sir Mark had, for more than thirty years, supplemented its resources with well-considered and valuable volumes. The Sykes collection was particularly focused on first editions of classical works, and among other important texts contained early works printed by Fust and Schöeffer, Sweynheym and Pannartz. Like most Roxburghe members he collected a variety of works produced by the early printers, especially those from the Aldine Press, of which he owned a number of perfect copies. As well as the expected incunabula he collected works of Elizabethan literature and early English poetry. Though not a committed collector of manuscripts, the small number he did purchase included some significant items, and, taken as a whole, his library was a rich but largely unsurprising collection, which eventually raised £18,700 at auction.

More unexpected perhaps is Sir Samuel Egerton Brydges, who, although known as an author, poet and critic, is not – interestingly given his membership of the Roxburghe Club – widely regarded as a significant book collector. He must, presumably, as a reasonably wealthy man of letters with a passion for seventeenth-century poetry, have owned a private library of some sort, but there is no mention other than in his own letters, of him frequenting the auction rooms or scouring the booksellers' shops and he is not mentioned in any of the usual volumes on book collectors. Probably he had no interest in the acquisition of particular volumes except as reference material and equally possibly very little spare money for collecting. He certainly haunted the reading room of the British Museum a great deal, and was very probably given ample research access to the collections belonging to his fellow club members. Possibly, though, his primary connection to the other men who formed the club was through his friendship and working relationship with Joseph Haslewood. Either way, Egerton Brydges's literary interests lay in directions other than collecting and most especially towards the redemption of early English works in danger of extinction due to their rarity and authors at risk of being forgotten by modern readers, a concern that would have firmly aligned him with the other members. His inclusion in the club confirms that it was not intended to be merely a meeting of book collectors but rather, as Dibdin stated, of

---

33 Leigh Hunt, *The Autobiography of Leigh Hunt* (London: Smith, Elder, 1870), p. 124.

enthusiasts for early literature who wished to reproduce rare pieces of poetry. By some means Brydges simply knew enough of the men who congregated for dinner and had enough to offer with regards to their shared interest to make his membership viable without possessing any substantial collection of his own.

In complete contrast to Brydges's apparent lack of collecting passion, stood Dibdin, who was arguably the driving force behind not just the Roxburghe Club but also bibliomania itself, or at the very least its most noteworthy chronicler. W. Powell Jones in 1940 stated that 'the Oxford English Dictionary credits Dibdin with the earliest usage of most of the biblio compounds in English', and that represents the most fitting of memorials for a man who lived and breathed books.[34] Never wealthy, although with a good income from his clerical positions, and towards the end of his life suffering from dementia, he became largely reliant on the generosity of his friends. The difficult combination of an obsession with books, a moderate income and a family to support apparently created problems for others beyond his domestic circle. He made full use of the early nineteenth-century gentleman's prerogative to live on credit to the detriment of tradesmen, and when he not only failed to honour the massive debts that he had incurred with the bookseller and publisher John Major but also involved him in his precarious business ventures, it eventually led to the publisher's bankruptcy.

Dibdin had collected from a relatively early age and often acted as a book agent for others, most notably for Earl Spencer, a role that took him onto the Continent in search of desirable volumes. It is unclear why he acted in this capacity: whether for straightforward financial gain, out of friendship and to gain patronage, or because it allowed him to attend auctions and visit booksellers, buying beautiful books and being involved in the arena he loved, but without expense to himself. It became necessary in 1817 for him to sell his library to cover the printing costs of his lavish volumes on book collecting, and it is notable that, when he presented a reprint as his contribution to the Roxburghe Club, it was a reproduction of a book taken not from his own collection, which may not perhaps by that point have contained anything that he considered of sufficient rarity or significance, but from the Duke of Devonshire's library. He was artistic by nature, and naturally drawn to the typographic and decorative elements of printing. Dibdin himself, however, argued strongly for the curbing of merely fashionable and superficial bibliomaniacal enthusiasms by calling for a concentration on the intellectual elements of texts alongside the aesthetic.

---

34 Jones, 'Three Unpublished Letters of Scott to Dibdin', p. 477n2.

Sir William Bolland, the host of the dinner party the night before the auction of the Valdarfer Boccaccio, was a lawyer, a Recorder of Reading and an amateur poet. Although his obituary in the *Gentleman's Magazine* describes him as 'an ardent admirer of the literature of the olden times' and duly notes his membership of the Roxburghe Club, the obituarist is more preoccupied with listing his collection of paintings than his library.[35] Yet Bolland's library was large, containing many important and beautiful works which, when sold by the bibliomania's favourite auctioneer Robert Harding Evans, raised £3,019 and formed 2,940 separate lots. He owned items originating from the Lincoln collection, obtained, as previously mentioned, in one of those purchases from ancient archives which appear somewhat unpalatable to the modern mind. Bolland's bundle of texts, including the valuable *Rape of Lucrece*, had already attracted Dibdin. Indeed, Dibdin says he had assembled the package with a view to purchasing them himself, having 'entwined some whip-cord around – setting them apart for the consideration of the Dean and Chapter, whether, a *second* time, I might not become a purchaser of some of their book-treasures? I had valued them at fourscore guineas'.[36] He comments that he had considered at the time how interested 'Hortensius' (William Bolland's alter ego in Dibdin's works) would be in these tracts, only to find later that the Chapter had sold them to Wheatley and that Bolland now owned them.[37] Bolland's interest in books was serious and well informed, free from the taint of bibliomania. As a contemporary noted 'often have I heard him express his contempt for the coxcomb who computes the value of a book by its mere rarity. And of all maladies, that which is called the bibliomania is the worst, – the most estranged from the rational and liberal pursuit of a scholar'.[38] It is striking how many individual members of the club were clearly recognized by their contemporaries as unsympathetic to the excesses of bibliomania, a necessary corrective to the myth that the club as a whole represents the apex of bibliomania.

Moving on from this point, Francis Freeling had a typical, if particularly well-appointed, book collection for that period. It did, however, have a particular area of splendour, which was that of witchcraft and demonology, in which Dibdin describes it as being so well represented that 'even the late Sir

---

35 'Sir William Bolland', *Gentleman's Magazine* 14 (1840), pp. 433–34; italics in original.
36 T. F. Dibdin, *Bibliomania, A Bibliographical Romance in Six Parts* (London: Messrs Longman, Hurst, Rees, Orme and Brown, 1811), III, pp. 588–89.
37 Hortensius, a friend and orator, appears in Cicero's *Hortensius*, which argues for the pre-eminence of philosophy: the name doubtless complements Boland's profession as an advocate.
38 Thomas Campbell, 'The Philosophy of Clubs', *New Monthly Magazine* 22 (January 1828), 261–73 (p. 270).

Walter Scott might have gathered more than one relic wherewith to enrich the many shrines of this description which he has erected within his fascinating performances'.[39] Hazlitt says, rather cryptically, that 'through his official connection with the Post-Office he procured many prizes from the country districts'.[40] Did Freeling make legal if unorthodox use of his position? Did he get reports from Post Office employees of likely documents or rural informants? What is certain is that he was able to buy these volumes at costs far lower than those commanded by London booksellers' prices.

Edward Utterson, a barrister, appointed a clerk in the Court of Chancery in 1815, is mostly remembered as an accomplished amateur artist who produced some attractive landscapes in watercolour. As well as having an interest in English early poetry he collected Italian, Spanish and French chivalric romances, and his bookish activities (especially through his own printing venture, the Beldornie Press) inspired the poet Charles Townsend to write the following, somewhat underwhelming, verses:

> A man of taste and learning he,
> And manners well refined,
> And what was best and worth them all,
> A heart most warm and kind.
>
> His books were choice – and very old,
> (By Pynson and de Worde)
> And bound so well they opened flat,
> Almost of their own accord.
>
> And from his own Beldornie Press,
> What treasures we obtain!
> 'Sam Rowlands' buried years in dust,
> Comes into life again.
>
> His ancient prints in Gothic style,
> Old Ballads in black letter,
> With wood-cuts, and the more grotesque
> He loved them all the better.[41]

---

39 Dibdin, *Reminiscences*, II, p. 936.
40 W. Carew Hazlitt, *Book Collector* (London: Grant, 1904), p. 269.
41 Charles Townsend, 'Ballad', in *Letters of a Literary Antiquary*, p. 14.

His library was sold in two lots, the first being auctioned in 1852 and the second, after a long gap, in 1857; the two sales raised around £8800 in total.

Examining the collection of the sixth Duke of Devonshire takes us again to another of those vast, inherited libraries owned by the aristocrats of the Roxburghe Club. The Duke acceded to his title and an immense fortune (as well as the massive gambling debts of his mother, the scandalous beauty Georgiana) in 1811 at the age of 21. He immediately set about collecting Italian marbles, art and a massive library of rare books that would eventually rival that belonging to his uncle, Earl Spencer. An unknown to the collecting world then, his purchases at the Roxburghe sale, made both in person and by an agent instructed by him, were so great as to lead to rumours that his agent was buying on behalf of Napoleon Bonaparte. According to Dibdin these purchases, a part of which consisted of 'clusters of Caxtons', included the *Recuyell of the Histories of Troy* for which he paid £1060.10s.[42] The Duke, like many of the period's wealthiest book collectors, purchased entire libraries to speed up the onerous task of building up his own cabinet. In 1812 he purchased the library of Dr. Damper, Bishop of Ely, for a little less than £10,000, whisking it from under the nose of Earl Spencer, who had prevaricated during the negotiations Dibdin was carrying out on his behalf. Another already formed library was the collection of dramatic works that had been amassed by Kemble, the actor and playwright. This was not the famous actor's entire library but rather a selection of the rarest items cherry-picked by the Duke before the remainder went to auction and for which the Duke paid 2,000 guineas. He continued to add to the collection, and the most important volume later purchased was the first edition, 1603, of *Hamlet*, believed at the time to be the only one in existence. Like Earl Spencer, the Duke was generous with his library, welcoming its use by authors and saying of the Kemble collection that it was 'on my first acquiring it placed [at Chatsworth House]; but for the sake of reference by living authors, as well as for convenience in attempting to complete the series as much as possible, they were removed to Devonshire House [i.e. in London]'.[43] Describing the formation of his entire collection, the Duke wrote,

> In that attempt, the unwearied diligence and unexampled knowledge of this subject displayed by Mr. J. Payne Collier have been of invaluable service to me; and the pleasure has indeed been great (besides that of possessing so many treasures) of finding that a pursuit, which may have had a good deal of bibliomania in its composition has been of real use

---

42 De Ricci, *English Collectors of Books 1530–1930*, p. 72.
43 Fitzgerald, *The Book Fancier*, p. 266.

to several men of letters, and especially that it has assisted in the completion of the best and most satisfactory edition of Shakespeare that exists.[44]

This presumably refers to the *Works of William Shakespeare* edited by John Payne Collier, with the dedication, 'to his Grace the Duke of Devonshire, K.G. This edition of the works of the greatest dramatic poet of the world, which could not have been completed without the aid of His Grace's matchless collection of the original impressions of William Shakespeare's plays, is, with permission, inscribed, by his devoted and grateful servant, The Editor'.[45] In the preface Collier describes the Duke's collection of early Shakespeare editions as 'notoriously the most complete in the world: his Grace has a perfect series, including, of course, every first edition, several of which are neither at Oxford, Cambridge, nor in the British Museum'.[46] Collier, of course, later became notorious himself when he stood accused of a number of literary forgeries concerning supposed discoveries that he had made about Shakespeare's life and works, the Duke, however, had died before the accusations of forgery came to light. He may have been a little self-deprecating when writing of his indebtedness to Payne Collier. While there may have been 'a good deal of bibliomania' in his collecting, he was also a committed and knowledgeable collector who accumulated with a purpose rather than indiscriminately. As Dibdin wrote, '[The Duke's] book-propensities had been scarcely developed to the public knowledge, but his more intimate acquaintance were well aware of his zealous attachment to the pages of Debure, Renouard, and Herbert. How frequently he would turn his back upon the gaieties of the "flaunting town," and consume the midnight oil in making himself acquainted with such libri desiderati as might at once add to the splendour and value of the library left him by his ancestors'.[47]

Back on less exalted ground, George Hibbert's library has been aptly characterized as 'a collection formed to illustrate the history of printing, and therefore offering the most splendid and unique examples', though this description could equally apply to most of the Roxburghe members' collections.[48] Hibbert's collection contained the familiar roll call of early printed Bibles, including a *Gutenberg Bible*, Fust and Schoeffer's *1462 Latin Bible*, the *Complutensian Polyglot Bible*

---

44 William Spencer Cavendish, *Hand Book of Chatsworth, Hardwick and Kemp Town, MS. and Proofs* (Devonshire Collection, 1844, CH1/2/48).
45 John Payne Collier, *The Works of William Shakespeare* (London: Whittaker, 1844).
46 Ibid., pp. v–vi.
47 Dibdin, *Reminiscences*, I, pp. 356–57.
48 Fitzgerald, *The Book Fancier*, p. 233.

reported to have belonged to Cardinal Ximenes, the first edition of Luther's copy of his translation of the *Bible* with his own autograph and the 1479 *Bible* printed by Jenson. He was also a collector of block books. According to Dibdin in his *Reminiscences*, Hibbert's library sold for £21,700; however, other sources put the sum raised at somewhere in the region of £23,000, and given the large discrepancy between these sums, it is possible that Dibdin in 1836 was unaware of an auction that had yet to take place at the time of his writing.

John Arthur Lloyd, another unfamiliar name today, was a wealthy landowner who had inherited a country estate at Leaton Knolls in Shropshire. He was proposed to the club by Henry Drury, his former tutor at Harrow, and Dibdin describes the man as 'a gentleman in all respects qualified by his scholarship and attainments – and, above all, by his unwarped and unwarpable attachment to the *Bibliomania*' and admires his collection, saying that 'I scarcely know, for its limits, so choice and so enviable a collection as his'.[49] This is confirmed by the details of his library, which contained editions of the most valuable bibles, including the *Mazarin Latin Bible* of 1455 and the *Aldine Bible* of 1518. He also owned a first edition of Homer from 1488 and the Aldine first editions of Herodotus, Thucydides and Pausanius.[50] In other words, his library contained the same rare, expensive and irreplaceable sorts of volumes that appear in so many of the collections of this period, volumes that are now mostly and fittingly held in public collections, and that a modern collector, however wealthy, could only ever dream of owning.

In this period clergymen seem to have been disproportionately represented among book collectors. One such, the Venerable Archdeacon Wrangham, was an avid reader, a prolific writer, a respected scholar and a passionate collector of books on a wide variety of subjects. At his death Wrangham's library contained around 300 manuscripts and an impressive collection of works printed by the Aldine Press and amassed using the most extensive and accurate bibliography of the time, produced by the bookseller Antoine-Augustine Renouard, as his guide.[51] Following the sale of much of Wrangham's library at auction, the British Museum purchased the manuscript collection for £2,000 following private negotiation with the executors of his estate. A keen writer and collector of pamphlets, in 1842 he donated 10,000 pamphlets to Trinity College, Cambridge. Alongside the books that he collected out of personal intellectual interest and to further his studies, Wrangham, in the spirit of a true bibliomaniac, loved collecting rare books just for the sake of their rarity. The elusiveness of these volumes was for him the sport, and apparently

---

49 Dibdin, *Reminiscences*, I, pp. 396.
50 Ibid., pp. 396–97.
51 De Ricci, *English Collectors of Books 1530–1930*, pp. 114–15.

'the harder they were to obtain (almost irrespective of their contents) the better he liked them'.[52] His multifaceted approach to book collecting illustrates the primary problem in dismissing a collector as a bibliomaniac with all the derogatory assumptions inherent in that term. A love for the trivialities of the book chase can, and in most cases does, dwell alongside a serious love for the text, without any contradiction at all. One volume may be bought for its contents, another for its rarity or binding and a happy third for containing all the admired qualities, and this holistic approach to books was the defining characteristic of the men who made up the Roxburghe Club. In most cases the increasing financial value of the book was of interest and satisfaction but incidental, not least because they had no intention of selling the volumes, although some may have hoped that their collections would help provide for their families after their death.

The Archdeacon was a correspondent of long standing with Sir Samuel Egerton Brydges, and a series of letters that span from 1812 to 1829 display both his ardent collecting spirit and his equally fervent desire to be a member of the Roxburghe Club. He writes, 'I wish my friend Heber and yourself would one day find a niche for me in the Roxburghe. I go on collecting with unabated ardour, and have really some curious books. In number my shelves hold about 12,000'.[53] And again later, 'if I belonged to the Roxburghe – an ambition I hinted when I last wrote to Mr. Heber – I should think Hornby would be a good subject for a reprint'.[54] His impressive rate of purchasing is apparent from yet another letter to Egerton Brydges, written in 1821, which states that 'I go on collecting with undiminished industry, my present number of volumes must be near 15,000'.[55] This indicates that in five years alone he had bought 3,000 books. He evidently had the required book-collecting credentials, and he was elected a member of the club in 1822.

Another example of the susceptibility of a man of the cloth to coveting the rare volume of his neighbour was that of the Venerable Archdeacon Butler. A respected scholar and author, he was renowned for his knowledge of a wide range of subjects including history, antiquities and classical literature. He composed verse and penned prose in Latin and Greek and was feted for his precision and quality in both. Unsurprisingly his collection contained a great many editions of classical works, but he also collected more widely and was, judging from the descriptions given of his collection in *Reminiscences*, a collector after Dibdin's own heart with a library full of rare early printed books and

---

52 Sadleir, 'Archdeacon Francis Wrangham: a supplement', p. 447.
53 Ibid., p. 432.
54 Ibid., p. 431.
55 Ibid., p. 436.

fragments. Furthermore, he apparently had tastes that ran to areas of collecting that even Dibdin could not appreciate:

> If Dr. Butler have not the *finest* Collection of Aldines – in regard to *vellums* and *large papers* – he has certainly the largest and most complete; [...] this Aldine passion is carried to extravagant, and to me unintelligible, limits. I cannot comprehend why forgeries are to be mixed up with genuine commodities. I cannot comprehend why the authors of such base stuff are to sit down upon the same bench with the original manufacturers. Would you knowingly travel one post in the same chaise with a notorious forger? And yet, my excellent friend, the Archdeacon, stuffs the pockets and seats of his own carriage with a very host of *Lyonese Counterfeits!*[56]

Turning to a collector with less perplexing tastes, Sir Walter Scott needs little introduction as a man, as a writer or as a book collector. He assembled, as might be expected from his own works, a library comprising books on Scottish and Irish history, chivalry and romance, folklore, witchcraft, English and Scottish poetry and early literature from a variety of traditions. There is little in the catalogue of his library, presented to the Bannatyne Club by his son-in-law John Gibson Lockhart after Scott's death, to indicate that he had any great interest in collecting what was fashionable, but rather that in many ways he had collected his library as a resource for his imagination and writing. That is borne out by the brief introduction to the catalogue, which includes a quote, attributed to Lockhart, in which he says 'the nature and extent of the Collection throw light, in a remarkable manner, on the history of its founder. The reader has before him a faithful inventory of the materials with which the National Poet and Novelist had stored his mind before he began his public career'.[57] Scott had, however, had an extensive correspondence with Dibdin, prior to the founding of the Roxburghe Club, and certainly long before he became a member in 1823. Their letters show that he owned copies of Dibdin's books and used them as a guide in some of his own collecting activities, and this indicates an important acknowledgement of Dibdin's reputation as a writer who was knowledgeable about early books, not simply a proponent of the dictates of bibliophile fashion. Scott's library which is retained intact at Abbotsford, contains around 7,000 volumes.

These wonderful libraries were amassed during the golden age of collecting, and by the mid-1830s it was all but over. Gradually the rare volumes were

---

56 Dibdin, *Reminiscences*, II, p. 970; italics in original.
57 J. G. Cochrane, *Catalogue of the Library at Abbotsford* (Edinburgh: Constable for the Bannatyne Club, 1838).

making their way into British public collections, and overseas to the new collections being created in America and other countries where new money was plentiful. Discussing Heber's vast collection after his death, Dibdin describes the dispersal in a melancholy tone that could have equally described the bibliomaniac age of book collecting itself: 'it is now fast melting away. Seven successive snow-balls of enormous dimensions have already disappeared; and four more of equal size are quickly to fall into dissolution. Within six months to come, every volume will have also probably taken its departure for ever'.[58]

---

58 Dibdin, *Reminiscences*, II, pp. 938–39.

Chapter 6

THE PASSION FOR PRINT

The possession of a private printing-press is, no doubt, a very appalling type of bibliomania. Much, as has been told us of the awful scale in which drunkards consume their favored poison, one is not accustomed to hear of their setting up private stills for their own individual consumption. There is a Sardanapalitan excess in this bibliographical luxuriousness which refuses to partake with other vulgar mortals in the common harvest of the public press, but must itself minister to its own tastes and demands.[1]

When John Hill Burton made this tongue-in-cheek observation, he swiftly followed it up with a number of bibliophilic names to illustrate his point, including those of Sir Alexander Boswell and Sir Samuel Egerton Brydges. In fact the early Roxburghe Club contained among its members three men who were drawn to the ownership of a private printing press and the freedom that it gave them to pursue their own literary interests, both in terms of printing their own original work and of reproducing rare, largely forgotten works of early literature. As Hill Burton pointed out, the ownership of a private press perhaps indicates an interest in books that extends beyond the mere dilettante concern with novelty or the collector's obsession with fine bindings and auction prices; it certainly goes beyond a taste for the classics or any literature that could be termed mainstream as such tastes have long been amply catered for by the standard printing houses with their business eye on the requirements of the average consumer. While each owner will have his unique reasons for entering the printing world, it often indicates a deeper-than-average interest in unrepresented literature and in the art of typography, a desire to create, reproduce and broadcast literature – an aspiration to control the means of print production which goes beyond even that of employing a printer to work under the patronage of the customer at the printer's own establishment. These undertakings wholeheartedly fulfilled the description coined by Will Ransom when he wrote that 'freed from the confining strictures of details, a

---

1 Burton, *The Book Hunter*, p. 285.

private press may be defined as the typographic expression of a personal ideal, conceived in freedom and maintained in independence'.[2]

The Roxburghe Club as a whole was deeply concerned with the traditional methods of printing, and for the members of this particular group of bibliophiles, pioneering lovers of early typographic practices, there would have been little joy to be gained from producing the texts in their period's standard, modern editions that could easily have been provided by the normal publishing channels. As a club their motives and methods, because of their access to private funding, could also be gloriously free from the constraints of profit and intellectual property and serve literary (and embryonic academic) projects not often provided for by contemporary commercial publishing. As the works remained uncopyrighted, the opportunity existed for mainstream publishers to print modern accessible editions of any of the works if they believed that there was a sufficient readership to make it worth their while, and the club members were mostly very generous in lending items from their collections to authors, editors and publishers who required access to the original texts. Richard Heber especially, with his massive collection was, as has already been discussed, a generous lender of rare volumes to needy scholars and blackletter editors. For their own publications the club members were interested in doing something very different which was, very often, to reproduce the books as closely as possible to how they had first appeared.

In this pursuit the Roxburghe were embracing and celebrating the printer's art while insisting on retaining the individuality and personal eccentricities of each volume and maintaining an artisan approach to the creation of a book, in direct contrast to the methods of mass book production that were just developing. Each early book had its individual personality, which was to be maintained and reproduced as far as possible; the literary content was certainly important but so too were the typography, the woodcuts, the mistakes and the oddities. Even blank pages were sometimes retained in order to create copies that appeared as similar as possible to the original. Why produce a copy in a modern, unvarying roman type when you could have atmospheric black letter? Why force the text into an unhistorical uniformity when with a little effort (and a strong-minded willingness to ignore your critics) you could experience the book as its first readers experienced it in all its idiosyncratic and authentic glory, printer's contractions and all? Today, undertakings such as Google books display digital reproductions of volumes which have been scanned in by the libraries that own them, allowing a wide readership to gain access to rare or expensive books and to study and appreciate many of the features of older book production and the representation of texts without the necessity of

---

2 Will Ransom, *Private Presses and Their Books* (New York: R. R. Bowker, 1929), p. 22.

travelling to the actual library. While there can be many criticisms and reservations regarding the Google Books Library Project, it undeniably does allow the reader to view the book as a digital representation of the physical object rather than just as the disembodied text. It allows the observation of many details that might otherwise remain hidden from the online reader: ownership and library stamps, page numbering and illustrations, size of margins, the type used and much more is available from the original book in a way that is not available from a modern edition of the same text. Modern scholarly digitizations provide even more reliably accurate and finely detailed representations of manuscripts and early printed books (e.g. the Gallica Project at the Bibliothèque National, the British Library digitization projects and Early English Books Online). When the Roxburghe Club reproduced their rare volumes they also attempted to reproduce as much information from the original item as they could, given the restrictions imposed by the available technology. They were not just reprinting early works but also reproducing or cloning them, which to some degree, although in no way attempting to pass them off as the genuine early artefact, entailed a blurring of perception between the original book and its recreated modern version.[3] These items were not forgeries, and, as already mentioned, the prime consideration was not commercial or to limit general access to the texts (in several cases the club members willingly allowed their editions to become the basis for later editions produced for a wider commercial circulation and available freely for purchase), but they did create an entirely new form of rarity, that of the Roxburghe edition, and Dibdin certainly took satisfaction from the value of their editions when they did occasionally come to auction.

They were in love with typography and early technology, admirers of the late-medieval innovators of movable type whose names they honour in their annual toasts and the practical workmanship of the press, not the idealized bucolic or chivalric dreams of mainstream romanticism. Dibdin certainly wrote in an overblown romantic style when he was gushing about his 'book-knights', but this was his own literary tic and obviously one that sold well, proving that he knew his wider audience. It was not representative of how the interests of the Roxburghe collectors presented themselves when it came to their own productions or even illustrative of how the other members approached the black-letter books that they collected, and it is certain that some members did not approve of Dibdin's style of communication, even if they simultaneously approved of the message being imparted. Theirs was

---

3 A fascinating discussion of nineteenth-century facsimiles can be found in current Roxburghe Club member David McKitterick's work *Old Books, New Technologies* (Cambridge: Cambridge University Press, 2013).

the romance of discovering and appreciating the authentic talent both literary and artisanal that was largely going unrecognized by other people at this time, combined with an excitement about the invention of the technology of printing, verging on what would now be summed up as 'boys and their toys'. Alongside a love of the traditional methods they were simultaneously keen, when it appeared advantageous to their aims, to embrace the newest, most cutting-edge technologies of the day such as lithography, which now allowed them to reproduce more exactly the workmanship that they loved; a simultaneous recognition of ancient craftsmanship and an avid early adoption of new technologies to better display what they had learnt. This was not a politically and socially reactionary notion of creating romanticized visions of feudal times but a highly personal reaction to the literature and technology that came together in the black-letter volumes.

Club members were obviously involved with and supportive of the incipient area of facsimile production, employing those printers who were leading the field in such work. One instance was the firm of Joseph and George Smeaton, specialist printers in type facsimile, and here again the connection is through Haslewood, where we see his close association with the important developments of early English, and (as is more usual with Haslewood) a re-evaluation and promotion of Elizabethan texts. Another example of this willingness on the behalf of the club to look forward technologically, while seeking to retain the authentic qualities of the early printers, can be seen in the volume presented to the club by John Dent in 1818. His offering was *Solempnities and Triumphes doon and made at the Spousells and Marriage of the King's Daughter the Ladye Marye to the Prynce of Castile, Archduke of Austrige*, which appeared as a facsimile reprint of a tract originally printed by Richard Pynson in 1508. It was another occasion where a club member arranged for the reprinting of a unique copy, the publishing of which safeguarded its future and made it more available (although obviously still to a restricted number of people) through its presence in at least 31 libraries. Rarity aside, however, the real significance of this reprint in the context of the club publications is that of the cutting-edge methods that Dent utilized in 1818 by having it printed by way of the recent invention of lithographic reproduction. This was a technology which had been invented in 1798 in Germany, and which Rudolph Ackermann brought to London and began to offer at his press from 1817 onwards. Obviously the Roxburghe membership had their finger on the pulse of modern developments in publishing. This is significant because not only does it support the argument that they were not simply backward-looking nostalgics, overromanticizing the past and dabbling in amateur recreations of relics of chivalry, but also that they were firmly entrenched in the onward progression of the printing arts and had an intelligent, up-to-date knowledge of the state of the art during their period. Dent was by no means a trendsetter in the rest of his life; in fact, he was generally agreed to be a staid, rather dull man, a pillar of the banking world and in no way likely to be at the cutting edge of new crazes. When it came to his passion for books, however, he was obviously keeping up with the very latest developments in the printing world. It should also be noted that it can have only been advantageous to the development of printing techniques at this time to have had the backing of the significant wealth and influence available to the men of the Roxburghe.

And so, returning to the question of why the club declined to produce texts edited in a more contemporary fashion, it was also certainly not the case that the founders of the Roxburghe Club failed to understand the utility, readability and scholarly importance of more modern, accessible, Roman-type editions of black-letter books. Many members were also instrumental in editing and publishing editions of Early English literature that conform much more closely to modern standards. The methods of production used for early Roxburghe volumes were not, it seems, used because of lack of knowledge of alternatives but rather as a rejection of the mass-produced aesthetic and the cultural push towards the mechanization of the printing process, where the printer became simply the operator of the machine rather than the craftsman whose aesthetic values and skill are reflected in the volume produced. For the collector early printed books had never been just books but took on the personality of the printer becoming a Caxton, a Valdarfer or an Aldine, and that identity needed to be preserved and expressed if the book was to be reprinted. This was a conscious act, designed to reproduce the works as closely as possible to the originals, and in so doing ensuring the continued existence and reading of rare works, increasing the number of readers who could in effect access the original as an artefact in all ways that mattered and also giving back to the book its identity as a valued artefact in its own right, rather than just the carrier of the text, interchangeable with any other bundle of paper that could hold the ink.

Given this affinity for the fruits of the printing press it was almost inevitable that some of the members might choose to explore its arts for themselves. Among the three early Roxburghe members who owned private printing presses, there were of course a range of differing reasons for their forays into press ownership, but none of the three appear to have been driven by financial considerations. At least one printing entrepreneur, Sir Egerton Brydges, seems to have found the experience to be an expensive mixture of vanity publishing and patronage during the short-lived adventures of his Lee Priory Press. At the other end of the scale was Boswell, who appears to have been successful both financially and in literary terms in his endeavours at the Auchinleck Press, an undertaking cut short only by his untimely death. The Beldornie

Press, the personal project of E. V. Utterson is of the three perhaps the most hobbyist, and provides an intimate reflection of the literary tastes of its owner. It served to provide both himself and a close circle of like-minded friends with reproductions of relatively unknown seventeenth-century poems and satires, and apparently only ran during the summer months.

The Lee Priory Press

Brydges established the Lee Priory Press in 1813, at a house belonging to his eldest son, T. B. Brydges Barrett, at Ickham, near Canterbury. It remained in production until 1823, printing during this time around 40 books and a large number of pamphlets and single leaves on a variety of literary subjects. According to his own accounts, he did not start out with the express intention of owning a printing press, but was rather attempting to support two printers in their endeavours, while presumably also hoping to enjoy the benefits and enhancement of status that might proceed from an extended act of patronage. One of the master printers associated with the Lee Priory Press was the compositor John Johnson, the author of *Typographia: or the Printer's Instructor*, published in 1824 and dedicated to the president and members of the Roxburghe Club.[4] The dedication of the two-volume work to the club can be seen as proof of his recognition of the club's position as experts and proponents of historical typographical skills. The first volume carries not only the dedication but also an engraving which portrays the coats of arms belonging to Roxburghe members surrounding a bust of Caxton. The bust sits upon a plinth bearing the date of the first Roxburghe dinner and the club's name (see Figure 6.1). This is obviously an expensive, commissioned engraving. While this could be viewed as Johnson's attempt to gain work from the club (which in itself would indicate how prominent the club must have been in the field to make it worth Johnson putting all his advertising eggs in one basket), it seems unlikely that this was his primary purpose as he would have already been well known to the club. The other printer who worked for Brydges was the pressman John Warwick, and both he and Johnson were previously known to Brydges through their long-standing employment in the offices of Thomas Bensley, a respected printer who produced a number of the early editions presented by members to the Roxburghe Club, including *Caltha Poetarum* in 1815 and *A Roxburghe Garland*, *The Glutton's Feaver* and the *Chester Mysteries*, all published in 1817.

Brydges had supplied the premises, which he described as a 'vacant room at the extremity of the offices and looking into a spacious stable-yard' and

---

4 J. Johnson, *Typographia: or the Printer's Instructor* (1824).

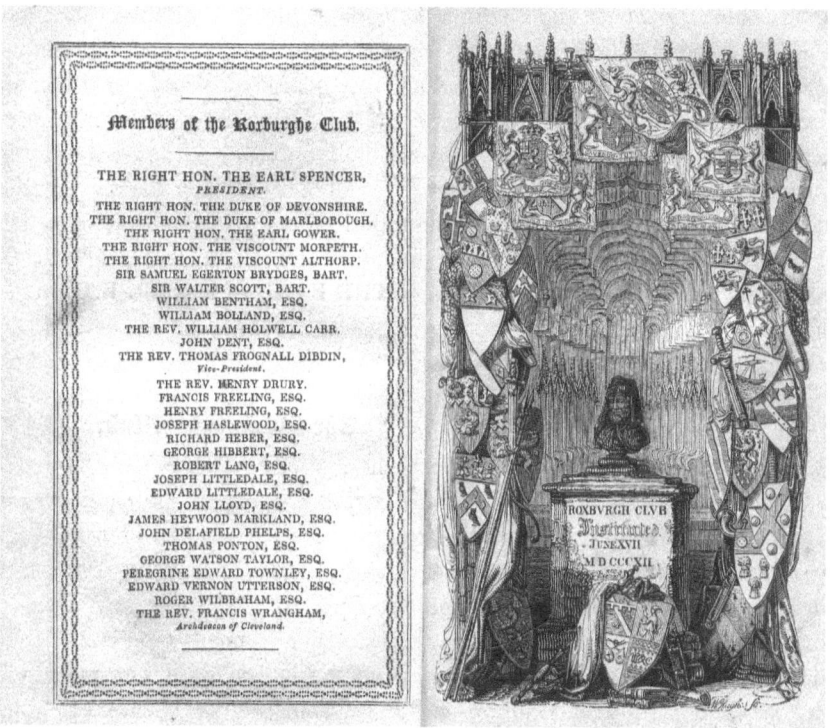

Figure 6.1 The dedication pages from Volume I of Johnson's *Typographia*.

kept the printers regularly supplied with material to print.[5] This took the form of literary items written by Brydges himself, or selected items of interest to antiquarian book collectors for the printers to reproduce. The consumable materials such as paper and more specialist items such as the typefaces and ornamental elements were to be their own responsibility to provide. The Press was not a financial success, as Dibdin explained: '[h]is first intention was to assume no financial responsibility, insisting that the printers, Johnson and Warwick, "must run all hazards, and, of course, rely on such profits as they could get," but he later admitted the necessity of supplying funds to keep the press in operation'.[6] It did stay in operation, at least temporarily anyway, producing regular work until in 1818 Brydges left England to live on the Continent and was no longer able (or perhaps willing) to supervise the working of the press room. He was also experiencing financial difficulties

---

5 Dibdin, *The Bibliographical Decameron* (London: Bulmer, 1817), II, p. 464.
6 Dibdin, *Library Companion* (London: Harding, Triphook, and Lepard, 1824), p. xix.

that would have made underwriting the costs of the Press difficult. The final demise of the Press has been ascribed to the printers no longer having ready copy to work on and instead spending their copious free time in drinking. During the Press's most productive period, however, the work produced was acknowledged to have been of a fine standard, and even at the later and less productive period some of the output was still of a sufficient standard that it could elicit the admiration of the contemporary bibliographer and bookseller John Martin, who described one of the later volumes, *Woodcuts and Verses*, as 'good evidence of the justice of a qualification to such censure – or a proof, in spite of Dr. Franklin, that tippling is not always injurious to the craft of men of type'.[7] Edward Quillinan provided Warwick with the verses to accompany the woodcut illustrations for the volume. Quillinan was a poet and the husband of Brydges's daughter Jemima until her death in 1822, after which he married Dora Wordsworth. He was the author of *Dunluce Castle, A Poem; Stanzas by the Author of Dunluce Castle; Consolation; Elegiac Verses* and *Woodcuts and Verses*, which were all printed at the Lee Priory Press. By 1817, when *Woodcuts and Verses* was produced, Johnson had already left the Press, citing 'cruel and unjust treatment', which was presumably connected in some way to Warwick's drinking.[8] The Press eventually closed in 1823, but during its short existence it produced a catalogue of important works of Early English literature, including works by Elizabethan authors such as William Browne, Nicholas Breton, Robert Greene and Walter Raleigh among others. The first book printed at the Press, but not made available for purchase, was *Poems of Margaret, Duchess of Newcastle*.[9] It was a royal octavo edition, and only 25 copies were printed, partly as a personal favour and partly to display the quality of production from the Press. Lee Priory publications were usually limited to 100 copies or fewer. Haslewood's contribution to the Roxburghe Club, *Two Interludes: Jack Jugler and Tersites*, was printed at Lee Priory in 1820 by Warwick.

It appears that Brydges also gained some personal amusement from the operation of the press beyond that of the more worthy literary pursuits. An anecdote, allegedly told by Quillinan, indicates that occasionally items were printed that were not intended for circulation but for more private motives:

> Among them was a little pungent moral of four octosyllabic quatrains, addressed by a very lovely young lady, the daughter of an amicable and venerable bishop, 'to him who will best understand them' a spruce,

---

7 Martin, *A Bibliographical Catalogue of Books Privately Printed*, p. 380.
8 Johnson, *Typographia*, p. viii.
9 Margaret Cavendish, *Poems of Margaret, Duchess of Newcastle* (Ickham: Lee Priory Press, 1813).

grey-headed gentleman, whose gallantry was rewarded by this effusion, ending with the flattering proverb, 'A fool at fifty is a fool indeed'. Only two rough proofs, and one copy were struck off; Sir Egerton Brydges and a friend stood by, to witness the whole process and saw the letters dispersed and restored to their several alphabetical places in the printers' boxes. The single impression was sent to the fair author, and the two rough proofs carried off by Sir Egerton Brydges and his friend.[10]

But by July 1817 Brydges admitted in a letter to Dibdin to having difficulty in maintaining his original enthusiasm in the Press, saying that 'as to what little I have done myself, either in original composition, or in the way of prefaces, &c. from this press, it is not such as I could wish. The variety of my concerns and pursuits always brings to every subject a distracted mind, and a wild and fugitive memory. My spirit evaporates with the violence of its first ardours. My fancy catches flame; and is almost immediately out again. [...] It has always been with me a main aim to bring taste and sentiment in aid of the heaviness of literary antiquities'.[11] This difficulty on Brydges's part in maintaining enthusiasm for projects was sadly not confined to his printing press but formed a constant motif throughout the tenor of his life. In the *Bibliographical Decameron*, Dibdin assessed works produced by the Lee Priory Press by that time and, while considering some of the larger types used to be 'perhaps too bold and heavy', the ink to have 'frequently too foggy a surface' (the red ink especially to display 'too uniform a failure') and the page borders to be 'objectionable', he also admitted that there was 'consummate taste in the setting up of *title-pages*, and perhaps unrivalled beauty in the working of the wood-cuts'.[12] His overall impression of the products produced at Lee Priory Press were that 'the beauties infinitely counterbalance the defects of the productions of the *Lee Priory press*; and we may compliment the amiable and able conductor of it, upon setting an example worthy of being more generally followed'.[13]

The Auchinleck Press

If Brydges was apparently a somewhat reluctant and beleaguered owner of a printing press, Boswell was by his own admission 'infected with the *type* fever'.[14]

---

10 John Martin, *A Bibliographical Catalogue of Books Privately Printed* (London: J & A Arch, 1834), II, p. 381.
11 Dibdin, *Bibliographical Decameron*, p. 465.
12 Ibid., p. 467; italics in original.
13 Ibid.; italics in original.
14 Ibid., p. 454; italics in original.

Boswell took a keen, if intermittent, interest in the running of his press, which was in operation from 1815 to 1818 at Auchinleck House in Dumfriesshire, Scotland. Boswell's account of the setting up of his Press is quoted in Dibdin's *Biographical Decameron* and ascribes his initial impulse to the desire to produce a facsimile reprint of a black-letter volume from his own collection, titled *The Disputation between John Knox and the Abbot of Crossraguel*, which was one of a number of texts that Boswell printed before the Press was officially established in 1815. At this point he owned a 'portable press', which he chose to exchange in 1815 for 'one of Mr. Ruthven's full sized ones', an upgrade necessitated by the wish of his brother James to have his first Roxburghe Club contribution printed at the Press.[15] James's presentation volume was an edition of *Poems* by Richard Barnfield, a collection which included the *Encomion of Lady Pecunia, or The Praise of Money*, printed in 1598, and considered by the often critical Payne Collier to be an accurate reprint of the earliest impression of the work. Boswell used the Press to print editions of his own compositions, including 'The Tyrant's Fall' in 1815 and 'Skeldon Haughs; or, The Sow is Flitted' in 1816. In all, at least according to a Victorian commentator, the products of the Press amounted to around 40 items which ranged 'from the most recondite treatises to rare old chap ballads besides a multitude of scarce tractates and leaflets bearing on history, social economy, philosophy &c, the number and titles of which it is almost impossible now to trace'.[16] Boswell employed 'Jamie' Sutherland as compositor and printer, and Patrick Simpson to correct proofs in his absence, and, according to Dibdin, Sutherland came to Boswell 'by the obliging accommodation of Mr. George Ramsay, one of our most respectable printers'.[17] Boswell also carried out some of the printing work himself, and presented to Walter Scott a book of his own composition that he had also printed and bound by his own efforts. The Auchinleck Press inevitably closed with Boswell's death in 1822.

The Beldornie Press

The third Roxburghe member who was moved to own a press was Edward Vernon Utterson, who founded the Beldornie Press at one of his residences, Beldornie Tower, on the Isle of Wight. Utterson was well known as a barrister, a book editor and an accomplished watercolour artist as well as an antiquarian book collector. He was married to the author Sarah Elizabeth Utterson who,

---

15 Dibdin, *Bibliographical Decameron*, p. 454.
16 Robert Howie Smith, *The Poetical Works of Sir Alexander Boswell* (Glasgow: Maurice Ogle, 1871), p. xxxiii.
17 Dibdin, *Bibliographical Decameron*, p. 455.

in 1812, had translated and published the collection of gothic stories *Tales of the Dead* from the French and German editions, in which as well as translating the stories she had undertaken to edit the collection, leaving out a number of stories and including a story written by herself titled 'The Storm'.

The first proof sheet produced by the press was printed on 21 June 1840, and it continued its intermittent production only until 1843. During its short existence four printers were employed: J. N. Lydall, George Butler, G. E. Palmer and James Jolliffe. Lydall was declared bankrupt in July of 1843, although whether the closing of the Beldornie Press had any bearing on the matter (or vice versa) is unclear. The press was largely used by Utterson to reprint rare pieces of sixteenth- and seventeenth-century poetry, and these he presented to his friends, rarely producing more than 20 copies of each item. These items had a high collectability for those lucky enough to receive them as not only were they produced in extremely limited numbers but they also contained interesting choices of texts with significant literary value. The publication *Catalogue of Books Printed at the Beldornie Press*, lists 16 printed items plus a number of pamphlets and other ephemera.

During 1841 Utterson's press got off to a prolific start. Of the 16 items printed at the Beldornie Press in total, seven were reprints of works by Samuel Rowlands, a writer of pamphlets, usually employing satirical verse, who lived between 1598 and 1628. These works by Rowlands were all printed in the first year, starting with the *Knave of Harts: Haile Fellow Well Met*, of which 15 copies were printed and distributed to friends, a typically representative number for editions from this press. Two more Rowlands texts, also with playing-card motifs, followed quickly: *The Knave of Clubbs* from 1609 and *More Knaves Yet? The Knaves of Spades and Diamonds*, first published in 1620. Other works by Rowlands printed in this year were *The Night-Raven, Looke to It: For, Ile Stabbe Ye*, and *The Melancholie Knight*. Rowlands was a writer who evidently also interested other Roxburghe members as Scott had also edited an edition of his work in 1814. In 1841 Utterson also produced an edition of *Cynthia; and the Legend of Cassandra*, by Richard Barnfield, which he printed from a version held in the Malone Collection at Oxford. *The Catalogue of Books Printed at the Beldornie Press* states that it was the same version 'from which the Auchinleck Press No. 3 was derived and in which they [the two poems contained in *Cynthia: and the legend of Cassandra*] do not appear'.[18] Payne Collier says of the collection that

> I was the more obliged to him for the reprint of *Cynthia*, because it contains the twenty sonnets, which were addressed by Barnfield to a person he calls *Ganymede*. Most of these are of a questionable character, and

18 Catalogue list reprinted in Ransom, *Private Presses*, pp. 212–13.

were cancelled by Mr. Utterson, after they had been composed by his printer; so that, at least, twelve of the copies struck off were without them. Moreover, unusual mechanical care was evinced about them, – a circumstance which may be attributed to the fact, that Mr. Utterson himself looked over the press, before he decided that he would not insert them. He sent them to me with a separate note, and wrote "cancelled" upon them.[19]

Collier also mentions the inaccuracies contained in many of Utterson's volumes and sheds some light on the cause of the errors, saying that the items were usually from originals that were either unique or extremely rare, and were usually held in public or private collections rather than in Utterson's own library. In an uncharacteristically forgiving mood, Collier explains that 'many allowances ought, in such cases, to be made' because in order to obtain copies of the originals Utterson was often reliant on the services of a scribe who would carry out the necessary copy work for him and who was not as precise in his work as might be desired. Utterson 'trusted too much to his fidelity', and in this way inaccuracies were introduced.[20] In part due to the difficulties of travel, it was common practice at this time for editors to employ a researcher who would visit the collection where the original manuscript or volume was held, in order to make a copy, but, as Collier points out, this left the editor somewhat at the mercy of the conscientiousness and accuracy of the transcriber. This was not the only factor. Collier continues, 'of course the printer too was now and then in fault, and I do not think that Mr. Utterson engaged a very good compositor. Those are commonly the best compositors who have most to do; and the person or persons who put together the letters for a private press, were not very likely to have enough work to keep them in constant employment. Hence they did not acquire a habit of accuracy'.[21] Collier later adds, in reference to *Cynthia; and the Legend of Cassandra*, that while there are errors in the censored version that was distributed, the full, uncensored version that Collier received had benefited from Utterson's more careful adherence to the original text: 'that Mr. Utterson himself took particular pains with this little work is clear, because, in my copy, he has introduced more than one MS. emendation, to remedy the inaccuracy of his printer'.[22] Collier raises another interesting point here: that mistakes were often introduced by the printers of the works and that the club members, such as Utterson in this case, may have often had

---

19 Collier, 'Reprints of Early English Poetry', pp. 6–7.
20 Ibid.
21 Ibid.
22 Ibid.

a far better sense of accuracy regarding the volumes reprinted than is necessarily reflected in the end products.

It is apparent that Utterson considered there to be different levels of readership for whom he was producing texts: the more learned, and perhaps sophisticated, friend who would appreciate an accurate, unaltered reprint of the original and a more general readership, less discerning perhaps, who would be more suited to receive a censored, more socially acceptable, if less accurate, edition. Utterson's most potentially controversial choice of text was *Micro-cynicon: Sixe Snarling Satyres*, a satire first published in 1599 and sometimes attributed to Thomas Middleton because it is signed T. M. This dealt with a number of socially dangerous themes including homosexuality. It is a curious piece that has accrued a superstitious reputation since its creation claiming madness, death and general bad luck for anyone who has appeared in the play or had a connection with it, but it has also elicited the wry observation that 'Utterson did not seem to suffer any ill effects from the book's production, and a series of mysterious ship wrecks around the [Isle of Wight] in the middle of the 19th century is not generally attributed to any known *Micro-Cynicon* performances'.[23]

Whatever the shortcomings of the editions published at the Beldornie Press, it does appear that Utterson's impetus for printing them was a genuine love of the poetry he reproduced and a desire to share this literature with like-minded enthusiasts. In Collier's opinion, 'Mr. Utterson's sole object was to benefit others by the communication of valuable materials, within the reach of few, I am confident that his first wish would have been that defects of the kind should, as far as possible, be cured; and when I have formerly made him aware of their existence, he always expressed his obligation and his regret: adding a desire, that if I ever made any public use of his little volume, I would take care not to omit the correction of errors. In my intercourse with him, I always found him kind, liberal, and disinterested'.[24]

The printing activities of the Roxburghe Club can be viewed as inhabiting an early pre–Arts and Crafts stage of romanticism. Although it would be another 60 years before William Morris and the Pre-Raphaelites gave a definite shape to the movement, many of the underlying tenets can already be seen to be present in the early nineteenth century. Augustus Pugin and John Ruskin, key theorists, were both born during this formative, turbulently changing period. As the Industrial Revolution gathered momentum, so did the desire to hold on to what was human and creative in an increasingly mechanized world,

---

23 Lavie Tidhar, 'The Curious History of the Micro-Cynicon', Fortean Bureau available at http://www.forteanbureau.com/jan2004/Tidhar/index.html.
24 Collier, 'Reprints of Early English Poetry', pp. 6–7.

and the typographic aesthetic of the Roxburghe reprints provided a window to the more human-scale work of the early printers. From the first Roxburghe dinner, where the toasts were proposed to the seminal printers, the Club's dual aims were set down: promoting early literature and, equally, promoting early typographic skills. The club placed a pioneering value on the craftsmanship and artistry of the early printers, which laid an important foundation for later nineteenth- and twentieth-century acceptance of printing as a central aesthetic educative model. This burgeoning interest in printed books is reflected by collections such as the Cardiff Books Collection deposited with SCOLAR at Cardiff University. This collection reflects the ambitions of the Cardiff City Council and its benefactors, to provide books of the highest quality, representing the whole history of the printer's art, to help train and educate young printers at Cardiff College of Art between the 1890s and 1920s.

Private presses including the Beldornie, Lee Priory and Auchinleck sustained a thread of practical typographical and artistic endeavour during a period when private presses were scarce, that could link the artisan of the pre-mechanized era with the idealistic art printer of the Victorian age and beyond. The Roxburghe Club, in their reprints of early books and initial concentration on facsimile reproduction, provided not only concrete examples of the early methods of book production but also helped form an aesthetic of artisan authenticity that would later inspire and inform people involved in the small printing press movement and the Arts and Crafts movement, influencing in turn artists such as Eric Gill and David Jones. The catalogue of William Morris's library mentions his ownership of a copy of Haslewood's edition of *Dialogues of Creatures Moralised*, highlighting the interest displayed by the later Arts and Crafts movement in these volumes produced by the early nineteenth-century antiquarians, and the link created by the editors of these texts between the early printed or manuscript forms of these texts and the later influential cultural movement.

Chapter 7

THE LITERARY WORKS OF THE ROXBURGHE CLUB MEMBERS

The early nineteenth century was an age of letters; the written word was everywhere, in both published and private form. The construction of a reliable postal service made personal communication easier than ever before. On the wider public stage, the increase in the production of books, newspapers, periodicals and other printed matter created a heady atmosphere in which ideas and opinions could be made concrete with relative ease and swiftly transmitted to a public eager for the newest information. In this fertile environment of literary possibilities it is perhaps unsurprising to find that the men who made up the Roxburghe Club were authors, almost to a man, although this aspect of its membership has seemingly been overlooked.

This chapter looks at the texts written by club members in some detail, and illustrates how many of the men who belonged to the Roxburghe Club were not simply consumers of printed matter but also the producers of a surprising variety of publications. It is, of course, to be expected that in any large group of individuals there will be a distribution of abilities across a given spectrum, and the Roxburghe Club was no exception. The literary distinction of the members ranged from professional authors like Sir Walter Scott through to enthusiastic and often surprisingly talented, but strictly private, writers like the Duke of Devonshire. Between these extremes were gentlemanly semi-professionals, scholars writing on academic subjects, professional men writing poetry as a hobby. There were also men, like Dibdin and Haslewood, who were employed in other fields but who made a significant part of their income or reputation from literary pursuits. Some members of the club, such as E. V. Utterson, did not write anything themselves (beyond introductory material) but instead preferred to act as editor, on their own behalf or in the employ of others, and in a related vein are those members who carried out labours of interpretation and transliteration such as George Neville Grenville who, as master of Magdalene, Cambridge, was instrumental in the efforts to decipher Samuel Pepys's shorthand, an undertaking which eventually enabled the diary to be published in 1825. Lastly, the Roxburghe members' literary offerings sometimes inhabited the interesting area that lay between personal letters and commercial publication, in which pieces of writing that originated in private correspondence, or formed open letters, were published for public consumption, often as part of an ongoing intellectual dialogue.

Dibdin, without doubt the foremost chronicler of the book-collecting circles, is familiar as the author of books such as *Bibliomania*; *The Bibliographical Decameron*; and *Reminiscences of a Literary Life*. Other titles by him are less familiar and include *Poems; Sermons, Doctrinal and Practical: Preached in King Street, Brompton; Quebec and Fitzroy Chapels; Sermons*; and the *Sunday Library; Or, the Protestant's Manual for the Sabbath-Day*. In 1808 he produced an edition in translation of Thomas More's *Utopia*. While his bibliographic texts have often been criticized or ridiculed for his hyperbolic, baroque style of writing, his abilities as an author go beyond these works and show very different sides to his personality. His sermons, for instance, reveal him to be capable of writing in a clear and robust manner, devoid of flowery mannerisms and affectations. Far from being the foolishly excitable cataloguer of superficialities that he is often painted, he instead appears to have been a skilfully versatile author who knew his target audiences and adapted his style accordingly. If the fashionable collectors of the day were pleased to speak in the ornate slang of the 'ton', then his books were equally pleased to reflect that language and tone. This elite usage of language delineated the world of the fashionable and excluded those who languished amongst the hopelessly outré as effectively as a 'cut' from a nobleman or being omitted from the list at Almacks. The difference here was that not only did the aspirant need to understand the fashionable vernacular but they also needed to be familiar with the jargon of book collecting and selling, making entrance to this rarefied world doubly exclusive. This desire to prove his credentials as one who existed on the inside of the fashionable world can be seen in the subject matter of Dibdin's bibliographical books as well as the language used to write them. He repeatedly mentions the beautiful libraries and homes of his friends and acquaintants and, by implicit or explicit suggestion, his frequent entry into those areas reserved for the personal use of those who orbit within the owners' exclusive social circles. To see him as merely a social climber is, however, to do him a grave disservice because alongside his more publicized activities in fashionable circles, he was active in other, more solidly antiquarian circles and, like many of the other members of the Roxburghe Club, belonged to many of the foremost societies of the day. His acknowledged presence in serious circles is illustrated by his appearance in the Cruikshank cartoon titled 'The Antiquarian Society', where he is shown standing to the left of the picture, wearing an oddly shapeless hat that makes him stand out in a room of otherwise bareheaded men and carrying a copy of his *Bibliomania* (see Figure 7.1). This caricature of another

Figure 7.1 The Society of Antiquarians by Cruikshank. Reproduced by kind permission of the Society of Antiquaries of London.

learned and antiquarian society is especially interesting as it would have been exactly contemporary with the founding of the Roxburghe Club, appearing in the *Scourge* only 16 days before the club's inaugural dinner. Dibdin's reputation was in the ascendant.

Dibdin's excitable gush of enthusiasm towards the more superficial or aesthetic attractions of rare books did not mean that he placed no value on the contents of the volumes that he collected. It is, of course, possible that this accusation could be levelled at other collectors who caught the 'bibliomania' from his paeans to the auction room. Rather than reflecting a superficial approach to books, Dibdin's writing is a consciously fey expression of what was for him a deeply held passion for every facet of books, in other words, treating a subject that he believed in wholeheartedly in a lightly entertaining way that would appeal to a strata of society that expected to be amused. He was also trying to divert himself, writing his expanded version of *Bibliomania* as an attempted distraction from his profound grief over the death of his youngest son.

For Dibdin, the extrinsic and aesthetic values of a volume's surface beauty and rarity were in addition to its intrinsic textual value, not instead of it. If people mistook his point, then it was not for want of his having made it clearly enough in his writing:

> In the first place, the disease of the Bibliomania is materially softened, or rendered mild, by directing our studies to useful and profitable

works; whether these be printed upon small or large paper, in the gothic, roman or italic type. To consider merely the intrinsic excellence and not the exterior splendor or adventitious value, of any production, will keep us perhaps wholly free from this disease. Let the midnight lamp be burnt to illuminate the stores of antiquity – whether they be romances, or chronicles, or legends, and whether they be printed by ALDUS or CAXTON – if a brighter lustre can thence be thrown upon the pages of modern learning! To trace genius to its source, or to see how she has been influenced or modified, by the lore of past times, is both a pleasing and profitable pursuit.[1]

As unscholarly or lacking in rigour as his works often appear to the eye of the modern bibliographer, he can nevertheless be credited with making pioneering contributions to the interface between bibliophilic and literary interests. Dibdin has always polarized opinion among other writers, book collectors and especially academics. Many have dismissed his works, emphasizing the innumerable errors and omissions that they contain. Others have praised his writing and ignored the message, by highlighting the style rather than the content, an approach exemplified by one description of his work as the 'amiable ravings of this honest collector, who by living in one long dream came at last to persuade himself that he was dealing with precious stones, and all that was rare and costly in the world! His style, from this generous ardour, was passionately expressive – full of quaint and gorgeous turns, with a power of delineating character that wins his readers. His career and story is valuable as exhibiting the very highest and most expressive form of which bibliophilism is capable'.[2]

Whatever the final judgement on Dibdin's bibliographical writing, the books themselves were beautifully printed and illustrated. They were expensive, often limited edition items when new, and are still much sought after by collectors today. As Edwards pungently phrased it, 'his well-known books have had the curious fortune to keep their price, without keeping their reputation. They are lustily abused, and eagerly bought', and little has changed.[3] Dibdin's less frivolous writings, however, have not fared so well. Although free of the ornate linguistic tics that have caused so much criticism of his bibliographical works, they are conversely perhaps too staid, too earnest and too commonplace to interest the modern reader or even perhaps many of his own contemporaries. His sermons are sensible, high-minded but tolerant of

1 Dibdin, *Bibliomania* (1811), pp. 607–8.
2 Fitzgerald, *The Book Fancier*, p. 227.
3 Edwards, *Libraries and Founders of Libraries*, p. 418.

human weakness in common with so many sermons published at that time, and although obviously written with sincerity they do not carry the same spark of lunatic enthusiasm that makes his bibliophilic writing so compelling and exasperating in equal measure. Similarly, he made occasional unsuccessful forays into journalism that failed to make any significant mark, either at the time of writing or on posterity. One such attempt was a short-lived venture as the editor of the *Director*, a weekly magazine launched in 1807 which only ran to two editions. Overall his writing did not secure him any regular financial support, and even with his ecclesiastical income, his financial position was one of extreme difficulty, especially in later life.

Moving on to the other club member who is well known as a proponent of bibliophilic pursuits, Sir Walter Scott, whose literary career is too well documented to need much elaboration here, was already the most popular writer of his age by 1823 when he took up the invitation to join the club, coyly addressed to 'the author of the Waverley novels'. His books often contained references to antiquarians and book collectors, and he displayed an intimate knowledge of the world of the bibliomaniac in works including the *Antiquary*, in which a character expounds on the anxieties of book collecting:

> "How often have I stood haggling on a halfpenny, lest, by a too ready acquiescence in the dealer's first price, he should be led to suspect the value I set upon the article! – how have I trembled, lest some passing stranger should chop in between me and the prize, and regarded each poor student of divinity that stopped to turn over the books at the stall, as a rival amateur, or prowling bookseller in disguise! – And then, Mr. Lovel, the sly satisfaction with which one pays the consideration, and pockets the article, affecting a cold indifference, while the hand is trembling with pleasure! – Then to dazzle the eyes of our wealthier and emulous rivals by showing them such a treasure as this" (displaying a little black smoked book about the size of a primer); "to enjoy their surprise and envy, shrouding meanwhile, under a veil of mysterious consciousness, our own superior knowledge and dexterity these, my young friend, these are the white moments of life, that repay the toil, and pains, and sedulous attention, which our profession, above all others, so peculiarly demands!".[4]

He was well acquainted with a number of the Roxburghe members including, of course, Dibdin before he joined the club, and was especially a close friend

---

4 Walter Scott, *The Antiquary*, ed. David Hewitt (Edinburgh: Edinburgh University Press, 2010), p. 31.

of Richard Heber, to whom he had dedicated the sixth canto of *Marmion*. Heber was also mentioned in the introduction, where he writes, 'Adieu dear Heber! life and health, And store of literary wealth', which neatly encapsulates those qualities most necessary to the bibliophile.[5]

Moving away from the immense fame of the Wizard of the North, Dibdin's close friend Haslewood, although largely overlooked now, was during this period a well-known name in literary circles as one who appreciated early English texts and as the editor of a significant number of reprints, especially of Elizabethan poetry, including *A Paradise of Dainty Devices*, by Richard Edwards; *The Italian Taylor and his Boy*, by Robert Armin; and the Puttenham/Webster *Arte of English Poesie*. His choice of texts reveals the expertise that made him such a suitable, and valuable, member of the Roxburghe Club. For example, in 1813 Haslewood edited *Palace of Pleasure*, by Robert Painter, a collection of stories from which Shakespeare is believed to have taken inspiration, and Haslewood's reprinting of this volume provides evidence of a theme that is looked at more closely in the next chapter: that the Roxburghe Club, both collectively and individually, took a special interest in the topic of literary influences and sources. In 1810, Haslewood published *Tusser's Five Hundred Points of Good Husbandry*, a treatise on farming, in rhyming couplets, with a long printing history dating from 1557, and an author whom he also briefly covered for the *British Bibliographer*.

In 1811, Haslewood published his edition of the *Book of St. Albans*, a collection of treatises on blood sports and heraldry, attributed to Dame Juliana Berners in 1486. In the introduction, Haslewood assigns only the treatise on angling to Berners, believing the other parts of the text to be collected from other sources. A later owner of Haslewood's manuscript copy of the text writes that 'George Isted [...] presented it to Mr. Haslewood, a few months before he died in 1821. Mr. Haslewood added a paginary transcript for the convenience of reading this ancient MSS., and it was bound by C. Lewis in 1823'.[6] This short extract illustrates two important points: first, the members of the Roxburghe Club maintained close and amiable relationships, most significantly (in light of the *Athenaeum's* accusations) with Haslewood, and secondly, Haslewood, in producing a 'paginated transcript', was obviously familiar with scholarly frameworks and was highly capable in his handling of an early manuscript, producing a workable, more accessible, modern edition, and at the very least making an attempt to protect the original document while still being able to work with the text. In another clever piece of literary detective work,

---

5 Ibid., p. 311.
6 Edward Jesse, 'Dame Juliana Berners and her "Boke of Venerie"', *Once a Week: An Illustrated Miscellany* 4 (London: Bradbury Evans, 1867), p. 386.

Haslewood's *Barnabae Itinerarium: Or Drunken Barnaby's Four Journeys to the North of England*, sometimes also known as *Drunken Barnabee's Journal*, was published in 1818, and Haslewood was the first researcher to attribute this work correctly to Richard Brathwaite. Not surprisingly it appears to be a text that he took a great deal of pride in, and with which his name is most often linked.

Haslewood made several forays into reprinting Elizabethan translations in English of medieval works originally written in Latin or Middle English. Moreover, in 1814 he was involved in the publication of the early fifteenth-century Lollard work *Pierce the Plowman's Crede*, edited by Dr. Whitaker, and which included the *Plowman's Vision*. This was a medieval text, an anticlerical set of verses composed in the style of *Piers Plowman*. Whitaker had already published an edition of the *Creed* in the previous year which was reprinted as a companion to the *Vision*, and although it is unclear what Haslewood's connection was exactly with this enterprise, it is possible that he was involved with overseeing the printing as the proof sheets remained in his possession, later to belong to Sir Frederic Madden.[7] Another important reprint was his 1816 edition of *Dialogues of Creatures Moralised*, which, although far from a perfect copy, largely due to Haslewood's erroneous belief that all previously existing examples were themselves imperfect, was nonetheless a significant link in the publishing history of the long-neglected English translation of this work, which had not been reprinted in the 300 years previous to Haslewood's edition. In 1815 the indefatigable Haslewood compiled a two-volume anthology of Elizabethan criticism, *Ancient Critical Essays upon the English Poets and Poesy by Webbe, King James the First, Sir John Harrington etc*, and also in that same year published an edition of the important mid-sixteenth-century anthology *Mirror for Magistrates*, a collection of cautionary moral tales of famous lives. In 1820 he published *Two Interludes: Jack Jugler and Thersytes*, his presentation to the Roxburghe Club. Along with Brydges, with whom he had been friendly at least since contributing to *Censura Literaria* between 1807 and 1809, he edited a reprint of *England's Helicon*, the great Elizabethan lyric anthology. In 1827 he reprinted *Wyl Bucke, His Testament, a Poem*, first published by Copland without a date, but probably between 1548 and 1568. Haslewood's edition was produced at the Chiswick press in 40 copies that were printed not with the intention of resale but as presents, which hints that Haslewood's literary activities were not necessarily the result of financial imperative. This somewhat macabre work by John Lacy, a writer who, according to Haslewood, was not known to have written any other works, portrays the final words of a dying stag in which he bequeaths the parts of his body (with recipes because, as well as being a poem, it is a cookery book)

---

7 Thomas Wright, *The Vision and Creed of Piers Ploughman* (London: Reeves and Turner, 1887), pp. xxxvii–xxxviii.

to various people: the king, a lady, the raven, the robin. Haslewood also seems to have been involved during his frenetic career with a number of publications that relate to Joseph Ritson's work. *Gammer Gurton's Garland*, an anthology of nursery rhymes collected by Ritson and published in 1784, was edited and reprinted in 1810 by Haslewood, and this second edition contained additional material provided by Francis Douce. In 1824 he published *Some Account of the Life and Publications of the Late Joseph Ritson, Esq.*

Haslewood's interests, however, were not restricted to poetry and early criticism: in 1795 he had published the two-volume *Secret History of the Green Room*, the 'authentic and entertaining memoirs of the actors and actresses in the three theatres royal' and which included a short essay on the history of the English stage.[8] Theatre life and the established field of 'greenroom' books was a subject matter that obviously interested him, at the very least for the considerable financial gains to be made from such a popular genre, but his personal enthusiasm was also reflected in his collection of theatre ephemera. In 1809 he published *Green Room Gossip*, a mixture of true and fictional backstage anecdotes and comical stories. Surprisingly, as well as earning his living as a partner in his uncle's legal practice, editing manuscripts and early books for publishing, writing a high percentage of the articles used in the magazines that were nominally under the editorship of Brydges and trading as an agent for booksellers, he also found time to contribute regularly to the *Gentleman's Magazine*, using the pseudonyms 'Eugenius Hood', E. Hood, EU, Cristofer Valdarfer or J. H. Under the first alias he contributed a series of articles entitled 'Fly Leaves', which began their long run in July 1822 and continued to appear until around 1829. Besides this bewildering variety of literary output Haslewood apparently still had enough energy left over to keep up a spirited correspondence in the letters pages on a variety of subjects. The topics include, but are certainly not limited to, 'Remarks on Fairs', 'A Lullaby', 'Forde's Apothegmes', 'Notitia Dramatica' and 'Winstanley's Water-works'.

Haslewood appears to have been a more familiar name within the world of books than outside it. He received an entry in the 1816 *Biographical Dictionary of the Living Authors of Great Britain and Ireland* which refers to him as 'an editor of new editions of old works'.[9] Even the *Athenaeum*, which only a few months later ran such a scurrilous attack on his memory, carried an obituary in which he was described as being 'generally admitted to have few superiors in what is called bibliographical knowledge, especially in all that related to our early

---

8 Joseph Haslewood, *The Secret History of the Green Room: Containing Authentic and Entertaining Memoirs of the Actors and Actresses in the Three Theatres Royal* (London: J. Owen, 1795).

9 John Watkins, Frederick Shoberl and William Upcott, *A Biographical Dictionary of the Living Authors of Great Britain and Ireland* (London: Henry Colburn, 1816), p. 148.

poets and dramatists'.[10] The posthumous attack by the *Athenaeum* did some lasting damage to Haslewood's reputation, although researchers within his areas of expertise continued to value the editions that he was instrumental in reprinting. Where assessments exist of his various reprints, the verdict seems to be largely positive, usually mentioning the thorough scholarship of 'that careful student' and acknowledging his expertise in his field.[11] His general reputation, however, does not seem to have recovered, and it would be interesting to know to what extent his humble origin, as designated by the *Athenaeum* and echoed by so many later critics, has led to his bibliographic achievements being underestimated or eclipsed by the reputations of the well-born company with whom he sometimes collaborated. His work on the *British Bibliographer* is often viewed as that of a dogsbody or assistant to Brydges, or described in ways that imply that he inhabited an important but still subsidiary role. Dibdin, in contrast, in reference to this publication, wrote that 'the professed editor was Sir S. Egerton Brydges but the real staff of its support was held by my deceased friend [i.e. Haslewood]', wording which makes clear that Dibdin considered the publication to be more Haslewood's work than Brydges's.[12] The four volumes of the *British Bibliographer* certainly carry Sir Egerton Brydges's name on the title page, and an introduction written by him, but in that same introduction he himself explicitly states that 'it is to Mr. HASLEWOOD that the work owes the care of constant superintendence, and a most copious and never-failing supply of articles, as remarkable for their rarity, as for the curious matter in which they abound. The keenness of his researches, his industry, his accuracy, his memory, his opportunities, his extensive acquaintance, give a value to his numerous articles which cannot be too highly rated'.[13] A brief survey of the volumes confirms that the greater part of the articles carry the signature of 'J. H.', and his work has retained its reputation for precision and for its attempt to retain the original presentation of the text.

Haslewood's frequent collaborator Brydges was involved in many areas of literature; he wrote poetry, romances, criticism and edited rare pieces of early English poetry. He was also, unfortunately, a man of very uneven talents and unstable emotional foundations. His faults notwithstanding, he was undoubtedly genuinely passionate about early English literature and instrumental in printing editions of many neglected pieces of poetry dating from

---

10 *Athenaeum* (28 September 1833), p. 652.
11 'Richard Brathwaite', *Saturday Review of Politics, Literature, Science and Art* 47 (25 January 1879), p. 122.
12 Dibdin, *Reminiscences*, p. 295.
13 Samuel Egerton Brydges, *The British Bibliographer*, 4 vols (London: Triphook, 1810), rep. (New York: AMS, 1966), I, p. v.

the sixteenth century, mostly, as already mentioned, through the medium of his private printing press at Lee Priory. Lockhart, reviewing Brydges's autobiography, laments the lack of diligence and steadfastness that prevented Brydges from making better use of his literary gifts, but also writes of 'his antiquarian pursuits, in which he really did so much service to literature'.[14] These Brydges had more or less dismissed as dull to produce, saying that 'the books in which I was engaged for the press occupied much of my time; and the long transcripts necessary were laborious and fatiguing. They were enough to suppress my imagination and deaden my powers of original thought. [...] Meanwhile, I was not at all satisfied with the way I was making in the literary world: I was pursuing a humble path not suited to my fiery ambition, and this produced a self-abasement which had an evil effect upon my energies'.[15] His lack of enthusiasm for methodical, solid work and preference for more celebrated and instant forms of recognition have, perhaps inevitably, meant that he failed to leave any lasting impression on the literary world as a poet, but with Haslewood's more practical assistance did produce some interesting and valuable additions to the reprinting of early poetry.

In stark contrast to Brydges's somewhat haphazard attainments stand the achievements of Henry Drury, the son of Joseph Drury, the headmaster of Harrow and himself a master at the same school. A respected classical scholar, he edited several editions of the classics specifically for use at Harrow, and although this sort of editing and publishing by its nature leaves little conscious impression on the world of literary studies, his work was considered valuable by contemporaries and his obituary alluded to these works, saying that 'Mr. Drury's literary attainments were very great'.[16] Dibdin wrote with approval that 'his Latinity was perspicuity and accuracy itself', and while it may be easy to overlook his works, confined as they were to the education of schoolboys, it is important to remember that they would have been well-known texts, familiar to generations of students, which in itself allots them a certain degree of influence.[17] Drury perhaps also contributed to journals anonymously: an article in the *Quarterly Review* of 1814 is provisionally attributed to Drury on the basis of pencil notes carried in John Murray's archives, and Dibdin refers to another article, saying 'how [Drury] *could* criticize, sufficiently appears in an article on the *Musae Edinburgenses* in an early number of the Quarterly Review'.[18]

---

14 Lockhart, 'Autobiography of Sir Egerton Brydges', *Quarterly Review* 51 (June 1834), 342–65 (p. 356).
15 Quoted in Lockhart, 'Autobiography of Sir Egerton Brydges', *Quarterly Review*, p. 356.
16 'Rev. Henry Drury', *Gentleman's Magazine* 16 (September 1841), p. 323.
17 Dibdin, *Bibliomania*, p. 607.
18 Ibid.; italics in original.

Literary works among the Roxburghe members appear from far less expected sources as well. The Duke of Devonshire surprisingly turned his hand to writing with the *Handbook of Chatsworth and Hardwick*. This is no mere factual handbook of the houses as the title may imply, but an informal, spirited text that weaves architectural information with historical and personal detail, and the book is as much a memoir of recollected personal events connected with the two grand houses as it is a simple guidebook in the modern sense. The volume takes the form of letters written from the Duke to his sister Harriet, describing the renovation and improvements that he had made to Chatsworth, and how it now differed from the house in which they had spent their childhood. The Handbook contains gentle humour and an engagingly chatty style. To give a brief example, the Duke writes of one room that he had renovated, saying that 'from this description it might be supposed that this was not so bad a room and decoration; but my sister must know better, – and you, posterity, take my word for it, it was atrocious'.[19] The Duke obviously relished the process of writing the *Handbook*, although he at one point complains that 'I like my task; but at times it turns upon me, and I feel exceedingly ridiculous, and like an auctioneer when he makes his inventory, and puts the striking features into capital letters'.[20]

While the Duke was writing in a strictly private way with no intention of his privately published book being issued for public sale, another member, George Isted, had apparently nurtured some short-lived aspirations to literary or journalistic attainments and had been in his youth the co-writer and editor of the *Literary Fly*, a magazine published in partnership with the author Sir Herbert Croft in 1779. This venture unfortunately only ran to 17 issues between the January and May of that year. Another Roxburghe member who showed early literary promise was Sir William Bolland, who while at Trinity College, Cambridge, enjoyed some success as a poet. In 1796 he had won the Seatonian prize with his poem *The Epiphany*, and in 1797 he won the prize again for *Miracles*. In 1798 his *St. Paul at Athens* won the prize for yet a third time and was described as 'another academic exercise in blank verse that reflects credit on the talents which the author displays and affords fair promise of excellence in his future poetical undertakings'.[21] The same article goes on to say that 'Mr Bolland's versification is correct and smooth his language in general chaste and animated and the sentiments which he inculcates rational and

---

19 William Spencer Cavendish, *Handbook of Chatsworth and Hardwick*, manuscript in the Chatsworth archives (1844), p. 36.
20 Ibid., p. 50.
21 Andrew Kippis and William Godwin, *New Annual Register or General Repository of History, Politics and Literature for the year 1800* (London: G. and J. Robinson, 1801), p. 327.

edifying'.[22] Bolland later wrote a satire, *The Campaign, to His Royal Highness the Duke of York, Britannia in the Year 1800 to C. J. Fox*, which was published privately and anonymously. His satirical abilities were perhaps less developed, or at least less warmly received, than his religious verse, if the review from the *British Critic and Quarterly Theological Review* of 1802 is to be believed:

> As this poem is printed for the author who is unknown and is not by any publisher its sale is *properly* provided for. The first Canto is a very lame and bungling satire on the Royal Commander in chief; the second is still ironical both in praise and satire but is no less unpoetical than the former. The first Canto is about the war; the second about every body and every thing; but without connection in the sense or harmony in the verse. To justify what we have said and remove all suspicion of biassed [sic] opinion let us take the first ten lines that present themselves
>
>> The chinking gold no more our bankers tell,
>> Since the House votes – that paper does as well;
>> Pitt asks no vote – but ships the precious ore,
>> To sharp the sword, and bid the cannon roar.
>> What miracles our banish'd guineas work,
>> Shar'd by the Russ, the Portuguese, and Turk,
>> Faithful allies, though in discordant spheres,
>> The Mufti, Pope, Grand Lama, and Algiers;
>> All leagu'd by reason, on religion's plan,
>> Louis to crown, and crush the rights of man.
>
> Of this skimble skamble stuff there are more than a thousand lines.[23]

It is, of course, highly likely that the reviewer may have objected to the poem's potential pro-Fox political tendencies rather more than to the structure of the verse itself.

Less controversially, Roger Wilbraham was an antiquarian with a keen interest in etymology who composed *An Attempt at a Glossary of Some Words Used in Cheshire*. A member of the Antiquarian Society, he only appears to have published this one book which reflected his life-long interest in the subject. Similarly, James William Dodd also published one work, which collected together his fascination with Robin Hood and Archery (he was the club

---

22 Ibid.
23 'Art. 17', *British Critic and Quarterly Theological Review* 19 (London: Rivington, 1802), pp. 83–84; italics in original.

member noted as drunkenly singing Robin Hood ballads at midnight after a club meeting). Dodd was the son of the Drury Lane actors James and Martha Dodd, who were both members of David Garrick's company. The younger James Dodd, moving away from his theatrical background, was a clergyman and usher at Westminster School and the author of a volume of poetry *Ballads of Archery, Sonnets &c*, which, as well as the various anthology items, contains an extensive preface covering the general subject of archery and the history of the Royal Kentish Bowmen.

James Heywood Markland was a much more prolific author, and in 1818 he presented the Roxburghe Club with an edition of the *Chester Mysteries*. His edition is accompanied by a detailed preface which displays his extensive interest in and familiarity with the subject as well as his skill as an author. Markland indicates that he had originally intended this introductory material to be considerably more substantial, saying that 'it was the Editor's intention to have prefixed to these Plays a concise history of the origin and progress of religious dramas in Europe, with a view to ascertain, if possible, the precise period of their introduction into this country; and also to have some account of the several series of Mysteries acted at York, Coventry, and other places'.[24] He goes on to explain that, although he had amassed a great deal of information regarding the subject, 'each day's research tended to convince him that a still larger portion remained unexplored, and that the subject had hitherto received far less attention than it deserved. Sensible therefore of the impossibility of affording it common justice [...] he has been reluctantly compelled to abridge his plan, and to content himself with giving some particulars of the collection from which the present specimens are selected, with a few incidental remarks on others of a similar class'.[25] This depth of knowledge and attention to scholarly detail can be seen to be typical of Markland's writing, which ranges over his wide antiquarian and religious interests. He was an active churchman who was well known for his published works on antiquarian and ecclesiastical subjects, and in most cases the titles of his works speak for themselves: *A Few Plain Reasons for Adhering to the Church; Remarks on the Sepulchral Memorials of Past and Present Times, with Some Suggestions for Improving the Condition of Our Churches; On the Reverence due to Holy Places; Remarks on English Churches & on the Expediency of Rendering Sepulchral Memorials Subservient to Pious & Christian Uses; On the Ecclesiastical Architecture of England in Past and Present Times: Read at the Annual Meeting of the Worcester Eng. Diocesan Architectural Society, Sept. 25th, 1854; The Offertory the Best Way of Contributing Money for Christian Purposes;* and

---

24 Anon., *Chester Mysteries De Deluvio Noe De Occisione Innocentium*, ed. by J. H. Markland (London: Bensley, 1818), p. i.
25 Ibid.

An Inscription Upon a Chimney-piece, Recently Discovered in the Governor's House in the Tower of London.

Like many of the club members, Markland belonged to a wide variety of antiquarian organizations beyond the Roxburghe and was active in contributing essays and articles to their magazines. His primary interest was the journal *Archaeologia*, published by the Society of Antiquaries of London, of which he was director in charge of publications from 1827–29. One article contributed by him to *Archaeologia* was entitled 'Some Remarks on the Early Use of Carriages in England, and on the Modes of Travelling Adopted by Our Ancestors'. He also contributed to the *Archaeological Journal* (the publication of the Royal Archaeological Institute) and the *Journal of the British Archaeological Association*. In later life he retired to Bath and became the president of the Literary Club of Bath in 1858. His varied publications were acknowledged in a paper read before the club in 1854, in which the author writes that 'we can walk, hand-in-hand, through our venerable "English Churches," with our erudite, worthy, and excellent President, hear his judicious remarks on their architecture and archaeological histories, view their sepulchral memorials, and be charmed with his Christian Commentaries thereon, or learn how to live and how to die from his interesting memoir of the good, the wise, but persecuted Bishop Ken'.[26] He occasionally wrote on literary subjects as well and contributed an article examining the life of the poet William Mason to *Censura Literaria*, the periodical published by Brydges for the discussion of Old English books. Markland was a regular contributor to the same publication of a continuous stream of brief descriptive articles and reviews of various rare books which continued throughout the existence of the journal.[27] In the same period *Notes and Queries* published numerous articles from him on aspects of literary history. In 1837 he wrote a memoir of his father-in-law and fellow Roxburghe

---

26 G. Monkland, *Monkland's Literature and Literati of Bath: An Essay, Read at the Literary Club, November 13, 1852* (Bath: R. E. Peach; London: J. H. Parker, 1854), pp. 90–91. The essay is also dedicated to Markland.

27 These include among many other examples, 'ART. XIV. Newes of Sir Walter Rauleigh, with the true Description of Guiana', *Censura Literaria*, 5 (London: Longman, Hurst, Rees and Orme, 1807), pp. 169–71; 'ART. XVIII. The Booke of Honor and Armes', *Censura Literaria*, 5 (London: Longman, Hurst, Rees and Orme, 1807), pp. 287–89; 'ART.IV. A Choice of Emblemes, and other Devises, for the moste parte gathered out of sundrie writers', *Censura Literaria*, 5 (London: Longman, Hurst, Rees and Orme, 1807), pp. 233–35; 'ART. XIX. Ideas Mirrour Amours in quatorzains.' *Censura Literaria*, 5 (London: Longman, Hurst, Rees and Orme, 1807), pp. 289–90; 'ART. III. The benefit of the aunciente bathes of Buckstones, which cureth most greevous sicknesses, never before published', *Censura Literaria*, 10 (London: Longman, Hurst, Rees and Orme, 1809), pp. 274–81; 'ART.X. Paradoxical Assertions and philosophical problems,' *Censura Literaria*, 10 (London: Longman, Hurst, Rees and Orme, 1809), pp. 383–88.

member, *A Sketch of the Life and Character of George Hibbert, Esq*, privately published following Hibbert's death.

George Watson Taylor's publications included two plays: *England Preserved*, a highly political work already discussed in Chapter 4, and a comedy, the *Profligate*, which was privately printed in 1820 for distribution to members of the Roxburghe Club. It is obviously not considered an official Roxburghe volume as it does not fit the criteria for the member contributions and is not mentioned in the catalogue of club books, which interestingly points to the possibility that members occasionally used the club to distribute their own work in addition to making their more 'official' contribution. Other pieces of writing by Watson Taylor include a poem titled *Equanimity in Death*, 1813, reprinted in *Pieces of Poetry: With Two Dramas*. This collection of Watson Taylor's work included a reprint of his satirical poem 'The Old Hag in a Red Cloak, a Romance', which is a parody of Matthew Lewis's popular Gothic romantic poem the 'Grim White Woman'. Lewis's original poem had, coincidentally, appeared in the collection *Tales of Wonder*, to which Sir Walter Scott had also contributed a number of ballads. Although he makes no direct criticism on any other writer's work, Watson Taylor, evidently no follower of the fashion for Gothic romance, states in his foreword to his amusing parody that 'no personal motives whatever dictated their composition. They were directed against the new creation of poetical romances in general; and the Author of the Grim White Woman having taken the lead in that department, he consequently became the chief object of criticism'. He goes on to further vitiate the implied criticism by saying that 'a lively imagination, and an easy and elegant flow of versification, are worthy of higher subjects, and of nobler exertions, than those of vitiating the taste of the Public, or of supplying it, if already vitiated, with a species of composition, which has its principal, and, perhaps, only merit, in creating wonder, and which, by repetition, ceases even to be wonderful'.[28] Watson Taylor obviously enjoyed satire and another piece by him, *Cross-Bath Guide; being the correspondence of a respectable family upon the subject of a late unexpected dispensation of honours. Collected by Sir Joseph Cheakill*, is a poem which takes the form of a series of family letters, presenting a humorous treatment of what the author perceives to be the current social obsession with advancement. It mocks the abundance of new baronets appearing among the middle classes, especially those financially ill-equipped to support their new positions in life, and he may have felt it wise to write under a pseudonym on this occasion as so many of his own social circle are represented in the poem. The story ends with the financial ruin of the recipient of the title, which proved to be

---

28 Watson Taylor, 'The Old Hag in a Red Cloak', *Pieces of Poetry: With Two Dramas* (Chiswick: Whittingham, 1830), pp. 69–79.

sadly prophetic for Watson Taylor. By 1832 he had, through a combination of the devaluation of Jamaican property and extravagant spending, lost much of the wealth that he had controlled through his wife's property in the West Indies, and was forced to sell many of his possessions. He had not, however, accepted a baronetcy.

James Boswell is probably best known (apart from being his famous father's namesake) for his editing of Edmond Malone's extensive work on Shakespeare after Malone's death. Malone, through his connection with Samuel Johnson, had become a friend of the elder James Boswell, and had provided assistance with his *Life of Johnson*. In turn, Malone at his death bequeathed to the younger James Boswell the immense undertaking of collating and completing his amended second edition of Shakespeare, from the vast quantity of material that Malone had already prepared. Malone died in 1812, and Boswell completed the 21-volume work in 1821. It was a groundbreaking and extensive piece of research which as recently as 1992 was described as 'easily the most complete and valuable edition of Shakespeare yet to be published'.[29] That in large part was due to the Herculean task that James Boswell undertook on behalf of his deceased friend. Boswell died in the year following the publication of the work, and his obituary stated that

> to this edition, Mr Boswell contributed many notes, and collated the text with the earlier copies. In the first volume, he has stepped forwards to defend the literary reputation of Mr. Malone, against the severe attacks made by a writer of distinguished eminence, upon many of his critical opinions and statements; a task of great delicacy, and which Mr. Boswell has performed in so spirited and gentlemanly a manner, that his preface may be fairly quoted as a model of controversial writing. In the same volume, are inserted the memoirs of Mr. Malone, originally printed by Mr. Boswell for private distribution; and a valuable essay on the metre and phraseology of Shakespeare, the materials for which were partly collected by Mr. Malone; but the arrangement and completion of them were the work of Mr. Boswell; and upon these he is known to have bestowed considerable labour and attention.[30]

On the subject of Boswell's own authorial abilities (as distinct from his editorial talents), he is described as possessing 'talents of a superior order, sound classical scholarship, and a most extensive and intimate knowledge of our

---

29 Arthur Sherbo, *Shakespeare's Midwives: Some Neglected Shakespeareans* (Newark, NJ; London; Cranbury: University of Delaware Press, 1992), p. 154.
30 'James Boswell', *Gentleman's Magazine* (March 1822), p. 277.

early literature. In the investigation of every subject that he pursued, his industry, judgment, and discrimination were equally remarkable; his memory was unusually tenacious and accurate'.[31] Boswell was only 43 when he died, but it is tempting and realistic to believe that he would have produced a great deal more useful scholarship in the field of literature had he lived longer.

Alexander Boswell, Lord Auchinleck and elder brother to James, was a prominent figure in Scottish literature. He wrote poetry, mostly in Scottish dialect and using traditional forms and subjects, described in one account of his work as 'that kind of familiar vernacular poetry which Burns again brought into fashion'.[32] This was a description that would have pleased him as he was an ardent devotee of Robert Burns's work. Boswell seemed to have an ambivalent attitude towards the publication of his poetry, and much of it was distributed anonymously, including *Spirit of Tintoc*, which was published in 1803 and is based on the legend of the Tintock Mountain. This is the highest peak in Lanarkshire, and was allegedly possessed of a large stone at its summit that collected rain water in a depression said to have been caused by the imprint of William Wallace's thumb. Boswell's poem takes its theme from a nursery rhyme about this legend. Although in the introduction Boswell asserts that the verses were found among his family papers, James Paterson, the Scottish journalist and an author who published on a wide variety of Scottish literary themes, writing less than 20 years after Boswell's death, states that 'there is little doubt, however, that it is one of his own'.[33] Walter Scott mentions Boswell's poem *Clan-Alpin's Vow*, an inspiration for his own novel, in the introduction to *A Legend of Montrose* saying that it was 'printed, but not I believe, published in 1811'.[34] This was in fact the first of Boswell's works not to be printed anonymously. Also connected to his friendship with Scott was the poem *Sir Albon*, which was published in 1811. Paterson, who reprinted the entire piece, suggests 'this poem is intended as a satire on Sir Walter Scott's poetical romances', but it was also apparently 'subsequently suppressed', although no reason for this is given by Paterson.[35] *Skeldon Haughs; or, The Sow Is Flitted*, published in 1816, tells the tragic story of a bitter feud between two landowning families and ends with the death of the son of the defender. On a lighter note, *The Woo' Creel, Or the Bill O' Bashan*, described by Boswell in the dedication as 'a

---

31 Ibid.
32 Robert Chambers, *A Biographical Dictionary of Eminent Scotsmen* (Glasgow: Blackie, 1835), I, p. 279.
33 Paterson, *The Contemporaries of Burns*, p. 311.
34 Sir Walter Scott, *A Legend of Montrose*, Waverley Novels (Edinburgh: Robert Cadell, 1844), IV, p. 222.
35 Ibid., pp. 313–14.

versification of an old story' (as were many of his poems), is the humorous telling of a cuckolded husband and his sly wife who hides her lover in the wool creel.[36]

Among those of Boswell's works that do not take their subject from Scottish traditional tales is his *Epistle to the Edinburgh Reviewers* from 1803. The verses are written in the form of a letter to the eponymous reviewers, taking them to task for their rudeness and overly critical approach to authors and their works. Similarly, in his later poem *Edinburgh, or, The Ancient Royalty*, which was written under the pseudonym Simon Gray, the author contrasts the past of Edinburgh with its present and censures the commentators who 'cant against the moderns', at the same time relating anecdotes of the older city and remembering the characters and manners of the earlier time. Lastly, the *Tyrant's Fall* is a short poem, the first work printed at the Auchinleck Press after it was set up in 1815, and it commemorates the fall of Boswell's friend Lieutenant Colonel Miller at the Battle of Waterloo.

Boswell composed many popular songs, including 'Jennie's Bawbee', 'The Old Chieftain to His Sons' (most commonly known by its second line 'Goodnight and joy be with you all') and 'Jenny Dang the Weaver', which appeared in his book *Songs Chiefly in the Scottish Dialect*. A staunch supporter of the government and anti-liberal, he was a contributor to the *Beacon*, a Tory journal published in Edinburgh, and later to its successor, the *Sentinel*. Unfortunately his penchant for writing anonymous defamatory political squibs led to his eventual involvement in the duel with James Stuart that left him with injuries that resulted in his death. He died within a week of the death of his younger brother, and his final poem was a tribute to James:

> There is a pang when kindred spirits part,
> And cold philosophy we must disown;
> There is a thrilling spot in ev'ry heart,
> For pulses beat not from a heart of stone.
>
> Boswell! th' allotted earth has closed on thee;
> Thy mild but gen'rous warmth is pass'd away;
> A purer spirit never death set free,
> And now the friend we honour'd is but clay.
>
> His was the triumph of the heart and mind;
> His was the lot which few are bless'd to know;

---

36 Alexander Boswell, *The Woo' Creel, Or the Bill O' Bashan; a Tale* (Auchinleck: James Sutherland, 1816).

More proved, more valued – fervent, yet so kind;
He never lost one friend, nor found one foe.[37]

Rev. Edward Craven Hawtrey, the provost (chair of the governing body) of Eton, possessed a reputation as a linguist and translator of poetic works, and contemporaries labelled him the 'English Mezzofanti'.[38] Mezzofanti was a minor celebrity of the period, an Italian hyperpolyglot said to speak 39 languages perfectly plus an equivalent number imperfectly. Hawtrey certainly did not speak anywhere near as many languages as Mezzofanti, but it was alleged that his 'standard was higher and his direction different. Cardinal Mezzofanti had a miraculous command of the colloquial speech of many lands, but he has left no literary memorial of his vast attainments. Dr. Hawtrey had the gift of metrical composition in Greek, Latin, German, and Italian'.[39] Hawtrey's publications were mostly privately printed for circulation amongst his friends and for distribution and use at Eton, and included a selection of Johann Wolfgang von Goethe's verse, with a preface by Hawtrey. There was also a multilingual collection entitled *Il Trifoglio, ovvero Scherzi Metrici d'un Inglese*, translations of short poems and some original compositions in Greek, Italian and German, described in the *Quarterly Review* as 'all executed, if we may venture to judge on all these points, not merely with surprising accuracy of phrase, but with a graceful felicity in catching the turn and genius of each tongue'.[40] His 'Trochaics' were also included among the six Latin and Greek pieces he contributed to the first edition of *Arundines Cami*. Hawtrey produced as well *Two Translations from Homer*, which led Matthew Arnold, in 1861, to describe Dr Hawtrey as 'one of the natural judges of a translation of Homer'.[41] Lastly, and in keeping with his clerical credentials, he also produced a number of volumes of sermons between 1846 and 1854. These attainments appear considerable for a man whose pupils (as we saw in Chapter 4) affectionately but condescendingly considered his scholarly methods to be lacking in comparison to their own: a telling indication perhaps of Victorian attitudes towards the generation who had educated them.

Sir Stephen Richard Glynne is an interesting example of an author who did not publish any of his research during his lifetime, concentrating instead

---

37 Paterson, *The Contemporaries of Burns*, p. 325.
38 William E. A. Axon, 'Dr. Hawtrey's 'Nugae', *Notes and Queries* (4 October 1902), 261–63 (p. 261).
39 Ibid.
40 'Arundines Cami', *Quarterly Review* 69 (March 1842), 237–56 (p. 248).
41 Matthew Arnold, *On Translating Homer: Three Lectures Given at Oxford* (London: Longman, Green, Longman & Roberts, 1861), p. 77.

on producing the extensive source material which has formed the basis of works published posthumously. Glynne was an avid antiquarian, and his copious notes on pre-Victorian ecclesiastical architecture run to some 106 volumes covering over 5,500 churches. The first work to be published based on these notes appeared in 1877, a volume titled *Notes on the Churches of Kent*. It was edited by Glynne's nephew W. H. Gladstone, the eldest son of the prime minister, with the considerable assistance of Archdeacon Harrison and Canon Scott Robertson of the Kent Archaeological Society. In his preface Gladstone points out that 'neither is it known whether Sir Stephen Glynne intended to publish his Notes; but inasmuch as they were left in a state as to make publication possible, his relations have not hesitated to embark, at any rate by way of experiment, upon that enterprise'.[42] It appears that the notes are presented as written by Glynne, and Gladstone refers to his uncle's working method, saying that 'a very short time usually sufficed for the jotting down of brief memoranda respecting the fabric and appurtenances, to be afterwards drawn up into the full but compendious form in which they are here presented'.[43] This implies that little editing was carried out on the notes themselves, but that the exercise was rather one of collating the various short articles left by the author. If this is so, then Glynne's writing style is plain and precise, purely descriptive rather than poetic, and displays a depth of technical architectural and historical knowledge in a style described by one reviewer of the *Yorkshire Church Notes of Sir Stephen Glynne* as 'agonisingly factual and concise; yet reliably meticulous'.[44] Where footnotes have been added, usually to refer to architectural changes carried out after Glynne's death but occasionally to add information that Glynne had omitted, they carry the identifying initial of the supplementary author. Since that initial publication there appears to have been sporadic interest in Glynne's works. Two editions of his 'notes' were published at the end of the nineteenth century by the Chetham Society under the titles *Notes on the Churches of Lancashire* and *Notes on the Churches of Cheshire* and eventually followed in 1902 by an edition of *Gloucestershire Church Notes*. There then follows a long period during which the only interest shown in Glynne's work appears in articles published by various archaeological societies' journals, and this situation continued until fairly recently when there has again been a revival of interest. In the present day the works appear largely to be produced by local antiquarian and archaeological societies and include *Sir Stephen Glynne's Church Notes for Somerset*, published by the Somerset Record Society; *Sir Stephen*

---

42 Ibid., p. iv.
43 Ibid., p. v.
44 Judith Frost, Review of *The Yorkshire Church Notes of Sir Stephen Glynne (1825–1874)*, by Lawrence Butler, *Medieval Review* (November 2008), p. xxiv.

Glynne's Church Notes for Shropshire, published by the University of Keele; *The Derbyshire Church Notes of Sir Stephen Glynne*, published by the Derbyshire Record Society; and *Notes on the Older Churches in the Four Welsh Dioceses: Archdeanery of Cardigan*, which is a facsimile reprint of articles from *Archaeologia Cambrensis*. The most recent publication of Glynne's work is the *Church Notes of Sir Stephen Glynne for Cumbria* published by Cumberland & Westmorland Antiquarian & Archaeological Society.

The Venerable Archdeacon Wrangham was an active writer in an impressive range of genres, summed up by one biographer as 'a reputable poet, an epigrammatist, a translator from Greek, Latin, French and Italian, and an editor of classical texts, as well as a prolific writer of pamphlets on church and social matters'.[45] Unusually for a Roxburghe member Wrangham had very little interest in typography, but rather favoured rarity (although, as has already been noted, he almost alone among the club members was almost certainly a bibliomaniac in his collecting methods alongside his more serious collecting habits) and, when it came to his own works, he used a variety of undistinguished printers, presumably chosen on the basis of economy, and the end results were in many cases publications of predictably poor quality. Wrangham also had a predilection for books printed on coloured paper, and often his own works appeared with some copies printed in this fashion contrary to all the dictates of taste at this period. Wrangham may have possessed a whimsical side, but he was also undoubtedly a scholarly and industrious man. He published a great many sermons and ecclesiastical treatises, including the *Advantages of Diffused Knowledge, a Sermon*; *Thirteen Practical Sermons*; *Earnest Contention for the True Faith*; *Leslie's Short and Easy Method with the Deists*; *The Pleiad; or Evidences of Christianity*; and *A Sermon on the Translation of the Scriptures into the Oriental Languages*. The publishing of his sermons and essays was more than a vanity project and held concrete practical application, as many of these sermons related to his committed work with the poor of his parish. His desire was to spread information about the various social programmes that he had created to assist his parishioners. His hope was that by advertising the ideas, they might be taken up by other clergymen to be used in their own parishes.

Wrangham published an extensive range of poetry, including his *Poems, The Sufferings of the Primitive Martyrs*; *The Restoration of the Jews*; *The Holy Land*; *Poetical Sketches of Scarborough*; *The Raising of Jaïrus' Daughter*; and *Sertum Cantabrigiense; or the Cambridge Garland*, many of which were winners of the Seaton Poetry Prize at Cambridge and printed at the University's request. He also produced translations of classical poetry, including *Sonnets from Petrarch*, and the *Lyrics of Horace*. His interest in classical authors extended beyond verse, and he

---

45 Trevor Beeson, *The Canons: Cathedral Close Encounters* (London: Clowes, 2006), p. 23.

returned repeatedly to Plutarch, contributing to a translation of *Plutarch's Lives* in 1811 and in 1816 publishing *Humble Contributions to a British Plutarch*. Over a number of years he privately printed occasional volumes of *Centuria Mirabilis; or the Hundred Heroes of the British Plutarch Who Have Flourished since the Reformation*. In 1792 he had published *Reform: A Farce Modernised from Aristophanes* under the pseudonym S. Foote Jr, which was described as 'an anti-radical parody', a fitting description because, as already shown, Wrangham was extremely radical for a clergyman of his time. Among his miscellaneous publications were *Scraps*, in 1816; *The Virtuous Woman: A Tribute to the Memory of the Right Hon. Lady Anne Hudson, of Bessingby*, which was written in 1818; and *The Works of the Rev. Thomas Zouch*, which included a memoir written by Wrangham and which appeared in 1820. Wrangham's acquaintance with Brydges began around the autumn of 1811 and so predated their connection through the Roxburghe Club by 11 years. As a result of this friendship he contributed two articles to volume 2 of Brydges's the *Ruminator* in 1813, one on Mary Queen of Scots, the other on Sir William Jones.

Despite the bewildering variety and quantity of his published works and his evident scholarship, Wrangham, displaying characteristic modesty, still judged his abilities to be lacking, writing that 'in truth I have never been able to write with fluency, and am at all times so little satisfied with what I do write, that if I were to transcribe one of my own compositions a hundred times I should make a hundred times a hundred alterations'.[46] Others were not so critical of his abilities, and by way of balance, a memoir of Wrangham, published anonymously in 1831, described his writing in warmly approving tones, noting that as 'many and various as the productions of his pen have been, there is not one line which he need ever wish to blot' and considering his legacy to be 'distinguished by innocent gaiety, by an earnest desire to benefit his fellow-creatures, and by unaffected piety'.[47] The pressures on Wrangham's time (and, it must be supposed, the time of most of the men discussed in this chapter) are evident from a letter written by Wrangham to Brydges in which he describes himself as 'much occupied with various literary engagements, the care of my three parishes and the tuition of my five children'.[48] This demanding routine did not, however, prevent him from accepting Brydges's invitation to contribute an article to *The Ruminator*.

46 Ibid., p. 435.
47 Anon., *The Venerable Francis Wrangham*, reprinted and extended version of the article of the same name first published in *The Imperial Magazine*, 1831; no publishing information is included, but the book is owned by the Bodleian.
48 Sadleir, 'Archdeacon Francis Wrangham; A Supplement', p. 426.

Looking at the group as a whole, it is sobering to consider the level of literary activity that even the busiest of men managed to maintain at this time, especially when one considers the more mundane, but often prolific letter writing, both personal and professional, the keeping of journals and the score of other workaday writing that needed to be undertaken on a daily basis. Some of these books are banal in their subject matter or mediocre in the writing skills displayed, and occasionally it is obvious that the author did not have to concern themselves unduly with the taste of their readership or the necessity of turning a profit, freed as they were by their personal wealth to follow their own interests irrespective of the market and its requirements. However, the fact that these books were written at all indicates firstly the primacy of the printed word at this time and how common the desire was to communicate the rush of ideas going on in the literary world. Secondly, it indicates the exceptionally high percentage of the Roxburghe Club members who were, or at least felt themselves to be, sufficiently involved in the world of letters to consider it feasible to put their opinions, knowledge and creativity into print for the consumption of others. There is a vast chasm between being a mere bibliomaniac as portrayed in the public imagination, and that of being a collector of rare books who also reads, writes and publishes books. The first position is an aesthetic, financial or competitive state, while the second implies an understanding and endorsement of the value of the intellectual contents of books, often coupled with an appreciation of the book as an artefact. It is especially noticeable that, apart from Dibdin, none of the club members were writing books about the collecting of books, and as already discussed, even Dibdin's works were only partially about the more superficial values of book collecting. This emphasis on literary pursuits, and their centrality in many of the club members' lives, forms an important context for the works published by the Roxburghe. These club editions did not appear out of nowhere in a rootless, random and dilettante fashion but can be viewed as the logical extension of the previous literary endeavours of the men who presented them, given context and purpose by the knowledge and serious intent that we have already seen reflected in the collecting and writing activities of the founder members. In the next chapter the early club editions are examined in more detail with a view to forming a clearer picture of not only the literary value of these works but also how they fitted into an ideological framework that informed the choice of texts presented by the members. In turn, these antiquarian literary concerns can be seen to have since formed the basis of much modern study of English literature in academia and the outlines of the present-day canon can already be seen in what, at the time, constituted highly specialized and controversial choices of literary matter.

Chapter 8

THE CLUB EDITIONS

In the year that the Roxburghe Club was established, the first steam-driven printing press was receiving its initial trial for *The Times* and the true mass production of books was fast becoming a reality. During this period when many men of letters, including Isaac Disraeli, were voicing their concerns about the avalanche of books that was threatening to overwhelm the discerning reader, the Roxburghe Club were unconcernedly revelling in the printed word. While the Roxburghe members' collections did, of course, contain many rare and beautiful manuscripts, some of which later became important Roxburghe editions, the main focus of collecting for most of the members were blackletter works, and, tellingly, the first items that they chose to reproduce were not manuscripts but reproductions of early printed volumes. Public opinion towards the collecting and study of black-letter items, as we have seen, was not overall a positive one, and a heated debate was carried on in magazines of the day, with the Roxburghe Club soon being seen as the epitome of this desire to 'grub up all the trash', as it was dismissively described by one detractor.[1] James Beresford, in his satirical work *Bibliosophia*, wryly acknowledged the public view when he described the features of black-letter type as 'the uncouthly angular configuration – the obsoletely stiff, grim and bloated appearance of its characters', while asserting that it is exactly this lack of appeal to the general reader which recommends it to the collector.[2]

There are a number of possible reasons for this cultural antipathy towards early texts, especially those reproduced in black-letter facsimile. One possibility is that, at a time when Catholic emancipation was a highly contentious subject, black-letter volumes could be seen as somehow too reminiscent of medieval Catholic hegemony. While anti-Catholic sentiment has been perceived in antiquarian culture, it was certainly not present in the activities of the early Roxburghe Club, who as a group worked to produce a number of reprints of books and manuscripts of Catholic origin, that is, pre-Reformation,

1 J. K. Letter, *Gentleman's Magazine* (December 1813), p. 544.
2 James Beresford, *Bibliosophia* (London: William Miller, 1810), pp. 62–63.

including excerpts from Mystery cycles: the *Chester Mysteries*, edited and presented by James Markland, and *Judicium, a Pageant*, presented to the club by Peregrine Towneley. Both of these editions were volumes that the club was rightfully proud of, with Didbin describing the *Chester Mysteries* as 'a beautiful specimen of united graphical elegance' and relating with obvious satisfaction that 'the introduction to this work upon our earliest dramas, and which does so much credit to Mr. Markland, was reprinted in Mr. Boswell's edition of Malone's Shakespeare'.[3] The other mystery play presented in this period of the club's history, *Judicium, a Pageant*, is an extract from a Wakefield mystery play called the *Last Judgement* and taken from the unique Towneley manuscript of the Wakefield Cycle. The Towneleys were a Catholic recusant family whose library had sheltered the manuscript after the dissolution of the monasteries had necessitated its removal from Whalley Abbey in 1537. Previously in 1817 Viscount Althorp had presented the club with an edition of *A Proper New Interlude of the World and the Child, Otherwise Called Mundus et Infans*. This item is a morality play (an 'interlude') rather than a mystery play, and while it is possible that he inspired Markland and Towneley in their own choices of text, it also strongly hints that such works were a topic of discussion among the group. *The World and the Child* is based on a poem from the late fourteenth or the early fifteenth century, called *The Mirror of the Periods of Man's Life*, which may have influenced Shakespeare's *Henry IV, Part 1*, and the edition presented to the Roxburghe is taken from a unique copy printed by Wynkyn de Worde in 1522, the earliest surviving printed edition.[4]

Another volume that can be seen as broadly fitting this allegorical theme nested within the larger Catholic theme was the 1821 copy of the allegorical verse play *Magnyfycence: an Interlude*, edited and offered to the club by Joseph Littledale. It was written in around 1519, or perhaps slightly earlier (there is some dispute among scholars, but regardless of the date of creation it does not appear to have been printed until 1533) by John Skelton, the Poet Laureate to Henry VIII. The Roxburghe edition is printed in black-letter and is based on two copies of the play, one held by the British Museum and the other by the Cambridge University Library, but according to the introduction, only the title page and the page following it were taken from the Cambridge copy. As an early example of an 'interlude', the play has significance both in historical and literary terms and, as Peter Happé points out, '*Magnyfycence* still stands almost at the beginning of what was to become a powerful literary and

---

3 Dibdin, *Reminiscences*, I, p. 467.
4 Geoffrey Bullough, *Narrative and Dramatic Sources of Shakespeare: King John, Henry IV, Henry V, Henry VIII, Vol. 4, Later English History Plays* (London: Routledge and Kegan Paul, 1962), p. 173.

theatrical genre'.[5] Although Skelton died in 1529, before the Reformation, he had allied himself publicly with the enemies of Cardinal Wolsey, writing powerful satires against Wolsey. Therefore it may be possible to add this author to other signs of the easy acceptance within the club of reproducing Catholic texts during a time when Catholicism was a political hot potato as well as linking *Magnyfycence* with the other morality plays printed by the club in this early period. Haslewood also presented texts that fit with this theme. *Two Interludes: Jack Jugler and Thersytes*, his contribution in 1820 was an amalgamation of unique copies of each Interlude. The introduction by Haslewood mourns the earlier dispersal of the collection from which they came before they could be reprinted as a coherent 20-volume collection of 'old English Mysteries, Moralities, Interludes, Pageants and Plays'.[6] Also perhaps falling within this theme is *The Garden Plot, an Allegorical Poem, inscribed to Queen Elizabeth*, which was written by Henry Goldingham and was presented to the club in 1825 by Archdeacon Wrangham, who also contributed an introduction to the volume. It had not previously been printed and was taken from a manuscript contained in the Harleian Collection in the British Museum. It was published with the addition of a brief account of the author and a reprint of his *Goldingham's Masques*, which had been performed before the queen at Norwich on Thursday, 21 August 1578. Dibdin is jovially scathing of the work, describing it as 'unworthy of the "Elizabethan Chair" and its adjuncts', but as an allegorical poem it seems entirely in keeping with the recurring motif of such texts among the early works of the club.[7]

Returning to the overarching theme, early presentations to the club with obvious Catholic provenance include *Diana; or The Excellent Conceitful Sonnets of Henry Constable*; *The Lyvys of Seyntes; translated into Englys be a Doctour of Dyuynite clepyd Osbern Bokenam, frer Austyn of the Convent of Stocklare*; and the *Metrical Life of Saint Robert of Knaresborough*. The first *Diana*, which originally dates from 1592, was reprinted for presentation in 1818 by Edward Littledale. Henry Constable was an Elizabethan convert to Catholicism who was imprisoned twice, and eventually exiled for his personal conviction and public testimony that being a Catholic did not preclude loyalty to the English Crown. *The Lyvys of Seyntes*, the offering of Viscount Clive in 1835, the year in which he became president of the club, is a fifteenth-century collection of verses in Latin and English,

---

5 Peter Happé and Wim N. M. Hüsken, 'Skelton's Magnyfycence', *Interludes and Early Modern Society: Studies in Gender, Power and Theatricality*, (Amsterdam: Rodopi, 2007), p. 72.
6 John Heywood, *Two Interludes: Jack Jugler and Thersytes*, ed. Joseph Haslewood (Lee Priory, 1820), unpaginated introduction.
7 Ibid., p. 396.

recounting the lives of 12 female saints, adapted by Osborn Bokenham from the famous thirteenth-century *Legenda Aurea* by Jacobus de Voragine.

In a similar vein, the *Metrical Life of Saint Robert of Knaresborough* was presented by Rev. Henry Drury in 1824 and printed from a manuscript in his own collection. This is a Middle English life of the Yorkshire hermit saint, a renowned holy man, written by the head of the house of Trinitarian friars established on the site of Robert's hermitage. In the Middle Ages Robert was a popular saint, and Knaresborough attracted many pilgrims.[8] After the Reformation other, but equally widely known, fame was attached to it. A healing 'dropping' well attracted visitors, and from the seventeenth century on a spa was established which rivalled the popularity of Harrogate. It was noted in the seventeenth century as a place where many Catholic families settled. Knaresborough was also associated with the prophetess Mother Shipwell. At the time of the Roxburghe edition, therefore, this text was both a medieval poem with considerable interest in and of itself and associated with a still well-known tourist venue with quaint folkloric associations. The manuscript itself contained numerous Latin prayers to Robert, a prose Latin Life and accounts of his miracles, confirming how large his following was in the medieval period. The Roxburghe dedication to the edition describes the manuscript as being 'presumed to be unique', and the modern editor, Joyce Bazire, confirms this.[9] Haslewood transcribed the manuscript and oversaw the printing. It contains an introduction and annotations provided by Francis Douce, and four extra copies were printed which were donated to public libraries.

The New Notborune Mayd. The Boke of Mayd Emlyn was a publication created from two poems contained in the Caldecott Collection and presented to the club by George Isted. The original 'Nut Brown Maid' was a late medieval debate poem between a man and a woman. The man pleads his love while claiming that all women are unfaithful and says he must go into the woods as a banished man, an outlaw. The woman replies that women are not all unfaithful and that she herself will accompany him in his outlaw life. Satisfied about her sincerity he reveals that he is really an earl's son, and she reveals that she is also of high birth. The *New Nutbrown Maid* was a Catholic reworking of this popular piece. In it the banished man is Christ, and the faithful woman is the Virgin Mary. The century before its reprinting by the club had seen the (original) story of the Nutbrown maid become the basis of several popular

---

8 There is a good account of St Robert and his cult in Brian Golding, 'The Hermit and the Hunter', in *The Cloister and the World: Essays in Honour of Barbara Harvey*, ed. John Blair and Brian Golding (Oxford: Clarendon Press, 1996), pp. 95–117.

9 Joyce Bazire, ed., *The Metrical Life of St. Robert of Knaresborough* (London: Early English Text Society, 1953), p. 1.

compositions: a poem by Prior, *Henry and Emma*, and a play based on this entitled *Henry and Emma or the Nut Brown Maid*, by Sir Henry Bate, performed in 1774, with music by Thomas Arne. Additionally, a song called 'Ho Ro My Nutbrown Maiden' was made popular from the early 1800s onwards when it was performed on the London stage. It was an English translation of a Gaelic song, 'Ho Ro Mo Nighean Donn Bhoidhach', still well known today. This means that the term 'Nut Brown Maid' and the romantic story of a girl willing to follow her lover into an outcast's life would be familiar to people of the club members' generation. The reprinting of a hitherto unknown sixteenth-century religious allegory of this work must therefore have been particularly interesting, especially as Emily A. Ransom describes it as having 'dwelt in obscurity, even among scholars with a proclivity for antiquarianism'.[10]

All these works are in some way connected with Catholicism as well as laying claim to literary or contextual significance. There is, of course, nothing to imply that the club members were choosing these works expressly because of their Catholic origin (except perhaps in the case of Towneley's personal choice of text), but it does strongly indicate that they were not avoiding works through any anti-Catholic feeling or political consideration, even though a number of members were opponents of Catholic emancipation. This underlying complexity for some members between contemporary politics and antiquarian interest is perhaps best represented by the text contributed by James William Dodd in 1817 which was a sixteenth-century verse text, a piece of Elizabethan poetry, *The Funeralles of King Edward the Sixt* by William Baldwin. This rare example of Baldwin's work was reprinted from an edition dating from 1560, when it had been printed in London by Thomas Marshe, and is a fitting presentation for a Protestant clergyman in an era of controversy about Catholic emancipation and fear of the effects of Catholic power on national safety and stability. Baldwin was a Protestant author whose work combines moral and political themes. His poem looks at the death of Edward VI and lays the blame for his demise on the sins of the country, including the greed of the Catholic Church and abuses of justice. Excerpts from the poem can also be found in a later article by Haslewood in the *British Bibliographer*, 1834. Similarly ambivalent was the first contribution of 1822 presented by Viscount Morpeth: *An Elegiacal Poem on the Death of Thomas Lord Grey, of Wilton*, written by Robert Marston and printed from a manuscript in the library of Thomas Grenville. The subject of the poem was, as the title implies, an elegy on the life and death of Thomas Grey, a puritan layman, drawn into the Catholic Bye Plot, the unrealized conspiracy to kidnap James I of England with a view to forcing him to agree to religious tolerance. Raleigh was also implicated in the

---

10 Ransom, *Private Presses and Their Books*, p. 3.

plot. Thomas Grey, the Fifteenth Baron Grey de Wilton, eventually died in the Tower in 1614. The poem is sympathetic in tone, but the subject matter inevitably raises philosophical questions about the perceived dangers of Catholic political ambitions.

While it is interesting and informative to trace these various threads of interest and connection through the books produced by the early club, it is important to remember that they are secondary in importance to the main focus of the Roxburghe and that these topics represent merely one strand of what makes the output of the club so significant to the history of publishing and early English literature. A striking feature of the early days of the club is the extent to which the club members were, beyond the usual bibliomaniac aesthetic preoccupations, conscious of and focused towards the appreciation of books as artefacts that contained important information for the reader, beyond the text itself. This consideration of books as artefacts is a commonplace idea in modern scholarship, but did not yet have such widespread currency in the early nineteenth century. As already discussed, during the club's early days it was the focus of much criticism regarding its reprints and facsimiles of early printed books, with its critics unable to understand the desire to reproduce works in a form that was visually as close as possible to the originals as early nineteenth-century technology allowed. It was considered by many to be a sign of their lack of scholarly discipline and knowledge of literature that they would waste their time on a fruitless reconstruction of long-forgotten works rather than focusing their considerable financial means towards producing modern editions of the early printed works or, better still, manuscripts. Of course, in this period the term 'modern edition' typically meant a readable text, and eighteenth- and early nineteenth-century editions were often cavalier in their verbal and graphological representation of the original. Yet frequently, these early printed books contained remnants of earlier manuscripts that no longer existed in their original form, and the printed version may well represent our only means of knowing that the earlier work had existed at all, let alone having any knowledge of the actual text. Furthermore that early book itself might exist in dangerously low numbers. That is the case in Lord Spencer's first offering to the club, *The First Three Books of Ovid De Tristibus*, printed in 1578 and at that time believed to be the only surviving copy of Thomas Churchyarde's translation. Its future survival certainly became more assured once another 36 copies had been printed. Ovid had written what is now usually referred to as *Tristia ex Ponto* while in exile from the court of Emperor Augustus for reasons that are today unclear. Churchyarde was a skilful poet, and in his translation personalized Ovid's melancholy verses, which begin with a plea to his 'little book' to fly back to the city without him and beg for his pardon. Such translations of Ovid were common in the sixteenth century, reflecting this text's continuing popularity for use in schools, and while the text is worthwhile in its own right, the publication of this work by the Roxburghe Club can furthermore be viewed as fitting with another literary thread that runs through their editions, that of their exploration of texts that provide literary context and relevant background to the works of Shakespeare, to which I will presently return.

On the same themes of both subject matter and rarity is the facsimile reprint of *Six Bookes of Metamorphoseos in whyche ben conteyned the Fables of Ovyde, translated out of Frensshe into Englysshe by William Caxton*, which was printed from a manuscript in the Samuel Pepys collection held at the library of Magdalene College, Cambridge. It was the contribution of George Hibbert and includes an introduction written by him and also a woodcut picture of Orpheus. Dibdin, in *Reminiscences*, referring to an article previously written for his revision of *Typographical Antiquities of Great Britain*, notes that he had said of this text that 'it is a little singular, that this should not only be the *only* MS. with which I am acquainted, incorporating the name of Caxton as "Translator and Finisher," but the only presumed performance of that venerable Printer of which *no printed* copy is known'. Returning to the present, he continues, 'little could I have anticipated, at the period of making this remark, of the treat afforded to all lovers of curious literature by the publication of Mr. Hibbert'.[11] Here is an indication that, sometimes, even fellow members of the club, and knowledgeable ones at that, could be taken by surprise by the rarity and significance of the items that were being brought to light and reprinted by their colleagues.

With respect to their contribution to the knowledge of a wider literary history, too, their publications show concerns beyond the mere enjoyment of quaint books. They show a pioneering and informed mission to extend awareness of a number of areas of literature. These included poetry from the fifteenth century and the early Tudor period, and drama from the same period. They were far ahead of their age: it is only in the last 20 years or so that the world of literary criticism as a whole (there have always been enthusiasts) has taken seriously the achievements of John Lydgate and John Gower, for example. That appreciation of the literature between Geoffrey Chaucer and Shakespeare's lifetimes shows the Roxburghe as rejecting the then-conventional picture of English literary history as beginning with these two peaks. Instead, they brought back to the light of day much writing that was both important in its own right and also represented major genres of the intervening period.

---

11 Dibdin, *Reminiscences*, I, p. 466.

Returning to the subject of Shakespeare previously touched on, the club's desire to look at the literary context preceding and surrounding Shakespeare emerges as a very strong impetus throughout the period in question, and reproducing texts which provided contexts, analogues and sources for Shakespeare in particular, but also other writers, was an explicit aim, as articulated by Dibdin, in one of a series of lectures on literature that he gave at the Royal Institution in three series: in 1806, 1807 and 1808, and again at the London Institution in 1823. He defended the devotee of black-letter volumes by asserting that the 'black-lettered student – if he must be so denominated' had an important part to play in the tracing of earlier works which may have influenced better-known authors such as Shakespeare, John Milton, John Dryden and Laurence Sterne (he is here thinking of Sterne's typographical additions to *Tristram Shandy*), and furthermore that 'if he be not the discoverer of absolute and hitherto unknown merit, he oftentimes points out to us how a hint, or a sentiment, of one writer has been expanded into imagery, or strengthened into a maxim by another'.[12]

Making an additional practical point, he argued that it allowed the reader of black-letter works to search out plagiaristic tendencies in contemporary authors as by reading early authors 'he [the early author] shows us the slender and subtle materials of others, with which later poets and writers have built up a precarious reputation'.[13] Greater familiarity with the printed conventions of early books would assist in detecting not only plagiarism and fraudulent styles of writing but also the counterfeit paratextual features, the styling of titles and so on, that forgers frequently added to their compositions. This series of lectures, given before the Roxburghe Club was conceived, highlight how serious Dibdin was in his approach to promoting early British literature. During the 28-lecture series he covered the work of writers such as Lydgate and Gower, writers who would eventually take their places in the canon, but who were yet to be appreciated. One lecture addressed the 'importance of preserving national literature', taking as its example the works of the Earl of Surrey, a writer whose *Certaine Bokes of Virgiles Aenaeis, Turned into English Meter* was soon to be the first text published by the Roxburghe Club.[14] Looking at the outline of Dibdin's lectures it is easy to see already the blueprint of a programme that the Roxburghe Club would unofficially follow in its printing activities, underlining the argument that the club was not haphazardly printing items due to their rarity in book-collecting terms but rather creating a modern series of early British literature, albeit one that does not meet the standards of a

---

12 Dibdin, *Reminiscences*, II, pp. 239–44.
13 Ibid., p. 236.
14 Ibid., p. 243.

uniform, scholarly framework we might expect to see today in a similar undertaking. This vision was, incidentally, definitely about the literature of Great Britain, and not restricted to works of English literature. Dibdin's second lecture covered the topic of 'druidical learning', and he later covered Scottish ballads and the 'influence of the Welch and Scottish languages'. Dibdin did not claim to be the first to examine these authors, explicitly referencing previous critics such as Ritson and Thomas Wharton, who had been pioneers of the recognition and study of national literature as a serious historical investigation and narrative. But he did extend the reach of this school of thought, carrying it to a fashionable and influential audience at a period when these literary tastes and scholarly respect for vernacular literary texts were not widely accepted or appreciated. These issues were being addressed by Dibdin at a time when Samuel Taylor Coleridge, a fellow lecturer at the Royal Institution, in his public lecture tours of 1808–9 was largely restricting his subject matter to Shakespeare, Milton and Chaucer and showed no interest in other early modern dramatists or poets. Coleridge gives little historical context to Shakespeare's work, preferring to attribute all to Shakespeare's 'imagination', the interior source of genius.[15] Dibdin (and later the Roxburghe Club) prefers to emphasize the cultural and literary history into which such works of genius can be seen in context and not as exemplars of an ahistorical creative genius.

Of the Roxburghe publications of this foundational period offering a connection with, and context to, the works of Shakespeare, the most overt is William Holwell Carr's presentation in 1817, a poetic text titled *Istoria Novellamente Ritrovata di due Nobili Amanti, &c., da Luigi Porto*, which was first printed in Venice in 1535 under the title *La Giulietta*, and which is the source for Shakespeare's *Romeo and Juliet*. Other volumes that offer a Shakespearean context do so in a more subtle way and take a variety of forms. For instance, in 1816 George Freeling presented his copy of *Newes from Scotland*, a pamphlet describing a notorious witch trial, written by King James VI of Scotland and originally printed in 1591. Although at first sight this text may appear to be largely of historical rather than literary value it has been cited as a possible source for Shakespeare's portrayal of the witches in *Macbeth*.[16]

In the same year *Dolarny's Primerose or the First Part of the Passionate Hermit* from 1606 was reprinted by Francis Freeling from a rare edition in his own collection. This poem had been previously discussed by Haslewood in the *British Bibliographer* and would later be attributed to Raynold, a contemporary

---

15 Terence Hawkes, *Coleridge on Shakespeare: A Selection of the Essays, Notes and Lectures of Samuel Taylor Coleridge on the Poems and Plays of Shakespeare* (New York: Capricorn Books, 1959).
16 Manuela Sonntag, *William Shakespeare: Subject of the Crown?* (Morrisville: Lulu Enterprises, 2010), pp. 144–45.

of Shakespeare (Dolarny being an anagram of Raynold).[17] This work especially highlights the club's complex and open-minded approach to the shared wellspring of cultural and literary roots that feed into English canonical works which stands in stark comparison to their contemporaries such as John Payne Collier who, discussing the same work in 1820, alludes to what he calls plagiarism within the poem, because motifs were taken from the gravedigger scene in *Hamlet* (1600).[18] Another piece of verse with a minor connection to the works of Shakespeare is the Antony Scoloker poem *Daiphantus, or the Passions of Love*, which had originally been printed in or after 1604. This was the club contribution of Roger Wilbraham, and Dibdin rather censoriously says that 'what led a half-way septuagenarian and octogenarian to the production of *such* a work as "Daiphantus," it were difficult to conjecture'.[19] Politely ageist sensibilities on Dibdin's part aside, this piece alludes to Shakespeare's tragedies in its introduction and has been studied in the light of Shakespearean context by later scholars. One further item with an interesting connection to the works of Shakespeare is *Selections from the Works of Thomas Ravenscroft; a Musical Composer of the Time of King James the First* which was the gift of the Duke of Marlborough in 1822. At first glance a collection of songs may seem to be a strange selection to present to the club, but that would be to overlook Ravenscroft's significance to the preservation of the history of Elizabethan and Jacobean theatre and our subsequent knowledge of theatrical staging of that period. Ravenscroft was an English musician, composer, choral singer and publisher who was active from the beginning of the seventeenth century to 1635. Alongside the composition of his own works Ravenscroft was active in assembling, editing and publishing collections of the earliest printed English folk songs, broadside ballads, nursery rhymes and rounds. From Ravenscroft's original publications modern scholars have been able to identify 11 pieces of music for songs that were used in contemporary plays. As the lyric books of the period did not include a musical score and there were no collections of theatrical music printed, very few songs from Elizabethan and Jacobean plays have survived. Of this relatively small number of extant songs, the 11 songs contained in Ravenscroft represent a large share of this group.[20] The collection of Ravenscroft items represented in the Roxburghe edition features lyrics

---

17 John Payne Collier, *The Poetical Decameron* (Edinburgh: Archibald Constable, 1820), II, p. 15.
18 Ibid., p. 16.
19 Ibid.; italics in original.
20 Linda Phyllis Austern, 'Thomas Ravenscroft: Musical Chronicler of an Elizabethan Theater Company', *Journal of the American Musicological Society* 38 (Summer 1985), 238–63 (pp. 238–39).

in most cases but sometimes the musical score as well. That one of these surviving songs appears in Shakespeare's *Twelfth Night* inexorably leads us once more to the club preoccupation with Shakespearean context.

An example of this valuable attention to context in relation to authors other than Shakespeare appears in a piece of poetry contributed in 1818 by the Duke of Devonshire. This was a volume containing two texts, 'The Life of St Ursula' and 'Guiscard and Sigismund', a black-letter reprint from a volume originally printed by Wynkyn de Worde in 1532. 'Guiscardo and Sigismonda' is a tragic tale of love from Boccaccio's *Decameron*. Dibdin comments that the 1818 reprint is 'two exceedingly rare pieces of early English poetry' and that the original was contained in the Duke's own collection.[21] The text had a long history, being more than once rewritten both in the early modern period and the eighteenth century.[22] Walter Scott, in 1808, writing on Dryden's poem *Sigismonda and Guiscardo*, in his *Works of John Dryden*, says that 'this celebrated tale was probably taken by Boccaccio from some ancient chronicle, or traditional legend' and notes that a prose translation appears in Painter's *Palace of Pleasure*.[23] Scott also mentions the story having been rewritten by Robert Wilmot as a tragedy for presentation before Queen Elizabeth in 1568. Here we see the same recurrent preoccupation, not merely with private book collecting and book printing but also with tracing the origins and alterations in works that made their way from early texts to more recent literary works and writers. These concerns reflect the themes explored by Dibdin in his lectures at the Royal Institute.

One of the club's publishing programme's greatest achievements was a widening of the received canon of English literature. The Roxburghe Club displayed an interest in early English literature at a time when it was receiving relatively little attention, and the club was instrumental in preserving and giving value to many early works that might otherwise have failed to come to the attention of both scholars and readers. Under the weight of public indifference, or even hostility, unique copies of works were in a precarious position, both physically and in terms of acceptance. Despite this a recurrent criticism of the club has been that the volumes produced during the early years of its existence, that is, the books printed and presented by individual members rather than the later volumes paid for by subscription, are lacking in

---

21 Dibdin, *Reminiscences*, I, p. 463.
22 Helen Phillips, 'Aesthetic and Commercial Aspects of Framing Devices: Fifteenth and Sixteenth Century Printers' Frames; Bradshaw, Roos and Copland', *Poetica* 43 (1995), pp. 37–65.
23 Walter Scott, *The Works of John Dryden*, 18 vols, XI, p. 403.

significance. Dibdin, writing in 1836, had obviously heard this criticism many times and defends the club's publications with grace, if a little wearily:

> Such are the Flowers of which I consider the Roxburghe Garland to be composed. These flowers doubtless vary both in colour and in quality; and the Garland is as doubtless more picturesque in consequence. But considering these forty-four volumes as the production of a society of noblemen and gentlemen of only twenty-three years standing, put forth without the slightest probability of any *profit* but that of the satisfaction of adding to the Archaeological Curiosities of their country, they ought to stand well in the estimation of all honourable minds. Whatever may be the ultimate 'sway' of fashion, the Roxburghe Club – if it rest only upon its present oars of distinction – will have deserved well of the Republic of Literature.[24]

'Curiosities' at this period meant 'an object of interest', with qualities of intricacy and/or rarity, without the more pejorative and superficial senses the word would have today. He also concurred with the decision to produce club editions as a joint expense with the intention of increasing the overall standard of publication produced, saying that 'I adhere to the opinion expressed in a previous page, that it will be better to contribute our respective quotas to the supply of some such other performance as HAVELOK'.[25] This acquiescence may have been the consequence of seeing the quality of *Havelok* and his eventual acceptance of the benefits to be gained from a more organized approach to Roxburghe editions, especially in light of the advances being made by newer book clubs, even if that involved bringing in 'outsiders' and losing some of the club traditions. It could also have been an acceptance that this scheme was the most likely way to preserve the Roxburghe Club's existence at a time when its fortunes were looking uncertain. Alternatively, it may have been the results of his, never affluent but now painfully straitened, financial situation, which possibly would have inclined him to consider the prospect of shared expenditure as looking considerably more attractive than it may have previously appeared.

The Ancient English Romance of Havelok the Dane: Accompanied by the French Text, an important Middle English text printed in 1828, was the first of the club's editions to gain general critical approval. It was edited by Frederic Madden and included an introduction, notes and a glossary also provided by him. This was the first book printed for the club rather than as the contribution of any

---

24 Dibdin, *Reminiscences*, I, pp. 469–70; italics in original.
25 Ibid., p. 470.

one individual, and the first to bring in a paid editor (Madden received £100 and six copies of the book) from outside of the ranks of the members. Dibdin's description of the work, written in 1836, is interesting because it indicates his approval of an edition being produced by Madden for general commercial purposes, with Dibdin saying that 'a whisper is abroad, that, with permission of the club, and of Earl Cawdor, it is the intention of Sir Frederic Madden, the able editor of this work and of the Werwolf, to reprint them, with notes and an index, in an octavo form, as a companion to his forthcoming edition of the Brut of Wace – a rare treat for lovers of early English romance and history'.[26] There is no indication here of the club attempting to limit the numbers of the commercially published edition or jealously restricting Madden's access to the work he had previously been paid to carry out for the club. There is also no hint of the bad feelings supposedly held by Dibdin and Haslewood towards a non-member poaching on their editorial ground. Whether Haslewood felt put out by the hire of an outside editor is difficult to say, and professional envy would perhaps be a natural reaction and need not carry any hint of personal inadequacy, but on the evidence of this paragraph from Dibdin's *Reminiscences*, it would appear that if Dibdin had felt uneasy at the development, he had recovered from his animosity in the intervening eight years.

Havelok was printed at the joint expense of the members and was taken from the MS. Laud Misc. 108, which is dated c. 1300–25 and held in the Bodleian Library. In the introduction, Madden describes the manuscript as having been 'discovered by accident' among the large quantity of manuscripts that made up that particular collection. Until the point of discovery, the text, although alluded to by a number of historical accounts, had been presumed lost for good. The Roxburghe edition of the text was popular enough to be reprinted by antiquarians in France as early as 1833, with a French translation of the introduction written by Francisque Michel. The praise was not without an element of critical attention, and in 1829 the antiquarian author and scholar Samuel Weller Singer responded to the publication of *Havelok* with his 'Remarks on the Glossary'. Madden responded robustly and convincingly to the points raised, and the controversy between the scholars apparently ended amicably. The 'Werwolf' mentioned by Dibdin in his discussion of *Havelok* is the *Ancient English Romance of William and the Werwolf*, which was reprinted in 1832 from a unique copy in King's College Library, Cambridge, which as indicated was also edited by Madden and carried an introduction and glossary written by him. This time the volume was the contribution of Earl Cawdor rather than a club publication. The werewolf theme was obviously one that held personal interest for the

---

26 Ibid., pp. 467–68.

Earl and at least one of his friends, the Hon. Algernon Herbert, as the volume also contains two letters written by Herbert to Cawdor which explore the werewolf myths in some depth. Herbert was an antiquary and author on a number of eclectic subjects, and the letters are erudite yet accessible and entertaining on the history and literature of lycanthropy.

A look at the club's output between 1812 and 1834 shows that most of the volumes had far more than rarity value to their credit and contained significant literary and historic worth. William Bolland set the standard when he donated the first club edition, a black-letter reprint of Henry Howard, Earl of Surrey's translation in verse of the second and fourth books of the *Aeneid*. This is from several points of view a landmark in English literature. It is the first experiment in blank verse (the form Shakespeare used and developed so successfully and influentially in his plays). Just as Chaucer invented the iambic pentameter, which he used in couplets and stanzas, Surrey moved on to invent blank verse. He intended this to imitate the classical Latin unrhymed hexameters (e.g., in the *Aeneid* itself). For the late eighteenth century and the era of the Roxburghe edition, Surrey was also a major humanist pioneer in English literature, in Thomas Warton's words 'the first English classical poet'.[27] While this Roxburghe choice can be fully justified as both a powerfully beautiful translation and a major document of the history of English poetry, it is intriguing to note that it also seems to have a connection with that interest in writings and writers with links to Catholicism that can arguably be traced in a number of Roxburghe choices. Surrey was beheaded by Henry VIII in 1547, and the second printed text came out in 1557 by Richard Tottel, who was able to present Surrey as a martyr in the Catholic cause.[28] The Roxburghe edition was reprinted from the 1557 edition by Tottel, now in Dulwich College library. That the literary–historical significance of a text of this nature was for so long largely overlooked is underlined by an excerpt from Harold Williams, who in 1929 said of this volume that 'if, as a series, the first forty five [Roxburghe Club] volumes are unsubstantial, there are redeeming exceptions' and that with regard to this volume, although 'of interest and not discreditable', in his opinion 'a larger type and better spacing would have given the page more distinction'.[29]

---

27 Thomas Warton, *History of English Poetry* (London: Ward, Lock and Tyler, 1781), section xxxviii. On the significance of Surrey's translation, see pp. 260–87 in W. A. Sessions, *Henry Howard the Poet, Earl of Surrey* (Oxford: Oxford University Press, 1999) and also Henry Howard, Earl of Surrey, *Poems*, ed. by Emrys Jones (Oxford: Clarendon Press, 1964), pp. 35–62.

28 W. A. Sessions, *Henry Howard the Poet, Earl of Surrey* (Oxford: OUP, 1999), p. 273.

29 Harold Williams, *Book Clubs and Printing Societies of Great Britain and Ireland* (London: Curwen Press, 1929), p. 24.

If intended to defend the volume against accusations of insubstantiality this defence raises a strangely discordant note of aesthetic disdain, especially in the last line, and reminds us that a large percentage of the analysis of the club's editions carried out since its foundation has been based on the criteria of book collecting rather than literary studies. In the same piece Williams also describes the second book produced by the club, *Caltha Poetarum; or, The Bumble Bee*, by T. Cutwode, saying that the volume 'despite the *Athenaeum* editor's scorn, was worth reprinting', although he unfortunately does not substantiate this view with any particulars (see Figure 8.1). *The Bumble Bee* was a reprint of a poem from 1599, and was Richard Heber's first presentation to the Roxburghe. This poem had an interesting history as it had been one of the works banned by the Archbishop of Canterbury on publication during the 'Bishop's Ban' against satirical works in 1599. The name of the author, Cutwode, appears to be a pseudonym, and although it is a salacious allegorical poem, it is more likely to have been banned as a result of its political satire.[30] Whatever the real reason, printing of the *Bumble Bee* was stopped and any existing copies found were taken to be burnt along with a number of other works banned under the same edict. The Bishops' Ban would have had interest too for the club members because of its role in the history of printing and publishing: Forshaw argues that printers tended to ignore the ban, as did satirists and the start of the seventeenth century marked the end of the Anglican Church's power in censuring printing and literature.[31]

In club lore terms the item was also interesting because it was the subject of a bet, as related by Dibdin:

> The cause of the above reprint was this. A bet was laid (the winner of the bet to give the Roxburghe Club a dinner) between Sir M. M. Sykes and Mr. Dent, whether the Anniversary Meeting of 1815 were the third or fourth of the Club? Mr. Dent was the loser; when Mr. Heber promised to present the Club with a reprint of the above poem at the extra dinner in contemplation. Only nine days intervened; but within that period the reprint was transcribed, superintended at the press by Mr. Haslewood (without a single error), bound by Charles Lewis, and presented to the Members on sitting down to dinner. Mr. Haslewood was reported to have walked in his sleep, with a pen in his hand, during the whole period of its preparation.[32]

---

30 Richard A. McCabe, '"Right Puisante and Terrible Priests:" The Role of the Anglican Church in State Censorship', in Forshaw, p. 105.
31 Forshaw, pp. 125–26.
32 Dibdin, *Reminiscences*, I, p. 465.

Figure 8.1 *Caltha Poetarum*. Reproduced by kind permission of the Bodleian Libraries, the University of Oxford, Roxburghe Club 2, 3rd Title Page.

The poem fitted with the theme of allegorical works published by the club, and it should also be reiterated at this point that the majority of the first books presented by the members were verse, in keeping with the ethos which had been agreed at the first anniversary dinner: 'It was proposed for each member, in turn, according to the order of his name in the alphabet, to furnish the Society with a reprint of some rare old tract, or composition – chiefly of poetry.'[33] Whether this concentration on poetry at the beginning contributed to the perceived insubstantiality of the volumes is open to debate, but it would certainly have circumscribed the type of books being reprinted. Additionally it may well have been the case that, when members later chose to present a second volume to the club, it was perhaps because the restraint had been lifted and a greater choice of work to reproduce was by then an option. This is, of course, merely conjecture.

The *Bumble Bee* also denotes one of the works published by the early club that raises the possibility of another, albeit very faint, thread running through works presented by members to the club and also some of those printed at the private presses owned by its members. These are a number of works that had been previously censored or supressed in some way or which contained subject matter of a culturally sensitive or potentially transgressive nature, including the reprint of *The Satyricon*, published at the Beldornie Press by E. V. Utterson, which was discussed in more detail in Chapter 6. Another work that could feasibly fall into this category is *Poems*, by Richard Barnfield, first printed in 1598 and presented in 1816 by James Boswell in an edition printed by Alexander Boswell at the Auchinleck Press from a volume contained in Malone's collection. Barnfield's poems are sensual, often eccentric, some of them expressing homosexual love, and they raised a degree of controversy at the time of their original publication. As in the case of the works of Catholic provenance, there is no indication that the club members were choosing these works specifically because of their provocative histories, but they were certainly not avoiding them because of it.

Examining the remainder of the texts presented to the club during its first two decades illustrates not only how very prolific the members were in the presentation of these volumes but also clearly demonstrates that alongside the large leitmotifs running through the output of the club there is a bedrock of works written by authors who have gained in recognition over the past 200 years and for whom the club were pioneering cheerleaders. One such author was John Gower, and 1822 saw the presentation by Earl Gower of *Balades and Other Poems*. As if to emphasize how groundbreaking the Roxburghe Club often were in their selections, this choice was not without controversy among critics, but Gower's verses, printed here for the first time, contain considerable literary and historic value. They date from around 1400, when they were presented to Henry IV, and Gower, a contemporary of Chaucer, wrote in English, Latin and Anglo-Norman. He has only in the last 15 years or so attracted much critical attention, and the Roxburghe printing marks a step

---

33 Dibdin, *Bibliographical Decameron*, p. 72.

towards that very slow recognition. The first modern and complete edition of Gower's works would not appear until that by George Campbell Macauley in 1899. It has been suggested that Earl Gower's reasons for this edition were primarily those of genealogy and his (misapprehension of his family's) descent from Gower, the fourteenth-century poet, despite widespread awareness by that time that there was little or no connection. This seems unlikely. Although Leveson-Gower may have been stubbornly claiming that connection, there is little evidence for that, and given the long history of book collecting in the Leveson-Gower family it would be equally fair to assume that Leveson-Gower is more likely to have printed the manuscript because he believed it to be an important, rare and neglected example of an author who deserved recognition as a major medieval poet irrespective of family connection. Being lucky enough to be its custodian (as a result of the original misapprehension, no doubt), perhaps he saw a good opportunity to safeguard the miscellany's future appreciation. The Yorkshire Gower family was after all a very old and wealthy family who could easily make their case for their aristocratic status without recourse to a familial connection to a neglected medieval poet, and yet if they had so chosen, would that in itself not indicate a high regard for the poet's abilities?

Even more controversial at the time of printing was the Roxburghe edition presented in 1827: *Poems Written in English, by Charles, Duke of Orleans, during his Captivity in England after the Battle of Azincourt* was the gift of George Watson Taylor and was printed from the Harleian MS. No. 682 in the British Museum. It carried an introduction by Taylor, and Dibdin tells us that as well as the normal quantity of copies for distribution among the members, four copies were printed on vellum and that 'one, splendidly bound in Morocco, was destined for Charles X. late king of France; a second is in the library of Earl Spencer; a third in the British Museum; and the fourth, in the possession of the Contributor'.[34] This, however, was not the real significance of the volume. As was the case with so many of these early club presentations, this volume was the first time that the poems had been published in either French or English, and it would be another 15 years before there would be a French edition of his work.[35] Its reception, however, was mixed. Sir Thomas Croft, writing in the *Retrospective Review* in 1827, says,

> A few words are first necessary on the volume printed by Mr. Watson Taylor. That gentleman has entitled his book, 'English Poems by Charles

---

34 Dibdin, *Reminiscences*, I, pp. 468–69.
35 Barker, *The Roxburghe Club: A Bicentenary History* (London: The Roxburghe Club, 2012), p. 72.

Duke of Orleans': but there can be little doubt, that not a single line of them was the production of that distinguished individual. It will be seen from our extracts, that they are close, nay, almost literal translations of the French poems; hence, to assign them in their English dress to the duke, and to call them, as Mr. Watson Taylor has done in his preface, 'imitations', are unequalled specimens of critical acumen. We have done what we do not believe that gentleman or the person he employed ever took the trouble to do – carefully examine a MS. of selections from Orleans' works in the British Museum, among which are three original 'Rondels' in English, but they are so decidedly inferior to the translations in the MS. printed by Mr. Watson Taylor, that it is scarcely possible the duke could have been the translator of his own writings.[36]

The manuscript that Croft refers to is Harley MS. No. 682, the manuscript that Watson Taylor's edition originated from, and it is difficult to see why he should believe that the editor of the volume would not have viewed the manuscript in detail. It must be pointed out, however, that Sir Thomas begins his article by setting out his views on the Roxburghe Club in an apparently unprovoked attack on both the members and their activities:

> It may be unnecessary to state that the 'Roxburghe Club' is a society of gentlemen many of who are 'to fame unknown' and whose principle literary pretensions consist of a *soi disant* attachment to early literature and scarce books in its members; the one manifested by an absurd veneration for useless volumes, simply because they cannot be easily procured; and the latter by occasionally reprinting an old author, not, however, with the liberal and honourable view of extending the knowledge of his merits by an impression accessible to the public, but by confining it to the members of the club, few of whom have the disposition, and fewer still the ability, to make the least practical use of the contents of the precious gift, even, which is but rarely the case, if the article itself be deserving of a higher destiny than to light a fire.[37]

Given the virulence of his dislike for the club, it is perhaps not so surprising that he appears eager to dismiss the abilities and research of one of its members. Irrespective of the personal animosity displayed in this article, the controversy regarding the authorship of the English poems of Orleans continued well into the twentieth century, but eventually it appears that the weight of

---

36 Croft, 'Early English Poetry', pp. 148–49.
37 Ibid., p. 147.

academic opinion has largely sided with Watson Taylor and the Roxburghe Club.[38] It has been noted that during the nineteenth century there appeared to be a certain insistence, in both France and Britain, that the Duke's poetry should be viewed as exclusively French, despite the body of poetry written in English. A. E. B. Coldiron points out that there has been an impetus 'to deny that the poetry belongs or could belong to both canons. Literary nationalism is, in this case at least, a powerful force for marginalizing bicultural texts'.[39] If this is the case, it is extremely interesting that Watson Taylor should have taken the opposite course, going so far as to anglicize the Duke d'Orléans's name in what Coldiron refers to as a 'perhaps deliberately inclusive orthography', especially when considered in the context of Watson Taylor's anti-French political sentiments.[40]

The Roxburghe were of course also instrumental in publishing far less contentious but equally significant works, among them two important examples of Arthurian literature, both printed from manuscript for the first time. The first text, *Le Morte Arthur,* presented to the club in 1819, was the offering of Thomas Ponton and was printed from British Library Harley MS. No. 2252. This is the so-called *Stanzaic Morte Arthure*, a fourteenth-century romance. It is a lively work, going back to the French thirteenth-century romance the *Morte Artus*, which relates the last part of the story of Arthur and the Round Table. In the fifteenth century Sir Thomas Malory used the *Stanzaic Morte* as the basis for the later part of his own *Morte d'Arthur*. This demonstrates the club's printing of a lengthy text from a manuscript, and Dibdin recorded that it was produced 'with a fac-simile of the original text by Mr. R. Thomson, by whom the work was superintended at the press'.[41] The woodcut used on the title page is based on a drawing created by a fellow club member Utterson who, although a lawyer by profession, was also an artist of some renown.

The second Arthurian volume was *Gaufridi Arthurii Monemuthensis Archidiaconi, postea vero Episcopi Asaphensis, de Vita et Vaticiniis Merlini Calidonii Carmen Heroicum* and was presented in 1830 by George Neville Grenville, who had recently joined the club to replace John Dent following the latter's death. This is the 'Prophecies of Merlin', written in the early 1130s and, around 1136, incorporated into the *Historia Regum Britanniae*. It is described by Dibdin as 'an

---

38 For an outline of the main areas of contention, see Norma Lorre Goodrich's *Charles of Orleans: A Study of Themes in His French and in His English Poetry* (Geneva: Library Droz, 1967), pp. 20–31.
39 A. E. B. Coldiron, *Canon, Period, and the Poetry of Charles of Orleans* (Ann Arbor: University of Michigan Press, 2000), p.106.
40 Ibid., p. 105n81.
41 Dibdin, *Reminiscences*, I, p. 467.

heroic Latin poem (from a MS. in the Cotton collection) by Geoffrey Arthur, Archdeacon of Monmouth [...] on the Life and Prophesies of the Welch Merlin', and is the earliest and most renowned of the tradition of political prophecies, of which many circulated during the medieval and early modern period.[42] It was transcribed and printed from MS. Cotton Claudius B VII f. 224 in the British Library, which is a manuscript from c. 1150–70, with elegant decoration and illustrations which are unfortunately not reproduced in the Roxburghe edition.

The remaining Roxburghe editions published during this period are largely works illustrating the club's appreciation of fifteenth-century and early Tudor poetry. During the first decade of the club's existence, while the members soared on a wave of enthusiasm for their new enterprise, far more than one presentation was made per year. For instance, in 1817 eight separate volumes were presented at the annual dinner. Alongside those already mentioned such as Viscount Althorp's *A Proper New Interlude of the World and the Child* appeared works including *Cock Lorell's Boat, a Fragment,* an early sixteenth-century satirical poem, from the unique surviving print contained in the Garrick Collection. This witty poem, the gift of Henry Drury, tells the story of Cock Lorell, the leader of a gang of thieves who posed as a tinker to cover his tracks as a foot pad. Also presented was *The Glutton's Feaver,* written by Thomas Bancroft and originally printed in London in 1633, which was the offering of John Delafield Phelps. Lastly, *Hagthorpe Revived; or Select Specimens of a Forgotten Poet* was edited and presented by Sir Samuel Egerton Brydges with a woodcut inscription that reads 'a Roxburghe Apology in select Specimens of a Forgotten Poet'. The word 'Apology' here presumably means a justification for printing a forgotten poet, and the text is an extract taken from the poet John Hagthorpe's work *Divine Meditations and Elegies* and printed at Brydges' Lee Priory Press. Hagthorpe lived in the early 1600s and produced several works, including the *Visions of Things, or Foure Poems* and an elegy for Prince Henry. Similarly, in 1818, nine items were presented which included Sir Mark Masterman Sykes's gift of John Lydgate's Middle English translation from French, *The Chorle and the Birde*, which had originally been popular enough as to be printed by both Caxton and later Wynkyn de Worde and is a dialogue between a peasant and a bird discussing the role of peasants in society. In 1822 he went on to present a companion Lydgate fable, *The Hors, the Shepe, and the Ghoos*. Dibdin's gift in 1818 was *The Complaint of a Lover's Life. Controversy between a Lover and a Jay*, by T. Feylde, which is a Tudor 'love aunter' or dit amoureux, a late example of the popular medieval genre of debate which takes the nature of women as its subject.

42 Ibid., pp. 409–10.

The only non-poetical offering of 1818 was *Ceremonial at the Marriage of Mary Queen of Scotts with the Dauphin of France*, dating from 1557 and presented by William Bentham, reprinted from the original held at the British Museum. Although literature was always the dominant genre in the club books, occasionally a member would offer a piece such as this with historical interest rather than specifically literary value. Another such item was William Wey's *Informacōn for Pylgrymes unto the Holy Londe*. This was presented by George Freeling and printed from a manuscript belonging to the Library of the Faculty of Advocates at Edinburgh. The original text dates from 1498 and was printed by Wynkyn de Worde. Wey had travelled across Europe, in 1456, 1458 and 1462, noting customs, currencies, languages and places of interest, while on pilgrimages to Jerusalem and St James's shrine at Compostela. Wey, a Fellow of Eton College, had died in 1474. This is another example of the high quality of many of the Roxburghe choices. Wey's book is now regarded as one of the most important early accounts of pilgrimage, and it has been suggested, very plausibly, that Wey may have been a spy for the government of Henry VI.[43] Of course, sometimes a text could have both historic and literary significance such as the second offering of Earl Spencer: *La Rotta de Francciosi a Terroana novamente facta*. *La Rotta de Scocesi* is a reprint of two Italian poems dealing with the battles of Terrovane and Flodden Field. The author is unknown, but the poems date from around 1513 and are reproduced with prefatory comments by Earl Spencer.

The item distributed by Sir Walter Scott to the members in 1828, *Proceedings in the Court Martial Held upon John, Master of Sinclair, Captain-Lieutenant in Preston's Regiment, for the Murder of Ensign Schaw of the Same Regiment, and Captain Schaw, of the Royals, 17 October 1708; with Correspondence Respecting That Transaction*, was perhaps intended to fill such a niche. Unfortunately it appears to have been a lacklustre contribution that failed to kindle much enthusiasm among the members, and Dibdin later wrote that 'Sir Walter Scott's book-contribution as a member of the club is, strangely enough, among the least interesting and valuable in our Garland'.[44] The text is an account by the Clan leader John Sinclair of his life as a soldier and a Jacobite. The lively narrative may have appealed to Scott. Sinclair was a Tory before his court martial and exile to Prussia for the killing of two men in duels, which ended his political career, but whatever Scott's reasons for choosing this subject, they were obviously not shared by his fellow Roxburghers.

---

43 *The Itineraries of William Wey*, ed. by Francis Davey (London: Oxford University Press, 2010).

44 Dibdin, *Reminiscences*, I, pp. 401–2.

Finally it must be noted that, as serious as the club was in its purpose, not all of the presentations were solemn offerings, although the texts were always valuable. *La Contenance de la Table*, contributed by George Freeling in 1816, represented the first move away from pieces of Elizabethan poetry and is a fifteenth-century French guide for children, offering advice in verse on table manners. It was a humorous supplement to Freeling's more serious club offering of *Newes from Scotland, Declaring the Damnable Life of Doctor Fian, a Notable Sorcerer, Who Was burned at Edenbrough in Ianuarie Last,* which was presented at the same dinner. Although provided wrapped in a napkin and with a tongue-in-cheek dedication ('To the Roxburghe Club, this reprint of a rare Manual for the BEHAVIOUR OF YOUTH AT TABLE, is dedicated and presented for their Edification and Improvement by their faithful and obedient Servant, A Member'), this is a black-letter reprint of a rare pamphlet. The light-hearted nature of the extra volume was obviously not appreciated by everyone, and Dibdin refers to 'a spiteful notice of it, irrelevantly introduced, in a number of the *Quarterly Review* for 1825'.[45] In a more personal nod to club lore, the following year James Boswell produced his anthology volume *A Roxburghe Garland*, containing a number of pieces of drinking-related verse from seventeenth-century poets, together with a poem written by himself titled *L'Envoy* (see Figure 8.2). This volume, although quite a small book, has a remarkable presence that makes it feel very personal to the club of that time, and this intimate quality is underlined by the inclusion of 'L'Envoy', which, full of charm and humour, would serve well in the guise of an eccentric club Anthem.

From 1835 onwards, in common with so much else that was changing within the club, the items being presented started to branch out to encompass a wider variety of texts including more items of historical political and social interest. There were still many items of poetry being printed or reprinted, but following the example set by the printing of *Havelok* the focus was increasingly on items, especially manuscripts, perceived to be acceptable to the demands of modern scholarship and amenable to being edited by hired scholars. It is, however, as shown in this section, oversimplifying the matter, if not entirely wrong, to say that the early Roxburghe volumes were without value, and time has vindicated the choices of literary material made by the founding members. The last word, as ever when it came to the early Roxburghe Club and their activities, has to go to Dibdin, addressing the question of black-letter research versus contemporary scholarship and negating the polemical nature of the issue when he wrote, 'let the midnight lamp be burnt to illuminate the stores of antiquity – whether they be romances, or chronicles, or legends, and

---

45 Dibdin, *Reminiscences*, I, p. 464.

L'ENVOY.

To Boccaccio in Heaven, as he chatted one day,
   With Chaucer and Caxton and two or three more;
The news of our meeting went up, as they say,
   And it set the celestial Bard in a roar:
     Says he, " Well I ween,
     When these fellows convene,
My laurels look fresher, more lively their green;
So myself, from this hour, I exultingly dub,
The Patron, and friend, of the Roxburghe Club.

But since they of *Me* as their origin boast,
   I shall storm, like King Herowde as drawn by
       Jhan Parfre;*
Unless, as their first Anniversary toast,
   They drink in a bumper, my Printer Valdarfer :"
     Quoth Wynkin de Worde,
     " 'Twill be vastly absurd,
Unless Caxton's their second, and I am their third :

* See Candlemas Day, or the killing of the children of Israel, by Jhan Parfre.

Figure 8.2 *A Roxburghe Garland*, 'L'Envoy'. Reproduced by kind permission of the Bodleian Libraries, the University of Oxford, Roxburghe Club 12, p. 17.

whether they be printed by Aldus or Caxton – if a brighter lustre can thence be thrown upon the pages of modern learning! To trace genius to its source, or to see how she has been influenced or modified by the lore of past times, is both a pleasing and profitable pursuit.'[46]

46 Dibdin, *Bibliomania* (1809), p. 76.

Chapter 9

THE LEGACIES OF THE CLUB

As fascinating as all these different aspects of the early Roxburghe Club's activities are, they inevitably lead to the question of what effect it was having outside the realm of antiquarian book collecting. While it is, of course, difficult to prove categorically the effects on literature or culture that have proceeded directly from the activities of the Roxburghe Club, it can at the very least be stated that the club was in the vanguard of a number of changes that were going on at that time and that in some cases acted as the blueprint or inspiration for other pioneers in these fields. The most obvious, but also the most easily overlooked, way in which the early Roxburghe Club has influenced the modern literary world is in its longevity and continuity. Since its acclaimed publication of *Havelok the Dane* and despite a rocky period during which the club came perilously close to ending, it has attracted increasing praise for its volumes and continued to build on the legacy of the pioneers of its early days, gradually evolving into the more recognizably modern face of a club which produces editions acclaimed equally for their literary significance, scholarly value and typographic beauty.

While the present-day club has, no doubt, the satisfaction of having eventually received its due acclaim, scholars have remained slow to recognize the serious intent of the early club, often viewing its activities as uninformed, with shallow self-interest the prime motivation among club members and antiquarian literature acting as merely an excuse for forming a club. This is to overlook that the Georgian era, including its intellectual and scholarly life, was one of sociability and that it contained a multitude of easily accessible, fully established and socially approved clubs available to wealthy men in the early nineteenth century. Antiquarian societies, professional guilds, drinking clubs, sporting and gambling clubs, dining societies and clubs built solely on the qualification of class were all available and were indeed already frequented by the members of the Roxburghe. There was little reason to go to the expense and effort required to create a new club unless it specifically catered to an interest and answered a need not already being met by existing means. That these needs were not being met, either by clubs or by commercial printing, was later underlined by Benjamin Disraeli, who reminded the critics of his period that 'the sources of secret history at the present day are so rich and various; there is such an eagerness among their possessors to publish family papers, even sometimes in shapes and at dates so recent, as scarcely to justify their appearance; that modern critics, in their embarrassment of manuscript wealth, are apt to view with too depreciating an eye the more limited resources of men of letters at the commencement of the century'.[1]

From its inception the club has acted as a role model and trailblazer inspiring many subsequent printing clubs and societies, and by extension has influenced the types of books being published, the methods employed to disseminate early and special-interest texts and to some extent the manner in which literature has developed as a specific area of study. Once the Roxburghe Club had shown the way, making mistakes and falling short of perfection as leaders into unknown territory so often do, other printing clubs and societies were quick to follow its lead into such promising country. Each new club had its own area of specialist interest and its own agenda to be promoted through the printing and distribution of its club editions. That the Roxburghe was the inspiration and example to the clubs that came after has been freely acknowledged both by their contemporaries and by later critics, and by extension the benefits that have accrued to the literary world by this indirect path. Harold Williams defined a book club as a group that may have 'some, or nearly all, the characteristics more naturally to be associated with the learned academy or the printing society, or it may possess very few. But the true book club, whatever else its attributes, may be taken as regarding the book as an end in and for itself. It is not merely a tool, nor yet, as with the printing society, a text upon which to base further progress'.[2] This is an important distinction, and many of the later clubs that formed in the wake of the Roxburghe, while branching out into valuable and useful forms of publishing, cannot be said to be book clubs in this sense.

Scott, writing to Dibdin in 1823 to accept membership into the Roxburghe, mentions the formation of the Bannatyne Club, which is 'to be established here something on the plan of the Roxburghe Club', and says that 'their first meeting is to be held on Thursday when the health of the Roxburghe Club will not fail to be drank'.[3] Again, in a letter dated 1827, he indicates that he considers the Bannatyne to owe its existence, at least in part, to the example set by the Roxburghe, writing that 'you will I hope find we have not failed to

---

1 Benjamin Disraeli, *Life and Writings of the Author* (1848), in Isaac Disraeli, *Curiosities of Literature* (London: Routledge, Warnes and Routledge, 1859), I, p. xxviii.
2 Ibid., p. 8.
3 Grierson, *The Letters of Sir Walter Scott*, p. 342.

let the lamp which we lighted at that of the Roxburgh [sic] shine forth to the best of our power'.[4]

Dibdin obviously admired the methods used by the Bannatyne Club and wrote approvingly of their advances in publishing, admitting that their more systematic approach was reaping benefits. He also incidentally, in the same paragraph, mentions *Havelok* and seems to lay to rest any ideas held by critics that he was against the printing of this work or its method of production, writing that 'Havelok was the last performance of any note; and I am not singular in the expression of my regret that the plan adopted which led to that publication has not been rigidly followed up in subsequent efforts. The BANNATYNE CLUB seem, in this respect, to be very much shooting ahead of the parent-Society'.[5] Despite Dibdin's comments, and although the Bannatyne is sometimes held up as being superior to the Roxburghe in terms of scholarship (and that may be true of the formatting of the publications themselves which were professionally edited), it does not appear that the membership of the Bannatyne possessed the same expertise or interest in early books as that displayed by the Roxburghe membership. Robert Pitcairn, the editor responsible for the Bannatyne editions, later wrote that 'the committees are apt to swamp [their funds] by editing costly and often (with reverence be it spoken) useless books, which more than nine-tenths of the members do not relish, and fully as many cannot read'.[6] This opinion was also voiced by Lord Cockburn, who in 1832 wrote in his journal that 'very few of us can read our books, and still fewer can understand them, yet type, morocco and the corporation spirit make us print on, and this quite independently of the temptation arising from the marketable worth of what we get being far beyond what we pay'.[7] Clearly many of the Bannatyne members, rather than being more scholarly or discerning in their literary activities, were passive consumers of the items being produced by the club, and rather than displaying discrimination instead cheerfully admitted to the very faults for which the Roxburghe were often (and erroneously) placed in the critical pillory.

There is insufficient space here to cover in any detail the many diverse book clubs and societies that followed the example of the Roxburghe Club, and later groups did quickly start to designate themselves as societies rather than clubs.[8]

---

4 Ibid., p. 285.
5 Dibdin, *Bibliophobia*, pp. 47–48.
6 Robert Pitcairn, in Padmini Ray Murray, 'The Diversity of Print: Antiquarianism', *The Edinburgh History of the Book in Scotland*, ed. Bill Bell (Edinburgh: Edinburgh University Press, 2007), III, p. 282.
7 Lord Cockburn, ibid., p. 282.
8 Laurel Braswell-Means, 'The Influence of Romantic Antiquarianism upon Medieval English Studies', *University of Ottawa Quarterly* 52 (1982), (273–85), p. 283.

The term 'society' probably carried a suggestion of professional gravitas and helped disassociate them from the connotations of sociability inherent in the word 'club'. New clubs appeared which, like the Bannatyne, concentrated on aspects of Scottish literature. Among these were the Maitland, founded in 1828 and containing much of the same membership as the Bannatyne; The Abbotsford, inaugurated the year after Scott's death, which similarly shared many names from the other two registers; The Iona Club, its name a commemoration of the monastery of Iona, which printed items of Scottish history, literature and antiquities; and the Spalding Club, named for the historian John Spalding and founded in 1839 to cater to the literature of the north-east of Scotland. In England a wide variety of societies started appearing, providing for every taste in historical, topographical and literary material, but in practice none were focused on literary texts in a similar way to the Roxburghe Club and the Scottish clubs, and even the Scottish clubs were in many cases soon to change their focus to that of archaeology and history.[9]

Not until 1840, which saw the founding of the Percy, the Shakespeare, and the Parker Societies, were any other clubs inaugurated that were directly concerned with printing early literature. The Percy Society, named after Thomas Percy, editor of *Reliques of Ancient English Poetry*, was unsurprisingly committed to 'the discovery and publication of ancient and obscure specimens of ballad poetry'.[10] The Parker Club, named after Archbishop Parker, the Elizabethan antiquary and manuscript collector, also founded in this year, concentrated solely on publishing literary and theological works by early Church of England divines. Finally, the Shakespeare Society was especially interesting in the context of the earlier, pioneering activities of the Roxburghe because, rather than (as the name might imply) printing the works of Shakespeare himself, the society proposed to 'print and distribute books illustrative of Shakespeare and the history of his time'.[11] As already discussed, the Roxburghe, almost thirty years before, had displayed a strong interest in exploring and illustrating the context against which Shakespeare produced his works. Unfortunately, the first director of the Shakespeare Society was the ubiquitous John Payne Collier, who was also responsible for the closing of the club due to the resulting lack of public confidence in its publications following the forgery accusations which blighted the end of Collier's career.

The most interesting and influential literary society to be established on the lines of the Roxburghe Club is the Early English Text Society (EETS), founded by Frederick Furnivall (who edited several texts for the Roxburghe

---

9 Harold Williams, *Book Clubs and Printing Societies*, p. 62.
10 Ibid., p. 64.
11 Ibid., p. 67.

in the 1860s) in 1864. This society marked the turning point which Williams describes as 'a new date in the story of printing societies' and is largely credited with overseeing the process by which literary studies and editing in Britain gained its modern scholarly methods.[12] Furnivall's position in the world of literary studies has been described as being 'like a Victorian explorer or empire builder, mapping out territories, building railways and bridges, improving, facilitation access, preparing the way for others', but in some senses the Roxburghe Club could be said to have earlier signposted the way for Furnivall.[13] Most of these clubs (with the obvious exception of EETS) failed to last the course, often finding that the public had little taste for the works that they published. The limited numbers of copies printed by the Roxburghe, combined with the members' acceptance of covering expenses out of their own pockets, allowed volumes to be printed without having to raise public subscription, enabling its longevity and maintaining its original purpose. Other clubs, otherwise similar in framework, foundered on the shores of public indifference, not least it may be assumed because the need for public subscription would have entailed both substantial administrative requirements and, more damagingly, the need to publish works that would appeal to the most common denominator among the target audience. The necessity of both appealing to a wide enough readership, while simultaneously offending the fewest possible potential subscribers, must have been a tricky line to walk, ensuring that few boundaries of established popular taste could be pushed but also perhaps eventually sapping the pleasure out of the venture for the founders of the particular publishing venture. The men who made up the Roxburghe, however, through their ability and willingness to fund the venture entirely, coupled with each individual's utter freedom to present whatever item appealed to his own tastes without the need to comply with a set of rules laid down by committee, were able to retain their interest and passion for the books that had brought them together in the first place. The act of presenting volumes retained its joy without the necessity for planning meetings, advertising budgets, lengthy debates about the difficulties of distribution or adherence to club standards and deadlines. Nobody had to collect public money or sell the idea of an unusual volume to a sceptical public. Even when times (and personal fortunes) changed and the club started altering its method to one of annual subscription and organizational financing of the club publications, these subscriptions were still limited to within the group itself and all that had to be agreed was the question of a volume to

---

12 Ibid., p. 72.
13 Derek Pearsall, 'Frederick James Furnivall', in *Medieval Scholarship: Biographical Studies on the Formation of a Discipline*, ed. by Helen Damico and Joseph B. Zavadil (London: Routledge, 1998) II, pp. 125–38, (p. 135).

print that appealed to the majority of the members themselves. The fact that the club publications have continued to be sought after is evidence perhaps that the public is not always the best judge of what it wants or needs until it is presented with a fait accompli. This freedom of expression guarded by the club, especially in the founding years, allowed the books published to cover a range of literary and historical significance which it is difficult to imagine occurring under any other publishing mechanism. It may not have lent itself to a systematic dissemination of the works of a particular author or period, but it did preserve and promulgate a wide variety of rare and all but forgotten works that otherwise might have permanently disappeared from literary culture and helped give impetus to the emergence of a national literature and the appreciation of early English works.

Bibliomania as a general social phenomenon had largely ended by 1832, with book prices plummeting and celebrated collections being sold for a tiny fraction of the amount that they had cost to purchase. Dibdin, in his melancholy sequel *Bibliophobia*, attributes this sad ebb of bibliographic fortunes to the combined effects of concerns about upcoming reform and the cholera epidemic, which made people understandably unwilling to appear in public places, and even less keen to gather together in confined auction rooms and booksellers' stores. He wrote, with a touch of what may be bitterness or perhaps just bewilderment, 'in short, FEAR is the order of the day. To those very natural and long-established fears of bailiffs and tax-gatherers must now be added the fear of *Reform*, of *Cholera*, and of BOOKS'.[14] The Roxburghe managed to hold on, although Dibdin says that many of the members at this point had either retired to their estates (they were, after all, an ageing group), were busy with other concerns of life or, in the case of Heber (under his guise as *Atticus*), had gone abroad.[15] It can be argued that the withdrawing tide of high book prices now made it possible for scholars and public institutions to afford to buy those very volumes that bibliomania had brought to the public's attention. The taste for early English works had been created, and now the raw materials were becoming affordable, and as importantly, accessible. Nicolas Barker has pointed out that during bibliomania 'the black-letter book, after having passed from the country hall to the scholar's study, passed back from the scholar's study to the country hall'.[16] Once fashion moved on it could be further claimed that from the country hall the volumes often later made their way to the British Library, the Bodleian, the John Rylands Library and other institutions where they were once more available for scholars' use, if never

---

14 T. F. Dibdin, *Bibliophobia* (London: Henry Bohn, 1832), p. 6; italics in original.
15 Ibid., p. 37.
16 De Ricci, in Nicolas Barker, *Bicentenary History*, p. 70.

again their ownership. Dibdin himself saw that bibliomania had perhaps created the perfect conditions for these books to make their way to public institutions and in fact welcomed it. In *Bibliophobia* he poignantly mentions that following the auction of a friend's collection, 'if I look back at the sale of any one article, out of this extraordinary collection, with more satisfaction than another, it is in the acquisition of the Luther Bible by the British Museum'.[17] He had frequently displayed frustration at the inability or unwillingness of the leading institutions to make the most of these opportunities to buy texts he considered to be important at auction. Writing about the British Museum in 1834, he asks, 'and how that National Library, attached to the most knowing and the richest set of human beings upon earth, can let so many opportunities slip of essential aggrandizement to their book-treasures, is as unaccountable as lamentable. Can an establishment like that plead poverty? Forbid it, every succeeding Prime Minister'.[18] Dibdin was not alone in his views, and a similarly damning verdict on the state of early nineteenth-century British public collections is displayed in a letter from 1816 in which the writer laments 'of public libraries in London we have none worth mentioning, except the British Museum; the library of which is undoubtedly a huge collection of books, brought together without plan or arrangement'.[19]

Sometimes, luckily for the public collections, the works made their way directly to their stacks without the need to enter the auction room, and it is clear that the antiquarians of this period often acted in the interests of posterity, at least where financially viable for their heirs.

Looking again at the purchasing methods previously mentioned, although there may be something morally questionable in the thought of Earl Spencer procuring items from cathedral collections, it can also be argued that if the guardians of those libraries had decided, for whatever reason, to sell the volumes in question, then it was preferable that they should be bought for a British collection rather than risking their later sale to foreign collectors. This is one of the many morally grey areas within which book collectors and their agents, not to mention the administrators of public and venerable collections, operated during this period. The items were not just being purchased from British archives and books newly liberated from French aristocratic collections and libraries looted during the revolution and succeeding wars were making their way to British private collections through sometimes questionable channels. Kristian Jensen relates how one French book dealer, secretly acting on

---

17 Dibdin, *Bibliophobia*, p. 42.
18 Dibdin, *Reminiscences*, p. 412.
19 'Of Libraries, Both Public and Private, Foreign and Domestic', *The European Magazine, and London Review* 69 (1816), p. 203.

Spencer's behalf, purchased an edition of Homer printed by Aldine for 2,900 francs, thereby having to suffer the double guilt of not only allowing the book to leave France for the library of a British collector but also of having to do so while leading his fellow countrymen to believe that he had preserved the work for France. This was an especially telling transaction as the bookseller in question was Philippe Renouard, a historian who specialized in the works of the Aldine Press and who was opposed to the losses of rare French books to English collectors.[20]

Again, as reprehensible as such profiteering appears, it has to be acknowledged that France's loss was Britain's gain. The flow was definitely not all in Britain's favour. As the book-collecting frenzy reached its end, there came the risk of an even greater flow of volumes to foreign institutions and collectors than previously experienced, especially with the creation of new and extravagantly endowed institutions in America. It is very possible that the massive collections belonging to the members of the Roxburghe Club, by virtue of their unwillingness to stop collecting simply because the fad had moved on, retained many of these works long enough for cultural tastes to catch up, for public financing of institutions to improve and for public collections to be in a position to acquire many of the rare items either through direct purchase from the owner or at auction after the collector's death. Even the wealth of the Roxburghe Club could not hold back the tide of foreign buyers, but they could and did delay the inevitable in many cases and ensured that a large number of items remained for the national collections to buy.

As already touched on in earlier chapters, before many of these large collections went to auction they were already available for the use of authors and scholars. Richard Heber was notable for allowing a wide range of people access to his vast libraries, not only well-known authors such as Robert Southey (who seems to have made extensive use of many of the Roxburgher collections), William Wordsworth, and the writer and editor Thomas Park but also scholars including Charles Burney and Martin Routh. While these collections were not being thrown open to the general public and there was inevitably a highly selective approach regarding who was allowed access to the books and manuscripts (and as these libraries were situated within the private residences of their owners, it is hardly surprising, because who would be willing to throw open their home and expose their expensive private possessions to the general public), the value of this access for authors and scholars and, by extension, literary and academic culture, was still immense. The club's facsimile copies of rare works also added to the means by which scholars could access rare works that may otherwise have lay beyond all possibilities of access,

20 Jensen, *Revolution and the Antiquarian Book*, p. 41.

either because they were in the possession of a collector who was unwilling to allow admission to their library or because of the distances involved and the difficulties of nineteenth-century travel. This trickle-down effect of cultural pursuits and the dissemination of the ideas contained within the original texts ensured that society gained in this way as well as through the eventual direct commercial reprinting of the texts if and when that occurred. As Edward Edwards acknowledged, 'the common books which pass into the hands of almost the humblest owe something of their merit and vitality to the hoarding up of rare and costly books in such collections as the Spencer Library – created with a liberal hand, and imparted with a liberal heart'.[21]

The club was, as has been shown, reproducing texts that often had become either exceptionally rare or even unique since the time of their original printing. While the belief persisted among the public that if the chosen texts did not possess sufficient literary merit to have ensured a continuing and unbroken publication history they could not be considered worth reproducing for a discerning nineteenth-century readership, the absolute opposite was, of course, the true situation. In most cases these texts were most useful specifically *because* they were not the types of items that general publishers were printing and for which there was no present commercial demand. The Roxburghe Club luckily did not equate a lack of modern reputation with a lack of merit, nor the absence of a commercial readership as a valid assessment of inherent literary interest, and their insistence on a different measure of literary worth to that which was currently prevailing, irrespective of the profitability of the venture, provided a necessary stepping stone for the popularization and acceptance of these works. Book clubs, from the Roxburghe Club onwards, filled a vital position in the publishing world in producing books that contain a great deal of value to scholars and other interested parties, without necessarily having the potential to turn a profit for the publisher of that text. If such material is to be saved for future research or interest, or indeed, as has occurred with a number of the authors reprinted by the Roxburghe Club, for a posterity that may have revised its opinions on the literary value of those works, then the undertaking of a club such as the Roxburghe to ensure the texts' longevity is obviously of great value. The worth of such an undertaking can, as in this case, be obscured by contemporary prejudice, ignorance or indifference and may only become apparent at a much later date.

While all those perceived to be bibliomaniacs were criticized for their supposed preoccupation with superficial aesthetics and the rarity of the items they collected, this accusation was doubly vehement against the Roxburghe as they also stood accused not only of buying rarities but of reprinting texts

---

21 Edwards, *Libraries and Founders of Libraries*, p. 446.

in extremely limited numbers as well, thereby supposedly restricting the availability and retaining the rarity value of the items. Many of the volumes that the members presented to the club were reprinted from originals considered to be either extremely rare or unique, which meant that even once those original volumes had been stored in a private collection, safe from the cheese shop or the degradations of decay, they were still essentially only one country house fire away from extinction. Thirty copies of a text, while perhaps not ideal, is a significant improvement of a text's odds for survival. It should also be taken into consideration that there was an extremely limited readership during this period and that even modern popular books such as novels published through more normal, commercial routes were produced in quantities of only 500 to 800 units.[22] The Roxburghe, of course, were not coming even close to producing impressions of this size, but in relative terms the numbers of books printed for each item was not so very small either. It is important to retain a clear understanding (which often seemed to be missing in early discussions of the club's publishing record) that all volumes, certainly until the club started producing 'club' editions, were indeed presented *to*, not *by* the Roxburghe Club as it was a group of individuals acting autonomously within a rough framework, not an organization working to rules designed to produce a uniform item attaining consensual standards. Each volume was financed entirely by the individual who presented it, and to expect them to underwrite a print run of, for example, 500 books for wider distribution would have been absurd.

It must also be pointed out that despite the often dim view of the club's activity taken by modern scholars, the Roxburghe members of the early days were not acting without scholarly intentions. Dibdin, so often held up as the epitome of superficial aesthetic obsession, was intellectually a far more complex character than he is often given credit for, who understood and passionately cared about the necessity of creating a book science to examine and categorize what had previously been overlooked and neglected. In *The Bibliomania* he argued that 'to place competent Librarians over the several departments of a large library; or to submit a library on a more confined scale to one diligent, enthusiastic, well-informed, and well bred Bibliographer or Librarian, (of which in this metropolis we have so many examples) is doing a vast deal towards directing the channels of literature to flow in their proper courses'.[23] Far from being a plea for dilettante cultural practices, this is an explicit call for a greater degree of professionalism and specialization. During his own

22 Adrian Johns, 'Changes in the World of Publishing', *The Cambridge History of English Romantic Literature* (Cambridge: Cambridge University Press, 2009), pp. 377–402 (p. 378).
23 Dibdin, *Bibliomania*, p. 741.

lifetime, although his writing style frustrated many critics, he was taken very seriously in some circles as a knowledgeable advocate of literature, and much of his work was in the area of cataloguing and categorizing, with much useful fruit of his labour going on to form a basis for later work to build upon. In 1824 he published his *Library Companion*, often derided for its frequent inaccuracies and overestimation of his own abilities, but in it, among other useful information, he described 26 Shakespeare First Folios, which is considered to be the 'first such published description of extant copies' and surely a vital building block in any scholarly examination of the history of the printing of the works of the playwright, not to mention forming part of the fossil record of modern bibliography.[24] This deeply held belief in the value of indexing and cataloguing, while still in its infant stage, has been one of the foundations that modern scholarship has been built upon, and without such systematic forms of searchable listings the worth of large collections of volumes to the academic who wishes to access it would be severely limited.

An important but difficult to quantify contribution made by the club to the world of letters was that of widening the public debate: about the value of early English literary texts, about books and their history as artefacts and about the preservation of our national literary wealth. The activities of the founding years look frivolous to the modern viewpoint only if we fail to take into account how serious intellectual pursuits were often framed within a social context during the early nineteenth century. The romantics of this period often met in social settings although these tended to be private domestic spaces, but while the concerns of antiquarians at this time are often regarded as representing a facet of the prevalent currents of romanticism, the Roxburghe dinners do not easily fit into this context, and while in many ways they reflected the changing culture of the time, they can be more easily viewed as belonging to the receding Georgian world of fashionable sociability. There was certainly no question of the Roxburghe Club being inclusive to women or of allowing them access to the activities of the club in the ways becoming increasingly popular in romantic circles, and the club stayed firmly in the public or semi-public arena of taverns rather than the private spaces of the drawing room or clubhouse. The club did, however, provide an important platform for the exchange of ideas and act as an interface between men of widely differing social standing and profession. It is tempting to view the Roxburghe Club as the almost perfect example of the process that Russell and Tuite, utilizing arguments from Georg Simmel and Jürgen Habermas, are describing when they write that 'what distinguishes the bourgeois public

---

24 Harold M. Otners, *The Shakespeare Folio Handbook and Census* (Westport, CT: Greenwood Press, 1990), p. 13.

sphere from an aristocratic culture, where talk is its own medium, is the way in which an urban culture begins to shed its dependence on the authority of the aristocratic noble hosts and to acquire that autonomy that turns conversation into criticism and *bon mots* into arguments'.[25] We see the Roxburghe Club, very literally, carrying its private 'aristocratic' dinner table conversation into the semi-public environment of the tavern, and from there, extending the debate into the public sphere of literary criticism through books, periodicals, auction houses, schools, universities and learned societies.

The club, and Dibdin in particular, were similarly influential in the process of creating a linguistic awareness of book collecting and its specialist terminology and promoting its diffusion into the domestic discussion. While the journals of the day were discussing, mocking or decrying the activities of the bibliomania, they were also, consciously or unconsciously, educating the public. Discussions of social transformation are by nature often difficult to pin down to definite cause and effect, and, of course, the Roxburghe were part of a larger scene of cultural change: however, the high-profile activities of the club ensured that the titles and nature of the works of early literature that they reprinted were becoming a matter of common knowledge and alongside it the book dealers' descriptive specialist language was being introduced into the working vocabularies of nonbook collectors. Even if much of that awareness was framed as censure, it nevertheless provided a means for the slow absorption of the information into the minds of the readers and correspondents and a creeping process of familiarization. By the time society had become more willing to discuss early texts in the light of a shared cultural resource, the educated public was far more equipped with the necessary knowledge and terminology that they would require.

Within their own sphere, the Roxburghe were not just part of a general change but were resolutely creating their own path, one that often moved in the opposite direction to the general consensus. This is not only obvious in the types of literature that they collected and reprinted but also, as we have seen, in technological terms the club walked a complex path between the traditional and the cutting edge. The first steam-driven printing press, developed in 1812, had its inaugural public run in 1814. It had been commissioned by John Walter II and was installed amid great secrecy in Printing House Square at the headquarters of *The Times*, where it produced its first commercial print run on 29 November. Industrialization was gaining momentum in every area of human endeavour, and printing was no exception. Up to this point, despite advances and improvements in the methods used on a daily basis, much of

---

25 Simmel, 'Sociability', p. 52; Habermas, *Structural Transformation*, cited p. 31 in Russell and Tuite, p. 13.

the equipment and expertise that had been a part of the early printer's repertoire was still available in many of the present-day printer's shops, but all that was changing very quickly. The huge shifts occurring in the world of printing and publishing left the Roxburghe Club fighting a rearguard action against the loss of traditional printer's arts in an age of increasing mechanization. Many printers foresaw that the generalized use of automation would result in the lessening of the need for skilled printers, quickly leading to a downgrading of their role to one of factory operatives, and John Johnson, the printer employed at the Lee Priory Press, was a 'dedicated opponent of steam and stereotyping'.[26] The club, however, was not acting from a fear of progress but from a love of, and a desire to retain, what was valuable, and far from being Luddite in their outlook they were simultaneously cherishing and supporting the traditional printer's arts while embracing those new technologies such as lithographic reproduction that added to its utility. They appear to have been willing and eager to use whatever technologies were available, whether traditional or cutting edge, to attain their goals of reproducing early books in a manner that came close to the original experience of the contemporary reader of early texts. Significantly this desire appears to have applied only to the contents of the book rather than the bindings.

The Roxburghe's love of the early, artisan printer's craft was a celebration of the creative process with all its idiosyncrasies and difficulties over that of the uniform perfection of mass production, and the club can be seen as contributing both aesthetical appreciation and financial support to the techniques of hand printing, which continue to have an influence into the present day. At this pivotal time for the printer's craft, when mechanization was gathering momentum and poised to take over, and the skills necessary for the reproduction of these early works were already starting to die out, the club utilized the enthusiasm and wealth available to its members not only to employ artisan printers and engravers to recreate the necessary methods but also to start their own private printing presses motivated by an underlying ethos that would recognizably continue to underpin small printing ventures as far in the future as the private press movement and William Morris's Kelsmcott Press.

Any endeavour in the area of reprinting new editions of early works inevitably raises questions about editing methods, and while this is an area in which the early club has received extensive criticism, it is also an area in which they made significant contributions. Although the presentation of the early Roxburghe volumes was not as uniform or consistent as would later be the case, many of the works published at that time by the club showed an awareness of scholarly apparatus and displayed introductions, indexes, glossaries

---

26 Johns, 'Changes in the World of Publishing', p. 391.

and the like. The Roxburghe members themselves apparently believed that there was sufficient uniformity in the early volumes as to be readily ascertainable to a new member. This assurance is evident from the letter sent by Francis Freeling to Scott in which he states that 'every Member shall print, that the form shall be such as the Books now sent will point out', which instruction, vague as it was, indicated that Freeling was confident that merely seeing the books already printed would be sufficient guidance in the printing of Scott's own offering.[27]

While often criticized for their lack of scholarly editing (criticism, it should be stressed, which is made from the comfortable position of easy access to both source materials and documented knowledge of methods), the Roxburghe Club were commonly using editing methods and scholarly frameworks that had not yet become common practice. Some members possessed considerable ability and skill, and the editing of a text such as *The Owl and the Nightingale*, presented by Sir Stephen Glynne, represented quite an undertaking. It was edited from two manuscripts, and the poem is written in Early Middle English from around the late thirteenth century. The language would have been far more difficult for a nineteenth-century reader to understand than that of Chaucer, and the poem itself is a difficult piece to unravel. Glynne's willingness to address a difficult text of this nature indicates that the club were operating at a far more committed level of editorship than that for which they have been given credit. A lack of recorded guidelines or club rules has been held up as proof that the club was amateur and unfocused in its editing and printing. This may be more an omission of documentation than of philosophy as Markland, writing in *Notes and Queries*, said that 'it was declared by the Roxburghe Club that "The omission of an Index where essential, should be an indictable offence!"'.[28] A comment of this nature indicates that certain rules of editing had been discussed and agreed upon, even if they were not written down or formalized for posterity. The club did not exist in isolation, and the presence among its members of a number of men known for their work in the editing of early texts underlines its position at the centre of existing spheres of progressive publishing in a wide range of early literature. The club was simply a particularly well-funded and influential outlet for the interests and expertise of many of the foremost proponents of early literature at that time, and their editing skills, far from being slapdash or careless, appear often to be experimental and pioneering if regarded in the context of the period. The club's publications include some formidable scholarship, notably

---

27 Grierson, *The Letters of Sir Walter Scott*, p. 285.
28 J. H. Markland, 'Spence's Polymetis: Indexes', *Notes and Queries* 7, 180 (11 June 1859), p. 469.

in some of the introductions and notes provided to editions, and the waning, since the 1990s, of the hegemony of traditional belief in 'laws' of editing (e.g., in a renewed respect for best-text or single-text editions) makes the efforts of these early nineteenth-century editors, who often knew of only one surviving exemplar of a text, appear far more worthy of attention.

The Roxburghe Club did not have an overtly stated nationalistic intention behind the printing of their books, but it is not possible to look at the club's activities without setting them within the context of an interest in nationalist literature that was a growing cultural energy during this period. Dibdin himself certainly wrote in terms of patriotism in connection with the early English texts that the group were collecting, and his *Library Companion* has been described as '[seizing] every opportunity to parade its credentials as a work of public spirit, showing how taste is a patriotic duty and proposing that private consumption might advance the project of national definition'.[29] Because English traditions represented the dominant culture of the period (in relation to the other countries of the British Isles), it is easy to overlook the fact that the predominant culture was the product of an education that took its values from classical texts and that the early works in the English vernacular were, at this time, overlooked and often disapproved of as barbaric or uncultured. That the Roxburghe Club was exerting a positive effect on the cultural acceptance of English literature is borne out by Scott's remark in a letter to a friend that 'I flatter myself the [Bannatyne] Club has placed the old Scottish literature very high and that it may match even the Roxburgh [sic] of London in its beneficial effect on the old literature of the country'.[30] It is interesting that as nationalistically Scottish as Scott may have been, he here seems to be using 'the country' to signify Britain as a whole and viewing the early literature of the British Isles as a common wealth of culture. The history of printing itself could be adapted into a form of national heritage. Seth Lerer describes Caxton in the nineteenth century as the 'focus of a new spirit of bibliographic nationalism'.[31] This is borne out by the club's actions in the raising of a monument to Caxton, as previously discussed, and their unfulfilled desire to see it installed in Westminster Abbey, not only the original site of Caxton's press but also, of course, a sacred space for the veneration of the national literary heroes whose memorials are displayed there.

---

29 Lynch, '"Wedded to Books": Bibliomania and the Romantic Essayists', Romantic Circles, Praxis Series, Romantic Circles, University of Maryland, www.rc.umd.edu/praxis/libraries/lynch/lynch.html [accessed 25 June 2011], p. 13.
30 Grierson, *The Letters of Sir Walter Scott*, p. 63.
31 Seth Lerer, 'Caxton in the Nineteenth Century', in *Caxton's Trace*, ed. by William Kuskin (Notre Dame, IN: University of Notre Dame, 2006), pp. 325–70 (p. 327).

The club's activities in this period do not, however, point only to the development of a purely English literary identity, but rather to an interest in a more cohesively British literature. Dibdin, as we have seen, made a point in his lectures for the Royal Institution of discussing the literary traditions of Wales, Ireland and Scotland as well as those of England, and a similarly broad interpretation of national literature can be seen in the club publications. The interests of the Roxburghe Club in medieval balladry can be seen to link them, at least in broad terms, back to the work of Burns and the wider concerns of the romantic movement with its divergence of focus from the 'dominant "Augustan" eighteenth-century literary tradition'.[32] The popularity of Burns's *Poems, Chiefly in the Scottish Dialect*, published in 1786, has been viewed as signalling that the romantic period was willing to entertain a perception of the developing national identity that was far less rigid in its outlines than is often supposed.[33] Furthermore, this interest in ballads has been cited as a positive force in the growing cohesion of the British Isles and one that supplied an acceptable medium through which the differing traditions of the individual countries could be combined in a new model of what it meant to be British, while still retaining elements that expressed and reflected the different cultures now contained within that tricky concept.[34]

Other groups of antiquaries were forming around the focal points of national literatures. The Scottish book clubs have already been mentioned, and similar groups coalesced around the literary heritage of Wales and Ireland. Welsh literature especially had lost its visibility as a formative part of British literary history, not only through the decline of the Welsh language but also through its perceived political undesirability within the union.[35] Existing Welsh Societies in London, including the Cymmrodorion, the Gyneddigion and the Cymreigyddion, all founded in the second half of the eighteenth century as social and charitable groups, now began to take an increasing antiquarian interest in the literary history of Wales and often in editing older texts.[36] The shared currents running between antiquarianism, nationalism and

---

32 Jane Moore and John Strachan, *Key Concepts in Romantic Literature* (London: Palgrave Macmillan, 2010), p. 189.
33 Ibid., pp. 195–96.
34 Manning, 'Antiquarianism, Balladry and the Rehabilitation of Romance', in *The Cambridge History of English Romantic Literature*, ed. by James Chandler (Cambridge: Cambridge University Press, 2009), 45–70 (p. 56).
35 Sarah Prescott, '"What Foes More Dangerous Than Too Strong Allies?": Anglo-Welsh Relations in Eighteenth-Century London', *Huntington Library Quarterly* 69 (December 2006), 535–54 (p. 553).
36 Glanmor Williams, 'Language, Literacy and Nationality in Wales', in *Religion, Language and Nationality in Wales: Historical Essays*, ed. by Glanmor Williams (Cardiff: University of Wales Press, 1979), pp. 127–47 (p. 138).

romanticism during the period have been noted, sharing as they did an interest in early poetry and works of medieval literature and providing channels through which such texts could be published.[37]

None of this should be taken to imply that English literature was dominant in any simple, consistent sense. At the period when the Roxburghe Club was founded, early English texts were not universally valued as literature, failing as they did to conform to the taste formed by a classical education, and perhaps on some level holding too much association with forms of education considered to be more suited to the lower classes. Although never overtly stated in criticisms of the Roxburghe Club's choice of works to reprint, it is difficult to shake the impression that at least some of the vehemence with which their lack of taste is attacked is due to the association of early English texts with works considered useful educational material for the moral development of the mercantile classes. Yet not every early author had suffered the fate of obscurity; Shakespeare and Chaucer had continued to be printed through well-established channels and had escaped the censure meted out to other early vernacular authors and their works. For Chaucer this channel had been assisted by the championing of his works by Henry VIII, who had viewed Chaucer's anti-Catholic attitudes with approval and considered him to be an early Protestant poet. The Roxburghe Club's readiness to tackle daunting texts meant that some old works saw the light of day for the first time since the sixteenth century and also as a result eventually came into prominence as part of the canon of English literature. Although no such thing as a Department of English Literature existed yet in universities, histories of English literature were certainly being published, and the Roxburghe Club's efforts helped give a boost to an awareness of a wider range of English literature than had generally been known hitherto. Although the interest in early English literature existed before the Roxburghe Club itself, many of the members of the club were the very same people who had been operating in this area of literature during the past 20 years or more, and in some ways the founding of the club can be seen as the culmination of their drive and purpose rather than the beginning of their activities.

Much emphasis is understandably placed on *Havelok*, and it tends to be held up as the first important work produced by the club, but this does not detract from the substantial value contained in the earlier works published by the club, and it is striking that Madden, the brilliant young scholar brought in to edit *Havelok* for the Roxburghe, had initially approached them with the manuscript that he had discovered. Madden already knew Earl Spencer, and it was no surprise that he should approach such a wealthy bibliophile for funding,

37 Ibid., p. 139.

but he did not ask Spencer to act directly as his patron, instead soliciting the Roxburghe Club's support.[38] It is telling that he considered them to be the most receptive, influential and knowledgeable audience for his discovery. He recognized that the club were the men most willing and able to underwrite the publishing of this significant text. He understood their dedication to early literature and trusted them to appreciate the significance of his find, which they did, and they supported his aims even to the extent of changing their own long-established club procedures in order to achieve the best result.

When it came to Middle English texts, no one had previously been publishing the material that the Roxburghe Club was printing, and even after the well-publicized founding of the club had made their activities widely visible both to the public and to commercial publishers, they still remained the sole representatives for this type of literature until 1823.[39] The relatively small numbers of men who were involved in the promotion of these texts was a significant factor in its success. While of course unavoidably restricting the progress that could be achieved in a limited time span, it did ultimately allow an intense and ultimately fruitful exchange of ideas to evolve. Even when there was passionate and bitter disagreement between the men working in these areas of literature, leading to private argument and occasional vitriolic public exchanges in the journals of the day, there is still a sense of shared common purpose and respect. Dibdin, discussing the publication of *Havelok* and the resulting critical disagreement between Madden and Samuel Weller Singer concerning the glossary, admits that the men were 'both of too amiable a temper to take delight in literary fisty-cuffs' and relates how, after the matter was settled to the presumed satisfaction or at least acceptance of both parties, 'Assailant and Defender were seen cordially shaking hands across the same MS. in the British Library'.[40] It is too easy perhaps, from the distance of 200 years, to see the event in isolation, without putting it into the context of an ongoing relationship or collaboration between the devotees of early literature. Overall, looking at the development of the field, there is present a sense of excitement in the discovery, or rather rediscovery, of these early English works and authors. There is the impression that these men, even or perhaps especially when not in agreement, were enjoying the shared process of working on such fruitful and untrodden ground in which they were to remain pioneers for several decades. While it must have often felt a thankless task, there must also have been a certain freedom in the exploration of virgin territory, discovering,

---

38 Matthews, *The Making of Middle English*, p. 119.
39 Ibid., p. 90.
40 Dibdin, *Bibliophobia*, p. 48.

researching and circulating this rich, undiscovered literature that was so often dismissed by their contemporaries as simply 'that which is not classical'.[41]

It is important to acknowledge that the attainments made by the early Roxburghe Club are in no way invalidated by the later achievements of their successors. Each period of activity can only be judged in the context of its time and not by the later standards that perhaps owe much of their existence to the imperfect activities of these earlier contributors to the field. Much of the important work carried out by the club in its first two decades, and indeed of the work carried out by antiquarians in a more general sense, has suffered from a process of disassociation which has been apparent in some modern literary scholarship. The value of antiquarian research has often been devalued by an insistence on measuring its worth by more exacting modern standards, by applying benchmarks of excellence that are at best anachronistic. As the discipline of English literature developed during the 1840s, along with the gradual introduction and acceptance of Germanic methods of research and analysis, it (perhaps understandably) was keen to map out the exact boundaries of the field, discarding what might be perceived as an emotional response to the texts in favour of more precision, and a scientific method that could be applied to scholarly activities.[42] This is exactly the sort of book science that Dibdin had been so keen to see introduced, and the role of the antiquarians in this process was recognized by Arnold Schröer, who in 1925 (rather patronizingly) wrote 'how gratefully the English enthusiasts welcomed the old and young German academics and were ready to lend them a hand, full of joy that the "learned doctors" copied and edited their manuscripts', going on to acknowledge that 'the most astonishing and admirable thing was, however, the idealism and the energy with which these enthusiasts were capable of influencing the public interest'.[43] These developments were coming three decades after the Roxburghe Club had started the process, but those enthusiasts were their direct successors, finally passing on the torch of publishing English texts that the club had lit in 1812. These societies, the Roxburghe and the various groups that followed their lead, had carried the flame for early English literature for decades and were to finally have the satisfaction of seeing it taken seriously with the development of research tools that could set

---

41 D. R. Woolf, 'The Dawn of the Artifact: The Antiquarian Impulse in England, 1500–1730', in *Medievalism in England*, ed. by Leslie J. Workman and Kathleen Verduin (Cambridge: Boydell and Brewer, 1996) IV, 5–44 (p. 5).
42 Richard Utz, *Chaucer and the Discourse of German Philology* (Sydney: University of Sydney, 2002), p. 37.
43 Arnold Schröer, 'Aus der Frühzeit der Englischen Philologie' (1925), p. 34, quoted in ibid., p. 117.

the infant field of English literary studies on its path to scholarly acceptance. It was, perhaps, a somewhat pyrrhic victory; antiquarians succeeded in their aims, but at the expense of being disowned and repudiated by the posterity who had built on their efforts. Like so many pioneers they were ultimately made irrelevant by their own success.

This development of studies in early English works in this period was, of course, set alongside the more widely recognized context of romanticism, which was heavily influenced both by the texts themselves but also by the style in which they were expressed. The beautiful illustrative themes of manuscripts were obviously a huge influence on the romanticists, but the early printed page also played its part. A commonly held view about antiquarians of this period is that their interests were primarily centred on illustrated medieval manuscripts and were somehow intrinsically bound up with the romantic, chivalric ideals that they perceived in these texts. This view, while perhaps true of many other antiquarians, does not hold strong against what we know of the activities of the early Roxburghe Club. If antiquarianism was universally bound up with a romanticized picture of the religious scribe creating beauty by candlelight in his austere cell, then why was the early club so uniformly dedicated to reproducing early *printed* books? Most people, especially book collectors, will respond to the aesthetic appeal of illuminated manuscripts, and the members of the Roxburghe Club were no exception, but that did not appear to be the impetus behind the activities of their founding years. There is always the temptation to classify early nineteenth-century antiquarian activities as uniformly belonging to the emergence of romanticism when a closer reading of these activities shows a complexity of intent and opinion that cannot be easily classified. Commentators have often pointed to the emphasis placed on 'feeling' rather than intellect in many writings by the collectors of the bibliomania, but as noted previously, the volumes collected and produced by the Roxburghe were viewed simultaneously as extremely physical, artisan objects, as emotive elicitors of sensation but also as intellectual property and cultural wealth. There is no perceived contradiction here, merely the multifarious facets of the same artefact. Dibdin can fawn over the beauty of an engraving on a title page or the generosity of a margin and yet argue for a more organized book science without any sense of disjunction or contradiction. If the Roxburghe Club's interest in the literature of the Middle Ages and Elizabethan period is taken to denote their activities as falling generally within the realms of romanticism, their preoccupation with the artisan and technical aspect of the desired volume as well as its literary and aesthetic qualities may indicate that if their activities must be classified in this way, they operated more in a pre-William Morris/Arts and Crafts area of the romantic imagination than at the sublime, poetical end of the spectrum. There is no suggestion that the club, or its individual members, took any interest in romanticism as a movement beyond that of a topic of the day, and there is no indication that they even perceived any substantial degree of crossover between their own activities and those of the romantics.

The study of English literature only began to develop as an academic subject during the nineteenth century. Although through the eighteenth century the Dissenting Academies had become, according to D. J. Palmer, the 'cradle of English studies' where they 'encouraged the study of English authors for their stylistic and literary qualities', this interest in the vernacular literature did not spread to the wider educational curriculum.[44] Previous to the mid-nineteenth century, education in public schools was primarily based around the study of Latin and Greek, with emphasis on translation exercises and a concentration on the forms of writing found in the classical works. For the lower strata of society, the study of English literature was considered to be a positive way to teach boys from the mercantile (and later on the working) classes. It was considered to be morally bracing to study the classics, but for boys who would need to work for a living and had little use for Latin or Greek, it would be a waste to teach them the classics. Instead, it was postulated that the same moral lessons could be gained by studying English literature, using the same methods employed to study the classics and thereby hopefully gaining a socially useful degree of discipline and culture. The ascent of English literary studies took place in the vacuum being left by the decrease in demand for the traditional classical education. The mercantile classes were becoming a dominant force in society and in the more practical mind-set of the times, meaning that a knowledge of classical languages became an ornament rather than a necessity. Even as English literature gained a foothold in schools alongside Latin and Greek as a practical method for the teaching of skills such as composition, it retained its association with an 'anti-classical' approach to education.[45] The value of the literature, of course, was perceived as residing in its suitability as material for the acquisition of other, more practical skills rather than in its intrinsic literary worth. It took even longer for English literature to be considered worthy of study in its own right.

The universities were also slow to accept English literature as a focus for study, and when it was eventually, theoretically at least, being taught as a distinct subject at the University of London and Kings College, it was still liable to be treated with distrust and a degree of moral outrage. The first official professor of English felt it necessary to establish his appointment to the role

---

44 For a thorough discussion of the topic, see D. J. Palmer, *The Rise of English Studies* (London: Oxford University Press, 1965), p. 7.
45 Ibid., p. 13.

with vigorous criticism of the supposed moral iniquities of English literature.[46] This attack was delivered in the inaugural speech of T. D. Dale on taking up his role with the University of London in 1828, and includes assurances to the parents of the students he will be tutoring that although such early writing contains 'gems with which it is so copiously adorned' that he will be on his guard against any of the 'pollution', 'profaneness' or 'disgusting wantonness in which [works of early English literature] are too often incrusted'.[47]

In contrast to these social currents of distrust and antipathy towards English literature, we again see in the Roxburghe Club a willingness to cross cultural and class boundaries with regard to literary taste, and can perhaps detect another provocation for the anger and disapproval voiced in the letters pages of contemporary journals. Not only were the club willing to tolerate a range of social classes among their membership but they were also collecting and promoting that early English literature that was generally perceived as only suited to the education and tastes of the middle or mercantile classes. Their literary taste was one that was only just starting to find a foothold, and the sight of wealthy men of taste, possessed of classical educations, actually preferring to collect and reprint works considered to be worthless or at best vulgar was provocative. It must have been jarring to those less assured in their taste, and more familiar with the socially approved method of judging literary matters according to their adherence to an accepted definition of refined taste. The changes in education were more than merely stylistic; they carried profound significance for the national psyche and can be seen as underpinning much of the Victorian era's preoccupation with moral evolution and national destiny. English literature, viewed as an historical record as well as a moral blueprint, becomes not only a shared national heritage but also the story of Britain's creation myth and the signpost towards forging the expanding empire, both geographically and as a stereotype of national character. Against this context of developing acceptance of English literature within the British educational

---

46 Ibid., p. 21.
47 T. D. Dale, quoted in Palmer, p. 20: 'Nor to those parents who are acquainted with the earlier productions of English literature will such a declaration appear superfluous or misplaced. *They* know that the gems with which it is so copiously adorned, sometimes require to be abstracted and exhibited with a careful hand, lest they should convey pollution with the foul mass of daring profaneness or disgusting wantonness in which they are too often incrusted. [...] never will I suffer the eye of inexperienced youth to be dazzled by the brilliancy of genius when its broad lustre obscures the deformity of vice; never will I affect to stifle the expression of a just indignation, when wit, taste, and talent, have been designedly prostituted by their unworthy possessors to the excitement of unholy passions, the palliation of guilty indulgences, the ridicule of virtue, or the disparagement of religion.' (italics in original)

system, it becomes easy to see the significance of the Roxburghe Club members who worked in, and more often, headed, some of the most popular public schools of the period. As previously discussed, the men who recalled their schooldays under the tutelage of Roxburghe members often mentioned their exposure to English literature through the collections and interests of these men and the effect of their encouragement on their pupil's education and later careers. These individual headmasters provided an effective and direct means by which the promotion of English literature could make inroads into the hearts of the most influential seats of education, effectively bypassing any potential disapproval or antipathy displayed by society and the educational system towards such texts, a service that while largely invisible to society at large, carried with it the opportunity of enacting immense changes in the way that British society viewed its national literature and, by extension, itself.

CONCLUSION

The Roxburghe Club has enjoyed a rich, unbroken history spanning over two hundred years. This book has concentrated on the significance of just the first two decades of its existence and has hopefully established a clearer, more factual account of this period than has previously been available, one which provides a plausible counternarrative to that formerly available and underlines the need for a more complex view of the club demographic and motivation than has previously been acknowledged. It is apparent that in contrast to commonly held views the club membership, although mythologized as aristocratic, contained considerably more middle-class professionals and representatives of the gentry than nobles and that the members were not dilettante playboys but men of serious intent, committed to books, especially early printed texts. They were also politically active in their various spheres, and this was sometimes reflected in their choice of texts. Although, as might be expected, some were Tories, a surprisingly large percentage of the club were Whig, at least one was radical and most were unexpectedly sympathetic to political reform and Catholic emancipation, a position underlined by the club's willingness to reprint works of pre-Reformation Catholic provenance during a period when this could be considered provocative, and despite what has been seen as the wider anti-Catholic conservatism of antiquarianism at this time.

The club's genesis and the onset of its early members' association together for the investigation and discussion of early printing and texts are two other topics where the powerful existing myth – that the club owes its existence to the chance occurrence of a contested rare volume raising an extravagant auction price followed by an absurdly gluttonous dinner – proves to be misleading, and not just for the lack of seriousness it conveys. The men who would become the Roxburghe Club were in most cases already well known to each other, and the formation of the club can be seen as the result of their literary interests and the pooling of their individual expertise rather than as the fortuitous and frivolous genesis. Dibdin was the focus of the group as the author of the books which had come to most readily signify the building cultural interest in early texts, and already his interest and scholarship in bibliography had provided a nucleus around which a group interested in the collecting of early printed books had formed. His celebrity as the flamboyant patron saint of book collectors should not, however, obscure the expertise and commitment of the many other members of the club, whose names may be less familiar but whose solid involvement in the developing world of early English literature also underpinned the activities of the Roxburghe.

The early club did not stand apart from scholarship, a slightly risible affectation of conspicuous, perhaps even vacuous, consumption awaiting the eventual advent of their more serious Victorian successors (and the even more serious scholars whom they would employ) to find its purpose. Rather, from the very beginning it formed an important nexus between the authoritative purchasing power of the wealthy collector and the growing impulse towards practical conservation and the dissemination of antiquarian literary interests. A major area in which the club members represent valuable early nineteenth-century developments in book history is that of the knowledge of early printing and printers. While their meetings may have involved dining together, their toasts were, famously, in honour of the great early printers of Western Europe. The members of the club, as we have seen, were united by their fascination with and knowledge of typography and printing. Three of the members owned private printing presses prior to the mid-nineteenth-century growth in interest in small presses, and the club's pioneering interest in early printing and facsimile copies of early books provides a clear link between the work of the early printers and the late nineteenth-century revival of artisan printing exemplified by the Arts and Crafts movement.

As we have seen, the early history of the Roxburghe Club dispels the myth that it was a group that fits easily into the centre of the so-called bibliomania craze unless we reframe what bibliomania meant, at least to those caught up in the frenetic book-collecting activities of the period. The majority of the club were collectors who had purchased early books before it became a phenomenon and a fashion at the turn of the nineteenth century and who continued to collect them seriously after the craze had ended. Some of the Roxburghe, it is true, collected the rarities and status symbol volumes commonly regarded as the focus of bibliomaniacs, but it was not indiscriminate purchasing and in almost all cases they did so in addition to their primary collecting of early texts and other books with literary, rather than merely collectible, value. The club's history turns out to also confirm what has been emerging in recent research currents into intellectual life in the late eighteenth and the early nineteenth century, which have stressed the 'conversable', social and interactive nature of much debate and exchange of knowledge about literature and other subjects. This leads us to view as more serious the contributions of sociable networks to both knowledge and to the change and expansion in taste. Looking back from a perspective of modern university-housed English studies, it has been easy for commentators during the last century or more to discount the potential of a sociable network of connoisseurs for genuine advances in the subject of literary history. A similar retrospective blinker can be discerned when bibliographical scholars schooled in the laws of allegedly scientific methods of editing early texts, formulated in the nineteenth century and derived originally from Lachmann, dismissed early Roxburghe editions. It becomes possible in the modern age to respect the (varied) approaches taken by Roxburghe editions as productions of an era when principle and procedures for editing were in their infancy and subject to a variety of methods and experiments. The club's publications include some formidable scholarship, notably in some of the introductions and notes provided to editions. The waning, since the 1990s, of the hegemony of traditional belief in 'laws' of editing makes the efforts of these early nineteenth-century editors, who often knew of only one surviving exemplar of a text, appear far more worthy of attention. It also becomes clear that some Roxburghe reprints of then virtually unknown and certainly uncanonical writers (examples include Gower and Skelton) should be taken seriously as small steps in the long march of widening out the canon of English literature from the received notion of the great peaks of Chaucer, Shakespeare and Milton, for the period covered by the Roxburghe's interests.

The club's series of publications also had its own relationships with the ideological and aesthetic currents of the period. While the Roxburghe Club was obviously formed against the background of romanticism, their activities were not framed in the context of the chivalric medieval idealism found often in writings, visual arts and social attitudes in the romantic movement, but instead they approached early English literature in an avowedly practical and methodical manner. Although when the club's publishing has been lauded at all it has been usually for their medieval editions, most of the texts presented to the club in the early years were Elizabethan, and usually poetry; that is the literary area in which the early club excelled. The club, as the study of its editions suggests, was not simply offering random quaintly antique items of purely rarity value but rather displaying a focused attention to early literature, which included tracing themes and authors, not yet commonly valued, which lay between the peaks of popularly recognized genius. Moreover, most of them had been doing so, and gaining recognition for doing so, among fellow antiquarians long before the Roxburghe sale. The publications of the club at this time were concerned with a number of interesting and fruitful themes which included mystery and morality plays, allegorical works, sources that formed context for the works of Shakespeare and works that had been previously censored but showed no interest in the concerns of romanticism.

Romanticism was interested in the activities and texts of the club far more than the club was interested in romanticism.

The study of the history of the book has gained new momentum in the last 20 years. Gone, for many scholars now, is the traditional narrow focus exclusively on recording practical facts about volumes (printing types, binding, etc.). Book history has become a study of books, their origins, ownership and afterlives, as sociocultural, political and economic, aesthetic and literary phenomena, with much to tell us – about authorship, books production, readership and the history of taste. The history of the Roxburghe Club, its genesis and motivations in the early years, offers a narrative that addresses all of these topics in microcosm. Rather than viewing the early Roxburghe Club as being peripheral to changes in literary culture and their focus as being essentially inward looking and self-serving, the details of their history in all these various areas of literary culture, scholarship, education, national identity, literary heritage and the printing world during this period of rapid change and cultural evolution indicate that their activities have at the very least carried the possibility of influence far beyond the narrow world of book collecting. It is easy to discount the activities of pioneers as amateurish and dilettante in comparison to the later gains made on the foundation of earlier exploration, but like any foundation, if it is serving its purpose well it will be invisible beneath the tower of achievements that it supports. The early Roxburghe Club members built that foundation upon which rests not only the achievements of the later club but also so many far-reaching cultural and literary accomplishments and that contribution deserves to be acknowledged.

Appendix 1

THE CLUB MEMBERSHIP 1812–1835

Presented in alphabetical order with the title shown in square brackets being that held by the individual at the time of joining the Club.

Barnard, Benjamin

A Club member from 1834 to 1848, he was elected to replace a founder member.
He presented *Illustrations of Ancient State and Chivalry, from MSS. In the Ashmolean Museum,* with an Appendix to the Club in 1840.

Bentham, William

A Club member from 1812 to 1837 and one of the first 18 who met on the evening of the Roxburghe auction.
He presented *Ceremonial at the Marriage of Mary Queen of Scotts with the Dauphin of France* to the Club in 1818.

Bolland, William (1772–1840)

A Club member from 1812 to 1839 when he resigned and one of the first 18 who met on the evening of the Roxburghe auction.
William Bolland was a lawyer, a Recorder of Reading and a somewhat successful amateur poet. He appeared in T. F. Dibdin's works as 'Hortensius'.
Bolland was most notably the host of the meal held on the eve of the sale of the Valdarfer Boccaccio at which Dibdin alleges that the decision was first made to meet for dinner at the St. Albans Tavern the next evening. He was further instrumental in the direction that the Club would take as he is credited with the idea of reprinting rare items of early poetry for distribution among the membership (an idea he raised at the first anniversary dinner

held in 1813 and made concrete by donating the first Club edition at the dinner of the following year) and also with the notion of printing the alphabetical list of members' names in the front of the volume with the intended recipient's name in red, a custom adopted thereafter in Roxburghe Club volumes.

He presented *Certaine Bokes of Virgiles Aenaeis, turned into English Meter* to the Club in 1814.

Boswell, Alexander [Sir] (1775–1822)

A Club member from 1819 to 1822, he was elected to replace a founder member.

Alexander Boswell, Lord Auchinleck was the son of Johnson's biographer and elder brother to the younger James Boswell. He was a prominent figure in Scottish literature, especially known for his poetry, mostly in Scottish dialect and using traditional forms and subjects. Alexander Boswell founded and ran the Auchinleck Press, which was in operation from 1815 to 1818 at Auchinleck House in Dumfriesshire, Scotland. He was a staunch Tory and an unfortunately hot-headed politician. Boswell's untimely death was the result of a duel related to his political views and quick-tempered approach to political disagreement.

Boswell, James (1778–1822)

A Club member from 1813 to 1822, he was elected to replace a founder member.

James Boswell, the younger brother of Alexander was a barrister and commissioner of bankrupts. He is probably best known (apart from being his famous father's namesake) for his editing of Edmond Malone's extensive work on William Shakespeare after Malone's death. Like Alexander, he was a talented poet with a penchant for writing humorous ballads. He died a week before his brother from an infection of the throat.

He presented Richard Barnfield's *Poems to the Club* in 1816 and *A Roxburghe Garland* in 1817.

Brydges, Samuel Egerton [Sir] (1762–1837)

A Club member from 1812 to 1837 and one of the first 18 who met on the evening of the auction.

Samuel Egerton Brydges was involved in many areas of literature; he wrote poetry, romances, criticism and edited rare pieces of early English poetry.

He was instrumental in the editing and printing of many editions of neglected pieces of poetry dating from the sixteenth century, mostly through the medium of his private printing press at Lee Priory. In collaboration with Joseph Haslewood he published *Censura Literaria* and the *British Bibliographer*. Brydges attempted to claim the Barony of Chandos although it appears that he had little or no connection to the family that had previously held the title, but eventually, after a long period of humiliating failure, he was created a baronet in his own right in 1814. He presented *Hagthorpe Revived; or Select Specimens of a Forgotten Poet* to the Club in 1817 and *Laelii Peregrini Oratio in Obitum Torquati Tassi* in 1822.

Butler, Samuel [Venerable Archdeacon] (1774–1839)

A Club member from 1834 to 1839, he was elected to replace a founder member.

The Venerable Archdeacon Butler, Lord Bishop of Lichfield, who was headmaster of the Royal Free Grammar School at Shrewsbury, was a notable educational reformer who is credited with revitalizing and modernizing his school. He was the grandfather of the author Samuel Butler, who wrote the Archdeacon's memoir, *Life and Letters of Dr Samuel Butler* in 1896.

He presented *Sidneiana, Being a Collection of Fragments Relative to Sir Phillip Sidney, Knight, and his Immediate Connexions* to the Club in 1837.

Campbell, John Frederick [Earl of Cawdor] (1790–1860)

A Club member from 1830 to 1860, he was elected to replace a founder member.

He presented *The Ancient English Romance of William and the Werwolf* to the Club in 1832.

Cavendish, William George [Duke of Devonshire] (1790–1858)

A Club member from 1812 to 1858 and one of the six men whose names were put forward for membership at the dinner on the evening of the sale.

The Sixth Duke of Devonshire succeeded to his title (and all the associated wealth, debt and responsibilities) at 21 and shortly thereafter began collecting (books, of course, but also much besides, including the famous collections displayed at Chatsworth). When he joined the Roxburghe Club he was still only 22 years old. The Duke quickly built up his own collection, by buying extensively at auction (especially at the Roxburghe sale) but also by purchasing entire libraries from other collectors. In 1812 he purchased the library of Dr. Damper, Bishop of Ely and in 1821 the collection of dramatic works amassed by Kemble, which included around 4,000 plays on its purchase, adding to it until it contained around 7,500 plays.

He presented *The Life of St Ursula and Guiscard and Sigismund* to the Club in 1818.

Churchill, George Spencer [Marquess of Blandford] (1766–1840)

A Club member from 1812 to 1840 and one of the six men whose names were put forward for membership at the dinner on the evening of the sale.

Lord Blandford was the winner of the fierce bidding for the Valdarfer Boccaccio at the Roxburghe sale, beating his uncle Earl Spencer and securing its purchase for £2,260. His extravagant lifestyle led to mounting debts and the eventual loss of his estates. Despite the loss of his collection and his wealth, he remained a member of the Roxburghe Club until his death.

He presented *Selections from the Works of Thomas Ravenscroft: A Musical Composer of the Time of King James the First* to the Club in 1822.

Dent, John (1761–1826)

A Club member from 1812 to 1826 and one of the 18 men who met on the evening of the auction.

John Dent was a partner in Child & Co., a city bank. He was an independent MP, who attempted to introduce legislation in 1796 for the taxation of the ownership of certain dogs, a subject which caused hilarity among his colleagues and the press alike and led to his nickname of 'dog' Dent.

He owned one of the foremost collections of his day, which he augmented by his purchase of the Heathcote library, bought in its entirety in 1807. Dent's collection was sold in 1827 at two auctions held on 29 March and 25 April and raised only £15,040, a dramatic fall in book prices which heralded the end of bibliomania. He appeared in T. F. Dibdin's works as 'Pontevallo'.

He presented *The Solempnities and Triumphes Doon and Made at the Spousells and Marriage of the King's Daughter the Ladye Marye to the Prynce of Castile, Archduke of Austrige* to the Club in 1818.

Dibdin, Thomas Frognall [Reverend] (1776–1847)

A Club member from 1812 to 1843, when he resigned. He was the founder, vice president and secretary of the Club, and one of the 18 men who met on the evening of the auction.

Thomas Dibdin needs little introduction as the indefatigable and ebullient chronicler of bibliomania. He was a bibliographer, artist and a man of the cloth who, despite his flamboyant writing career, book collecting and social exploits, was surprisingly sincere in his vocation. He is perhaps best known for his long-standing connection with Earl Spencer and the library at Althorp and for his bubbling, often inaccurate, but enthusiastic and groundbreaking works on book collecting and other literary subjects. He was a man of talent with many facets to his career, and although his reputation has suffered since his death, he was sufficiently respected as a bibliographer during his lifetime as to be employed by the Royal Institute to present a series of public lectures on the history of literature.

He presented *The Complaint of a Lover's Life Controversy between a Lover and a Jay* to the Club in 1818.

Dodd, James William [Reverend] (1759–1820)

A Club member from 1813 to 1818 and one of the seven men elected to the Club at the first anniversary dinner.

Rev. James William Dodd was the son of the Drury Lane actors James and Martha Dodd, who were both members of David Garrick's company. The younger James Dodd, moving away from his theatrical background, was a clergyman and usher at Westminster School. He was the author of a volume of poetry *Ballads of Archery, Sonnets &c*, which as well as the various anthology items, contains an extensive preface covering the general subject of archery and the history of the Royal Kentish Bowmen.

He presented *The Funeralles of King Edward the Sixt* to the Club in 1817.

Drury, Henry [Reverend] (1778–5 March 1841)

A Club member from 1813 to 1841 and one of the seven men elected to the Club at the first anniversary dinner.

Rev. Henry Drury, the son of Joseph Drury, the headmaster of Harrow, was himself a master at the same school, becoming assistant master in 1801 and master of the lower school from 1833 to 1841. Drury had a somewhat stormy friendship with Lord Byron, and conducted the funeral for Byron's daughter Allegra. As a classical scholar Henry Drury rather predictably collected classical works in Greek and Latin, but his collection also contained more than 250 medieval manuscripts. His collection was sold in 1827 in 4,729 lots. He appeared in T. F. Dibdin's works as 'Menalcas'.

He presented *Cock Lorell's Boat, a Fragment* to the Club in 1817 and *Metrical Life of Saint Robert of Knaresborough* in 1824.

Freeling, Francis (1764–1836)

A Club member from 1812 to 1836 and one of the first 18 men who met on the evening of the auction.

Francis Freeling was the secretary of the Post Office and one of a number of officials who aided the government in the surveillance of the activities of radical groups.

He presented *Dolarny's Primrose or the First Part of the Passionate Hermit* to the Club in 1816.

Freeling, George Henry (1789–1841)

A Club member from 1812 to 1841 and one of the first 18 men who met on the evening of the auction.

George Freeling was the son of Francis Freeling and the commissioner of customs. He was married to the daughter of fellow Roxburghe member Sir Robert Lang.

He presented *La Contenance de la Table* and *Newes from Scotland, Declaring the Damnable Life of Doctor Fian, a Notable Sorcerer, Who Was burned at Edenbrough in Ianuarie* to the Club in 1816 and *Informacōn for Pylgrymes unto the Holy Londe* in 1824.

Glynne, Stephen Richard [Sir] (1807–1874)

A Club member from 1834 to 1874, he was elected to replace a founder member.

Sir Stephen Glynne was a Welsh landowner and an avid antiquarian whose notes on pre-Victorian ecclesiastical architecture have been published posthumously as works including *Sir Stephen Glynne's Church Notes for Somerset*, *Sir Stephen Glynne's Church Notes for Shropshire*, *The Derbyshire Church Notes of Sir Stephen Glynne* and *Notes on the Older Churches in the Four Welsh Dioceses: Archdeanery of Cardigan*. The most recent publication of Glynne's work is the *Church Notes of Sir Stephen Glynne for Cumbria*, published by Cumberland & Westmorland Antiquarian & Archaeological Society.

Grenville, George Neville [Honourable and Reverend] (1789–1854)

A Club member from 1827 to 1854, he was elected to replace a founder member.

George Neville Grenville was an eminent example of an absentee clergyman, that is, one who was ordained in order to gain a valuable living but with little or no intention of taking up their clerical duties, instead paying a curate a fraction of the income to carry out the duties on their behalf. He was the rector of Butleigh in Somersetshire, and Ellingham in Norfolk, and in 1840 he was appointed dean of Windsor.

He presented *Gaufridi Arthurii Monemuthensis Archidiaconi, postea vero Episcopi Asaphensis, de Vita et Vaticiniis Merlini Calidonii Carmen Heroicum* to the Club in 1830.

Haslewood, Joseph (1769–1833)

A Club member from 1812 to 1833 and one of the first 18 men who met on the evening of the auction.

Joseph Haslewood was not a wealthy man and, having originated from a humble background, was to a large extent self-educated through following his taste for early printed texts. He worked extensively with his close friend Sir Samuel Egerton Brydges, acting as an editor, researcher and writer for Brydges's various journals, including the *British Bibliographer* and *Censura Literaria*. During his own lifetime Haslewood appears to have enjoyed a solid reputation as an able and respected editor of early English texts, especially of Elizabethan poetry. He was a close friend of Dibdin's and one of the driving forces behind the founding of the Roxburghe Club. He appeared in T. F. Dibdin's works as 'Bernardo'.

He presented *Two Interludes: Jack Jugler and Thersytes* to the Club in 1820.

Hawtrey, Edward Craven [Reverend] (1789–1862)

A Club member from 1831 to 1862, he was elected to replace a founder member.

Rev. Edward Craven Hawtrey was the son of a vicar and educated at Eton, becoming in turn assistant master, headmaster and later provost of the school.

He presented *The Private Diary of William first Earl Cowper, Lord Chancellor of England* to the Club in 1833.

Heber, Richard (1773–1833)

A Club member from 1812 to 1833 and one of the first 18 men who met on the evening of the auction.

Richard Heber was a wealthy and ardent book collector who amassed a vast library that filled eight houses and who was known to buy multiple copies of a work. He was a close friend of Sir Walter Scott until his later life was marred by a scandal that resulted in his living in exile for a period. On his eventual return to Britain he lived largely as a recluse until his death. He appeared in T. F. Dibdin's works as 'Atticus'.

He presented *Caltha Poetarum; or, The Bumble Bee* to the Club in 1815.

Heber, Thomas Cuthbert [Reverend] (1786–1816)

A Club member from 1812 to 1816 and one of the first 18 men who met on the evening of the auction.

Thomas Heber was the younger brother of Richard Heber.

Herbert, Edward [Viscount Clive] (1785–1848)

A Club member from 1828 to 1848, he was elected to replace a founder member and became president of the Club in 1835 following the death of Earl Spencer.

Viscount Clive was a landowner who possessed large areas of land in Wales, including 3,127 acres in the area of Merthyr Tydfil. He was also the Tory MP for Ludlow.

He presented *The Lyvys of Seyntes; translated into Englys be a Doctour of Dyuynite clepyd Osbern Bokenam, frer Austyn of the Convent of Stocklare* to the Club in 1835.

Hibbert, George (1757–1837)

A Club member from 1816 to 1837, he was elected to replace a founder member.

George Hibbert, who came from a family that accrued its wealth from sugar plantations, acted as an agent for Jamaican planters and was the chairman of the West India Dock Company. He was MP for Seaford between 1806 and 1812.

He presented *Six Bookes of Metamorphoseos in whyche ben conteyned the Fables of Ovyde, translated out of Frensshe into Englysshe by William Caxton* to the Club in 1819.

Holwell Carr, William [Reverend] (1758–1830)

A Club member from 1813 to 1830, he was one of the seven men elected at the first anniversary dinner.

As well as collecting books, Holwell Carr is best known for his extensive collection of artworks, which he bequeathed to the nation.

He presented *Istoria novellamente ritrovata di due nobili Amanti, &c., da Luigi Porto* to the Club in 1817.

Howard, George [Viscount Morpeth] (1773–1848)

A Club member from 1812 to 1837, when he resigned. He was one of the six men whose names were put forward for membership at the dinner on the evening of the sale.

Viscount Morpeth was a Whig MP in the family's interest for Morpeth, Northumberland, and later for the County of Cumberland. Morpeth married the Sixth Duke of Devonshire's sister Georgiana in 1801.

He presented *An Elegiacal Poem on the Death of Thomas Lord Grey, of Wilton* to the Club in 1822.

Isted, George (1734–1821)

A Club member from 1812 to 1821 and one of the first 18 men who met on the evening of the auction.

George Isted was a barrister of the Middle Temple.

He presented *The New Notborune Mayd: The Boke of Mayd Emlyn* to the Club in 1820.

Lang, Robert

A Club member from 1812 to 1828 and one of the first 18 men who met on the evening of the auction.

Robert Lang was a West India merchant. His library, rich in ancient French poetry, raised £2,837 when auctioned in 1828.

He presented *Le Livre du Faulcon* to the Club in 1817.

Leveson-Gower, George Granville [Earl Gower] (1786–1861)

A Club member from 1812 to 1861 and one of the first 18 men who met on the evening of the auction.

George Leveson-Gower acted as MP for Newcastle-under-Lyme and later for Staffordshire.

He presented *Balades and Other Poems to the Club* in 1818.

Littledale, Edward (1779–1837)

A Club member from 1813–1837, he was one of the seven men elected at the first anniversary dinner.

Edward Littledale was a barrister at Gray's Inn.

He presented *Diana; or the Excellent Conceitful Sonnets of Henry Constable* to the Club in 1818.

Littledale, Joseph (1767–1842)

A Club member from 1813 to 1842, he was one of the seven men elected at the first anniversary dinner.

Joseph Littledale was the younger brother of Edward Littledale and was a prominent judge.

He presented *Magnyfycence: An Interlude* to the Club in 1821.

Lloyd, John Arthur (1787–1864)

A Club member from 1822 to 1864, he was elected to replace a founder member.

John Arthur Lloyd was a wealthy landowner who had inherited a country estate at Leaton Knolls in Shropshire.

He presented the elaborately titled *The Cuck-Queanes and Cuckolds Errants or the Bearing Down the Inne, a Comædie. The Faery Pastorall or Forrest of Elues. By W – P –, Esq* to the Club in 1824.

Markland, James Heywood (1788–1864)

A Club member from 1812 to 1845, when he resigned. He was one of the six men whose names were put forward for membership at the dinner on the evening of the sale.

James Markland was a parliamentary agent for the West Indian planters. He was an active churchman and published articles on a wide variety of ecclesiastical and antiquarian subjects. He belonged to a wide variety of antiquarian organizations beyond the Roxburghe.

He presented the *Chester Mysteries De Deluvio Noe De Occisione Innocentium* to the Club in 1818.

Masterman Sykes, Mark [Sir] (1771–1823)

A Club member from 1812 to 1823, he was one of the first 18 men who met on the evening of the auction.

Mark Masterman Sykes was an English landowner and Tory MP for York. He presented *The Chorle and the Birde* to the Club in 1818 and *The Hors, the Shepe, and the Ghoos* in 1822.

Phelps, John Delafield (1764–1842)

A Club member from 1812 to 1842, he was one of the first 18 men who met on the evening of the auction.
He presented *The Glutton's Feaver* to the Club in 1817.

Ponton, Thomas (?–1853)

A Club member from 1812 to 1853 and one of the six men whose names were put forward for membership at the dinner on the evening of the sale.
He presented *Le Morte Arthur: The Adventures of Sir Launcelot Du Lake* to the Club in 1819.

Scott, Walter [Sir] (1771–1832)

A Club member from 1823 to 1832, he was elected to replace a founder member and was initially elected as 'the author of Waverley', a situation which continued until 1827, when he revealed his identity as the author of the series to the public. He appeared in T. F. Dibdin's works as 'Sir Tristrem'.
Sir Walter Scott, as the most successful author of this period or as a book collector, needs little introduction. He only dined with the Club on one occasion but had corresponded with Dibdin since before the founding of the Club and was inspired to emulate the example set by the Roxburghe in his founding of the Scottish Bannatyne Club.
He presented *Proceedings in the Court Martial held upon John, Master of Sinclair, Captain-Lieutenant in Preston's Regiment, for the Murder of Ensign Schaw of the same Regiment, and Captain Schaw, of the Royals, 17 October 1708; with Correspondence respecting that Transaction* to the Club in 1828.

Spencer, George John [Earl Spencer] (1758–1834)

A Club member from 1812 to 1834, he was one of the first 18 men who met on the evening of the auction. He remained president from the first dinner until his death.
Earl Spencer, the Club president bought books on a prodigious scale. As well as purchasing books in the usual ways such as attending auctions or visiting booksellers, Spencer also bought a number of complete library collections. These included Count Karoly Reviczky's library in 1789, bought for £2,500;

Stanesby Alchorne's library in 1813, for £3,400; and the Duke di Cassano Serra's collection, purchased in 1820. His vast collection was purchased from his heirs in 1892 by Enriqueta Rylands, the widow of John Rylands, who used it as the foundation of the library that she endowed in Manchester in her husband's name.

He presented *The First Three Books of Ovid De Tristibus, translated into English* to the Club in 1816 and *La Rotta de Francciosi a Terroana novamente facta: La Rotta de Scocesi* in 1825.

Spencer, John Charles [Viscount Althorp] (1782–1845)

A Club member from 1813 to 1845, he was one of the seven men elected at the first anniversary dinner.

Viscount Althorp was the son of Earl Spencer but also a book collector in his own right. Like Earl Spencer, he had a lengthy and illustrious, if somewhat reluctant, political career and acted as leader of the Whig Party in the Commons.

He presented *A Proper New Interlude of the World and the Child, otherwise called Mundus et Infans* to the Club in 1817.

Towneley, Peregrine Edward (1762–1846)

A Club member from 1812 to 1846 and one of the six men whose names were put forward for membership at the dinner on the evening of the sale.

Peregrine Towneley presented *Judicium, a Pageant* to the Club in 1822, and this text is an extract from a Wakefield mystery play, *The Last Judgement*, taken from the unique Towneley manuscript of the Wakefield Cycle. The Towneleys were a Catholic recusant family, and following the dissolution of the monasteries they had maintained guardianship of the manuscript.

Watson Taylor, George (1771–1841)

A Club member from 1822 to 1841, he was elected to replace a founder member.

George Watson Taylor was the son of a West India plantation owner and an MP (for Newport in the Isle of Wight between 1816 and 1818; for Seaford between 1818 and 1820; for East Looe between 1820 and 1826; and for Devizes between 1826 and 1832).

He presented *Poems written in English, by Charles, Duke of Orleans, during his Captivity in England after the Battle of Azincourt* to the Club in 1827.

Utterson, Edward Vernon (1776–1856)

A Club member from 1812 to 1856, when he resigned, he was one of the first 18 men who met on the evening of the auction.

Edward Utterson was a barrister by profession but was also a talented watercolour artist of some renown. Utterson owned a house on the Isle of Wight, where during the summer months he operated a private printing press (the Beldornie Press).

He presented *Cheuelere Assigne* to the Club in 1820 and *A Little Boke of Ballads* in 1836.

Wilbraham, Roger (1743–1829)

A Club member from 1812 to 1829 and one of the first 18 men who met on the evening of the auction.

Roger Wilbraham was an antiquarian with a keen interest in etymology and the author of *An Attempt at a Glossary of some Words used in Cheshire*. Wilbraham was also the MP for Bodmin and Helston.

He presented *Daiphantus, or the Passions of Love* to the Club in 1818.

Wrangham, Francis [Venerable Archdeacon] (1769–1842)

A Club member from 1822 to 1842, he was elected to replace a founder member.

Venerable Archdeacon Wrangham was an avid reader, a prolific writer, a respected scholar and a passionate collector of books on a wide variety of subjects. Following his death, the British Museum purchased his manuscript collection for £2,000. He was a keen writer and collector of pamphlets, and in 1842 he donated 10,000 pamphlets to Trinity College, Cambridge.

He presented *The Garden Plot, an Allegorical Poem, inscribed to Queen Elizabeth* to the Club in 1825.

Appendix 2

ROXBURGHE CLUB EDITIONS 1812–1835

Presented in chronological order.

1. **Henry Earl of Surrey,** *Certaine Bokes of Virgiles Aenaeis, turned into English Meter*, **ed. by William Bolland (London: Valpy, 1814).**
   Originally printed in 1557. Presented to the Club by William Bolland.
2. **T. Cutwode,** *Caltha Poetarum; or, The Bumble Bee*, **ed. by Joseph Haslewood (London: 1815).**
   Originally printed in 1599. Presented to the Club by Richard Heber.
   This poem (a political satire) was one of the works banned by the Archbishop of Canterbury on publication during the 'Bishop's Ban' in 1599.
3. **Thomas Churchyarde,** *The First Three Books of Ovid De Tristibus, translated into English* **(London: W. Bulmer, 1816).**
   Originally printed in 1578. Presented to the Club by Earl Spencer.
   At the time it was reprinted it was believed to be the only surviving copy of Churchyarde's translation. Ovid had written what is now usually referred to as *Tristia ex Ponto* while in exile from the court of Emperor Augustus for reasons that are today unclear.
4. **Richard Barnfield,** *Poems,* **ed. by James Boswell (Auchinleck: Auchinleck Press, 1816).**
   Originally printed in 1598. Presented to the Club by James Boswell.
5. **John Raynolds,** *Dolarny's Primrose or the First Part of the Passionate Hermit* **(London: W. Bulmer, 1816).**
   Originally printed in 1606. Presented to the Club by Francis Freeling and reprinted from a rare edition in his own collection.
6. *La Contenance de la Table* **(London: W. Bulmer, 1816).**
   Presented to the Club by George Freeling.

The text is a fifteenth-century French guide for children, offering advice in verse on the subject of table manners.

7. **King James VI of Scotland,** ***Newes from Scotland, declaring the Damnable Life of Doctor Fian, a notable Sorcerer, who was burned at Edenbrough in Ianuarie*** **(London: W. Bulmer, 1816).**
   Originally printed in 1591. Presented to the Club by George Freeling. This is a pamphlet describing a notorious witch trial.

8. **Anon.,** ***A Proper New Interlude of the World and the Child, Otherwise called Mundus et Infans*** **(London: W. Bulmer, 1817).**
   Presented to the Club by Viscount Althorp. Originally printed by Wynkyn de Worde in 1522.
   A morality play based on a poem from the late fourteenth or the early fifteenth century called *The Mirror of the Periods of Man's Life*. The edition presented to the Roxburghe is taken from a unique copy of the earliest surviving printed edition.

9. **John Hagthorpe,** ***Hagthorpe Revived; or Select Specimens of a Forgotten Poet***, **ed. by Samuel Egerton Brydges (Ickham: Lee Priory Press, 1817).**
   Presented to the Club by Sir Samuel Egerton Brydges, it is an extract taken from the poet Hagthorpe's work *Divine Meditations and Elegies*.

10. **Luigi Da Porto,** ***Istoria novellamente ritrovata di due nobili Amanti, &c., da Luigi Porto*** **(London: W. Bulmer, 1817).**
    Presented to the Club by William Holwell Carr, this text was first printed in Venice in 1535 under the title *La Giulietta*, and is the source for William Shakespeare's *Romeo and Juliet*.

11. **William Baldwin,** ***The Funeralles of King Edward the Sixt*** **(London: G. Woodfall, 1817).**
    Presented to the Club by James William Dodd, this rare example of Baldwin's work was reprinted from an edition dating from 1560.

12. ***A Roxburghe Garland***, **ed. by James Boswell (London: Bensley, 1817).**
    Presented to the Club by James Boswell, this text contains a number of pieces of drinking-related verse from seventeenth-century poets and an original piece of verse by James Boswell titled 'L'Envoy'.

13. ***Cock Lorell's Boat, a Fragment*** **(London: W. Bulmer, 1817).**
    Presented to the Club by Henry Drury, this is a satirical poem, originally printed by Wynkyn de Worde in 1510 and taken from the unique surviving print contained in the Garrick Collection.

14. **Isabeau Faucon,** ***Le Livre du Faulcon*** **(London: W. Bulmer, 1817).**
    Presented to the Club by Robert Lang and taken from Lang's own collection, a black-letter reprint of a very rare tract, previously printed by Verard.

APPENDIX 2: ROXBURGHE CLUB EDITIONS 1812–1835   193

15. **Thomas Bancroft,** *The Glutton's Feaver* **(London: Bensley, 1817).**
    Originally printed in London in 1633 and presented to the Club by John Delafield Phelps.
16. **John Lydgate,** *The Chorle and the Birde* **(London: W. Bulmer, 1818).**
    Presented to the Club by Sir Mark Masterman Sykes, this is a Middle English translation from French and had originally been printed by both William Caxton and later Wynkyn de Worde. It is a dialogue between a peasant and a bird discussing the role of peasants in society.
17. **Antony Scoloker,** *Daiphantus, or the Passions of Love* **(London: W. Bulmer, 1818).**
    Originally printed in or after 1604 and presented to the Club by Roger Wilbraham.
18. **Thomas Feylde,** *The Complaint of a Lover's Life: Controversy between a Lover and a Jay* **(London: W. Bulmer, 1818).**
    Presented to the Club by Thomas Frognall Dibdin, this is a Tudor 'love aunter' or *dit amoureux*, a late example of the popular medieval genre of debate, and takes as its subject of the nature of women.
19. **John Gower,** *Balades and other Poems* **(London: W. Bulmer, 1818).**
    Presented to the Club by George Granville Leveson-Gower. Gower's verses date from around 1400 and were printed here for the first time. Gower, a contemporary of Geoffrey Chaucer, wrote in English, Latin and Anglo-Norman.
20. **Henry Constable,** *Diana; or The Excellent Conceitful Sonnets of Henry Constable* **(London: Woodfall, 1818).**
    Presented to the Club by Edward Littledale. Henry Constable was an Elizabethan convert to Catholicism who was imprisoned twice, and eventually exiled for his personal conviction and public testimony that being Catholic did not prevent loyalty to the English Crown. Originally printed in 1592.
21. **Anon.,** *Chester Mysteries De Deluvio Noe De Occisione Innocentium*, **ed. by J. H. Markland (London: Bensley, 1818).**
    Presented to the Club by James Heywood Markland.
22. **Francis II,** *Ceremonial at the Marriage of Mary Queen of Scotts with the Dauphin of France* **(London: Woodfall, 1818).**
    Originally printed in 1557 and reprinted from the original in the British Museum. Presented to the Club by William Bentham.
23. *The Solempnities and Triumphes doon and made at the Spousells and Marriage of the King's Daughter the Ladye Marye to the Prynce of Castile, Archduke of Austrige*, **ed. by John Dent (London: Ackermann, 1818).**
    A lithographic facsimile reprint of a unique tract originally printed by Richard Pynson in 1508. Presented to the Club by John Dent.

24. ***The Life of St Ursula and Guiscard and Sigismund*** **(London: W. Bulmer, 1818).**
Presented to the Club by the Duke of Devonshire.

25. ***Le Morte Arthur: The Adventures of Sir Launcelot Du Lake*** **(London: W. Bulmer, 1819).**
Presented to the Club by Thomas Ponton and printed from British Library Harley MS. No. 2252. This is the so-called *Stanzaic Morte Arthure*, a fourteenth-century romance going back to the French thirteenth-century romance the *Morte Artus*, which relates the last part of the story of Arthur and the Round Table. In the fifteenth century Sir Thomas Malory used the *Stanzaic Morte* as the basis for the later part of his own *Morte d'Arthur*.

26. ***Six Bookes of Metamorphoseos in whyche ben conteyned the Fables of Ovyde, translated out of Frensshe into Englysshe by William Caxton*****, ed. by George Hibbert (London: W. Bulmer, 1819).**
Presented to the Club by George Hibbert, this edition includes an introduction written by him and also a woodcut picture of Orpheus.

27. **Anon.,** ***Cheuelere Assigne,*** **ed. by E. V. Utterson (London: Publisher unknown, 1820).**
A Middle English romance translation from the French, which was printed from a manuscript in the Cotton Collection in the British Museum and presented to the Club by E. V. Utterson, with an introduction written by him.

28. **Anon.,** ***Two Interludes: Jack Jugler and Thersytes,*** **ed. by Joseph Haslewood (Ickham: Lee Priory Press, 1820).**
An amalgamation of unique copies of each Interlude presented to the Club by Joseph Haslewood.

29. **John Scot,** ***The New Notborune Mayd: The Boke of Mayd Emlyn*** **(London: W. Bulmer, 1820).**
A publication created from two poems contained in the Caldecott Collection and presented to the Club by George Isted.

30. ***Book of Life: A Bibliographical Melody*** **(London: J. Johnson, 1820).**
This item is unusual as it was not presented by a Club member but by Richard Thomson, an antiquary and librarian of private means who during his lifetime published a number of books relating to antiquarian topics.

31. **John Skelton,** ***Magnyfycence: An Interlude,*** **ed. by Joseph Littledale (London: Woodfall, 1821).**
Originally printed in 1533 and presented to the Club by Joseph Littledale. This edition is printed in black-letter and is based on two copies of the

play, one held by the British Museum and the other by the Cambridge University Library.

32. **Anon., *Judicium, a Pageant*, ed. by Francis Douce (London: Taylor, 1822).**
Presented to the Club by Peregrine Towneley, this is an extract from a Wakefield mystery play, *The Last Judgement*, and taken from the unique Towneley manuscript of the Wakefield Cycle. The Towneleys were a Catholic recusant family whose library had sheltered the manuscript after the dissolution of the monasteries had necessitated its removal from Whalley Abbey in 1537.

33. **Robert Marston, *An Elegiacal Poem on the Death of Thomas Lord Grey, of Wilton* (London: W. Nicol, 1822).**
Presented to the Club by Viscount Morpeth and printed from a manuscript in the library of Thomas Grenville. The subject of the poem was, as the title implies, an elegy on the life and death of Thomas Grey.

34. **Thomas Ravenscroft, *Selections from the Works of Thomas Ravenscroft; a Musical Composer of the Time of King James the First* (London: McMillan, 1822).**
Presented to the Club by the Duke of Marlborough (previously the Marquess of Blandford).

35. **Laelius Peregrinus, *Lælii Peregrini Oratio in Obitum Torquati Tassi. Editio Secunda*, ed. by Samuel Egerton Brydges (Publisher unknown, 1822).**
Presented to the Club by Sir Samuel Egerton Brydges. An oration on the life of Torquato Tasso, the sixteenth-century Italian poet who is best known for his epic poem *La Gerusalemme liberate*.

36. **John Lydgate, *The Hors, the Shepe, and the Ghoos* (London: W. Nicol, 1822).**
Presented to the Club by Mark Masterman Sykes. A companion piece to the fable *The Chorle and the Birde*, presented by the same member in 1818.

37. ***The Metrical Life of Saint Robert of Knaresborough*, ed. by Joseph Haslewood (London: Valpy, 1824).**
Presented to the Club by Rev. Henry Drury and printed from a manuscript in his own collection. This is a Middle English life of the Yorkshire hermit saint written by the head of the house of Trinitarian friars established on the site of Robert's hermitage.

38. **William Wey, *Informacōn for Pylgrymes unto the Holy Londe*, (London: W. Nicol, 1824).**
Presented to the Club by George Freeling.

39. **William Percy,** *The Cuck-Queanes and Cuckolds Errants or the Bearing Down the Inne, a Comœdie. The Faery Pastorall or Forrest of Elues.* **By W – P –, Esq, ed. Joseph Haslewood (London: W. Nicol, 1824).**
Presented to the Club by John Arthur Lloyd but taken from a manuscript belonging to Joseph Haslewood, who had also edited the text and provided the introduction.

40. **Henry Goldingham,** *The Garden Plot, an Allegorical Poem, inscribed to Queen Elizabeth* **(London: D. S. Maurice, 1825).**
Presented to the Club by Archdeacon Wrangham, who also contributed an introduction to the volume. It had not previously been printed and was taken from a manuscript contained in the Harleian Collection in the British Museum and was produced with the addition of a brief account of the author and a reprint of his *Goldingham's Masques*.

41. **Anon.,** *La Rotta de Francciosi a Terroana novamente facta: La Rotta de Scocesi* **(London: W. Nicol, 1825).**
Presented to the Club by Earl Spencer, this is a reprint of two Italian poems dealing with the battles of Terrovane and Flodden Field. The author is unknown, but the poems date from around 1513 and are reproduced with prefatory comments by Earl Spencer.

42. *Novelle Édition d'un Poème sur la Journée de Guinegate* **(Paris: 1825).**
Presented to the Club by the Marquis De Fortia, La Société des Bibliophiles Français of Paris

43. **C. Pichler,** *Zuléima* **(Paris: Didot, 1825).**
Presented by H. De Chateaugiron, La Société des Bibliophiles Français of Paris

44. **Charles, d'Orléans,** *Poems written in English, by Charles, Duke of Orleans, during his Captivity in England after the Battle of Azincourt* **(London: W. Nicol, 1827).**
Presented to the Club by George Watson Taylor and printed from Harleian MS. No. 682 in the British Museum.

45. **John Sinclair,** *Proceedings in the Court Martial held upon John, Master of Sinclair, Captain-Lieutenant in Preston's Regiment, for the Murder of Ensign Schaw of the Same Regiment, and Captain Schaw, of the Royals, 17 October 1708; with Correspondence Respecting That Transaction* **(Edinburgh: 1828).**
Presented to the Club by Sir Walter Scott.

46. **Anon.,** *The Ancient English Romance of Havelok the Dane,* **ed. by Frederick Madden (London: Nicol, 1828).**

This important Middle English text was edited by Frederick Madden and included an introduction, notes and a glossary also provided by him. This was the first book printed for the Club rather than as the contribution of any one individual.

47. **Geoffrey, of Monmouth,** *Gaufridi Arthurii Monemuthensis Archidiaconi, postea vero Episcopi Asaphensis, de Vita et Vaticiniis Merlini Calidonii Carmen Heroicum* **(London: Nicol, 1830).**
Presented to the Club by George Neville Grenville. This is the 'Prophecies of Merlin', written in the early 1130s and around 1136 incorporated into the *Historia Regum Britanniae*. It is the earliest and most renowned of the tradition of political prophecies, of which many circulated during the medieval and early modern period. It was transcribed and printed from MS. Cotton Claudius B VII f. 224 in the British Library.

48. **Anon.,** *The Ancient English Romance of William and the Werwolf,* **ed. by Frederic Madden (London: Nicol, 1832).**
Reprinted from a unique copy in King's College Library, Cambridge, and edited by Madden, with an introduction and glossary also written by him. This volume was presented to the Club by Earl Cawdor.

49. **William Cowper,** *The Private Diary of William First Earl Cowper, Lord Chancellor of England* **(Eton: E. Williams, 1833).**
Presented to the Club by Edward Craven Hawtrey.

50. **Osborn Bokenham,** *The Lyvys of Seyntes; translated into Englys be a Doctour of Dyuynite clepyd Osbern Bokenam, frer Austyn of the Convent of Stocklare* **(London: Nicol, 1835).**
Presented to the Club by Viscount Clive in 1835. This is a fifteenth-century collection of verses in Latin and English, recounting the lives of 12 female saints, adapted by Osborn Bokenham from the famous thirteenth-century *Legenda Aurea* by Jacobus de Voragine.

51. *A Little Boke of Ballads* **(Newport: Yelf, 1836).**
Presented to the Club by E. V. Utterson and selected by him from black-letter copies in his own collection.

52. *The Love of Wales to their Soueraign Prince, expressed in a true Relation of the Solemnity held at Ludlow, in the Countie of Salop, upon the fourth of November last past, Anno Domini 1616, being the day of the Creation of the high and mighty Charles, Prince of Wales, and Earle of Chester, in his Maiesties Palace of White-Hall* **(London: 1837).**
Presented to the Club by the Hon. R. H. Clive, the brother of the incumbent president.

BIBLIOGRAPHY

Works Written by Early Roxburghe Club Members

Bolland, William, *The Campaign, to His Royal Highness the Duke of York, Britannia in the Year 1800 to C. J. Fox: A Poem in Two Cantos* (London: Bensley, 1800).
—— *The Epiphany* (London: Rivington, 1799).
—— *Miracles* (London: Rivington, 1797).
Boswell, Alexander, *Edinburgh, or, The Ancient Royalty* (Edinburgh: Manners and Miller, 1810).
—— *Epistle to the Edinburgh Reviewers* (Edinburgh: Nundell, 1803).
—— *Songs Chiefly in the Scottish Dialect* (Edinburgh: Manners and Miller, 1803).
—— *The Spirit of Tintoc; a Ballad* (Edinburgh: Manners and Miller, 1803).
—— *The Tyrant's Fall* (Auchinleck: A and J Boswell, 1815).
—— *The Woo' Creel, or the Bill O' Bashan; a Tale* (Auchinleck: James Sutherland, 1816).
Boswell, James, *A Roxburghe Garland* (London: Bensley, 1817).
Brydges, Sir Egerton, *The Autobiography, Times, Opinions and Contemporaries of Sir Egerton Brydges* (London: Cochrane and McCrone, 1834).
—— *The British Bibliographer* (London: Triphook, 1810; repr. New York: 1966).
—— *A Catalogue of All the Works Printed. by at the Private Press at Lee Priory in Kent: from Its Commencement in July 1813, Till Its Termination in Jan 1823 [With a Ms Letter from Geneva by Sir E Brydges, Dated. by March 29, 1824, Respecting the Difficulty of Transmitting Books to England]* (London: John Warwick, 1824).
—— 'On Bibliomania', *Theatrical Inquisitor, and Monthly Mirror* (April 1819), 277–79.
Cavendish, William Spencer, *Hand Book of Chatsworth, Hardwick and Kemp Town*, MS and Proofs (Devonshire Collection, CH1/2/48), Chatsworth House (1844).
—— *Handbook of Chatsworth and Hardwick* (London: Privately printed, 1845).
Dibdin, T. F., *Aedes Althorpianae* (London: Bulmer, 1822).
—— *A Bibliographical Antiquarian and Picturesque Tour in the Northern Counties of England and Scotland* (London: Ruff, 1803).
—— *The Bibliographical Decameron; or Ten Days Pleasant Discourse upon Illuminated Manuscripts, and Subjects Connected with Early Engraving, Typography and Bibliography* (London: Bulmer, 1817).
—— *Bibliomania, or, Book-madness; A Bibliographical Romance, in six parts; illustrated with cuts* (London: Longman, Hurst, Rees, Orme and Brown, 1811).
—— *The Bibliomania: or, Book-madness; Containing Some Account of the History, Symptoms and Cure of this Fatal Disease, in an Epistle Addressed to Richard Heber, Esq.* (London: Longman, Hurst, Rees, and Orme, 1809).
—— *Bibliomania; or Book-Madness* (London: Bohn, 1842).
—— *Bibliophobia* (London: Bohn, 1832).
—— *Bibliotheca Spenceriana* (London: Bulmer, 1814).

―――― *Book Rarities, or a Descriptive Catalogue of Some of the Most Curious Rare and Valuable Books of Early Date, Chiefly in the Collection of George John, Earl Spencer, K G* (London: no pub., 1811).

―――― *Catalogue of the Books Printed in the Fifteenth Century Formerly in the Library of the Duke de Cassano Serra and now in Earl Spencer's Collection* (London: no pub., 1823).

―――― *Library Companion; Or the Young Man's Guide and the Old Man's Comfort in the Choice of a Library* (London: Harding, Triphook, and Lepard, 1824).

―――― *Poems* (London: Murray, 1797).

―――― *Reminiscences of a Literary Life* (London: Bloomsbury, 1836).

―――― *Sermons* (London: Harding, Triphook and Lepard, 1825).

―――― *Sermons, Doctrinal and Practical; Preached in King Street, Brompton; Quebec and Fitzroy Chapels* (London: Longman, Hurst, Rees, Orme, and Brown, 1820).

―――― *The Sunday Library; or The Protestant's Manual for the Sabbath-day* (London: Longman, Rees, Orme, Brown and Green, 1831).

Drury, Henry, *Arundines Cami* (London and Cambridge: Deighton and Parker, 1841).

Foote Jr, S. [Pseud. Francis Wrangham], *Reform: a Farce, Modernised from Aristophanes* (London: Edwards, 1792).

Glynne, Sir Stephen R, *The Church Notes of Sir Stephen Glynne for Cumbria*, ed. by Lawrence Butler (Kendal: Cumberland and Westmorland Antiquarian and Archaeological Society, 2011).

―――― *The Derbyshire Church Notes of Sir Stephen Glynne, 1825–1873*, ed. by Aileen Hopkinson and others (Chesterfield: Derbyshire Record Society 2004).

―――― *Gloucestershire Church Notes*, ed. by W. P. W. Phillimore and J. Melland Hall (London: Phillimore, 1902).

―――― *Notes on the Churches of Cheshire*, ed. by J. A. Atkinson (Manchester: Chetham Society, 1894).

―――― *Notes on the Churches of Kent* (London: John Murray, 1877).

―――― *Notes on the Churches of Lancashire*, ed. by J. A. Atkinson (Manchester: Chetham Society, 1893).

―――― *Notes on the Older Churches in the Four Welsh Dioceses: Archdeanery of Cardigan* (Cribyn: Llanerch Press, 2004).

―――― *Sir Stephen Glynne's Church Notes for Shropshire*, ed. by D. C. Cox (Keele: University of Keele, 1997).

―――― *Sir Stephen Glynne's Church Notes for Somerset*, ed. by Michael McGarvie (Taunton: Somerset Record Society, 1994).

Gridiron Gabble [Pseud. Joseph Haslewood], *Green Room Gossip* (London: Barker, 1809).

Haslewood, Joseph *Ancient and Critical Essays upon the English Poets and Poesy* (London: Bensley, 1815).

―――― Letter to an unknown recipient contained in a scrapbook (Roxburghe Club Archive) deposited with the Society of Antiquaries

―――― *The Roxburghe Revels*, manuscript (Roxburghe Club archives) deposited with the Society of Antiquaries.

―――― *The Secret History of the Green Room: Containing Authentic and Entertaining Memoirs of the Actors and Actresses in the Three Theatres Royal* (London: Owen, 1795).

―――― *Some Account of the Life and Publications of the Late Joseph Ritson, Esq.* (London: Triphook, 1824).

Hawtrey, Edward Craven, *Auswahl von Goethes Lyrischen Gedichten* (London: Eton, 1833).

────── *Two Translations from Homer (Iliad, iii 234–244, and vi 394–502), in English Hexameters, and the War-song of Callinus in Elegiacs, with prefatory remarks on the Versification* (London: Privately Printed, 1843).
Hood E. U. [Pseud. Joseph Haslewood], *Gentleman's Magazine* (July 1822), 15–17.
────── *Gentleman's Magazine* (August 1813), 121.
────── *Gentleman's Magazine* (December 1813), 648.
────── *Gentleman's Magazine* (April 1816), 309–12.
────── *Gentleman's Magazine* (December 1821), 603.
────── *Gentleman's Magazine* (January 1828), 36.
Langhorne, J. W. Langhorne, and F. Wrangham, *Plutarch's Lives* (Philadelphia: Brannan and Morford, 1811).
Markland, J. H., 'ART III The benefit of the auncient bathes of Buckstones, which cureth most greevous sicknesses, never before published', *Censura Literaria* 10 (London: Longman, Hurst, Rees and Orme, 1809), 274–81.
────── 'ART IV A Choice of Emblemes, and other Devises, for the moste parte gathered out of sundrie writers', *Censura Literaria* 5 (London: Longman, Hurst, Rees and Orme, 1807), 233–35.
────── 'ART X Paradoxical Assertions and philosophical problems,' *Censura Literaria*, 10 (London: Longman, Hurst, Rees and Orme, 1809), 383–88.
────── 'ART XIV Newes of Sir Walter Rauleigh, with the true Description of Guiana', *Censura Literaria* 5 (London: Longman, Hurst, Rees and Orme, 1807), 169–71.
────── 'ART XIX Ideas Mirrour Amours in quatorzains' *Censura Literaria* 5 (London: Longman, Hurst, Rees and Orme, 1807), 289–90.
────── 'ART XVIII The Booke of Honor and Armes', *Censura Literaria* 5 (London: Longman, Hurst, Rees and Orme, 1807), 287–89.
────── 'An Inscription upon a Chimney-piece, Recently Discovered in the Governor's House in the Tower of London' *Archaeologia* 23 (1831), 405–10.
────── 'Lives of Modern Poets No VI William Mason, A. M.', *Censura Literaria*, 5 (London: Longman, Hurst, Rees and Orme, 1807), 299–308.
────── *The Offertory the Best Way of Contributing Money for Christian Purposes* (Oxford: London: Parker, 1862).
────── 'On the Ecclesiastical Architecture of England in Past and Present Times: Read at the Annual Meeting of the Worcester Eng Diocesan Architectural Society, Sept 25th, 1854', *Associated Architectural Societies Reports and Papers* 3 (1855), 120–45.
────── *On the Reverence due to Holy Places* (London: John Murray, 1846).
────── *Remarks on English Churches & on the Expediency of Rendering Sepulchral Memorials Subservient to Pious & Christian Uses* (Oxford: Rivington, 1842).
────── *Remarks on the Sepulchral Memorials of Past and Present Times, with some suggestions for improving the condition of our churches* (Oxford: Rivington, 1840).
────── *A Sketch of the Life and Character of George Hibbert, Esq., F. R. S., S. A. and L. S.* (London: Parker, 1837).
────── 'Some Remarks on the Early Use of Carriages in England, and on the Mdes of Travelling Adopted by our Ancestors', *Archaeologia: or Miscellaneous Tracts Relating to Antiquity Published by the Society of Antiquaries of London* 20 (London: Nicols, 1824), 443–76.
────── 'Spence's Polymetis: Indexes', *Notes and Queries* 7 (June 11 1859), 469.
Scott, Walter, *The Antiquary*, ed. by David Hewitt, Edinburgh Edition of the Waverley Novels (Edinburgh: Edinburgh University Press, 1995).

—— *The Letters of Sir Walter Scott*, ed. by H. J. C. Grierson (London: Constable, 1936).
—— *Marmion; A Tale of Flodden Field, The Lady of the Lake, Rokeby*, 3 vols (Edinburgh: James Ballantyne, 1808–1913), I *Marmion, A Tale of Flodden Field* (1813).
—— *Waverley* (1829) rep. and ed. by Susan Kubica Howard (Peterbrough, ON: Broadview Press, 2010).
—— *Waverley Novels*, 12 vols (Edinburgh: Robert Cadell, 1823–44).
Scott, Sir Walter, and others, *Tales of Wonder* (London: Bulmer, 1801).
Taylor, George Watson, *The Cross-Bath Guide; being the correspondence of a respectable family upon the subject of a late unexpected dispensation of honours Collected by Sir Joseph Cheakill* (London: Underwood, 1815).
—— *England Preserved* (London: Longman, 1795).
—— *Pieces of Poetry: With Two Dramas* (Chiswick: Whittingham, 1830).
—— *The Profligate* (London: Bulmer and Nicol, 1820).
Utterson, E. V. *Letters of a Literary Antiquary*, ed. by A. T. Utterson (Oxford: no pub., 1938).
Wilbraham, Roger, *An Attempt at a Glossary of Some Words Used in Cheshire* (London: Bulmer and Nicol, 1820).
Wrangham, Francis, *The Advantages of Diffused Knowledge, a Sermon* (London: Mawman; Cambridge: Deighton, 1803).
—— *Earnest Contention for the True Faith, a Sermon* (London: Mawman, Cambridge: Deighton, 1809).
—— *The Holy Land, a Poem* (Cambridge: Burges, 1800).
—— *Humble Contributions to a British Plutarch* (London: Baldwin, 1816).
—— *The Pleiad; or Evidences of Christianity* (Volume 26 of *Constable's Miscellany*) (Edinburgh: Constable; London: Hurst and Chance, 1828).
—— *Poems* (London: Mawman, 1795).
—— *The Raising of Jaïrus' Daughter* (London: Mawman, 1804).
——, *The Restoration of the Jews* (Cambridge: Archdeacon and Burges, 1795).
—— *Scraps* (London: Baldwin, 1816).
—— *A Sermon on the Translation of the Scriptures into the Oriental Languages* (Cambridge: Cambridge University Press, 1807).
—— *Sertum Cantabrigiense; or the Cambridge Garland* (Malton: Smithson, 1824).
—— *The Suffering of the Primitive Martyrs: A Prize Poem* (Cambridge: Smith, 1812).
—— *Thirteen Practical Sermons: To Which Are Annexed 'Rome is Fallen!' and St Peter* (London: Mawman, 1800).
—— *The Virtuous Woman: A Tribute to the Memory of the Right Hon. Lady Anne Hudson, of Bessingby* (Bridlington: Galtrey, 1818).
—— *The Works of The Rev. Thomas Zouch* (York: Rivington, 1820).

Roxburghe Club Editions and Texts Edited by Club Members

Ames, J., *Typographical Antiquities: or the History of Printing in England, Scotland and Ireland* (1749), ed. and expanded by T. F. Dibdin, 4 vols (London: Bulmer, 1810–19).
Anon., *The Ancient English Romance of Havelok the Dane*, ed. by Frederick Madden (London: Nicol, 1828).
Anon., *Chester Mysteries De Deluvio Noe De Occisione Innocentium*, ed. by J. H. Markland (London: Bensley, 1818).

Anon., *Two Interludes: Jack Jugler and Thersytes,* ed. by Joseph Haslewood (Ickham: Lee Priory Press, 1820).

Baldwin, William, George Ferrers and others, *Mirror for Magistrates: in five parts,* ed. by Joseph Haslewood (London: Lackington and Allen, 1815).

Berners, Juliana, *Book of St. Albans* (1486), ed. by Joseph Haslewood (London: Harding and Wright, 1810).

Bodenham, John, *England's Helicon,* ed. by Joseph Haslewood and Sir Egerton Brydges (London: Triphook, 1812).

Brathwaite, Richard, *Barnabae Itinerarium,* ed. Joseph Haslewood, 2 vols (London: J. Harding, 1818).

Cavendish, Margaret, *Poems of Margaret, Duchess of Newcastle* (Ickham: Lee Priory Press, 1813).

Dodd, James William, *Ballads of Archery, Sonnets &c* (London: Evans, 1818).

Isted, George, Sir Herbert Croft, *The Literary Fly* (London: Etherington, 1779).

Leslie, Charles, ed. by Francis Wrangham, *Leslie's Short and Easy Method with the Deists,* ed. by Francis Wrangham (New Haven, CT: Sidney's Press, 1807).

Papworth, J. B., F. Wrangham and W. Combe, *Poetical Sketches of Scarborough* (London: Ackerman, 1813).

Pasquil, 'Palinodia', *A Roxburghe Garland* (London: Bensley, 1817).

Rowlands, Samuel, The *Knave of Clubbs,* ed. by E. V. Utterson (London: Beldornie Press, 1841).

——— *The Knave of Harts Haile Fellow, Well Met,* ed. by E. V. Utterson (London: Beldornie Press, 1840).

——— *The Letting of Humours Blood in the Head Vaine,* ed. by Walter Scott (Edinburgh: Laing and Blackwood, 1814).

——— *Looke to It: for, Ile stabbe ye,* ed. by E. V. Utterson (London: Beldornie Press, 1841).

——— *The Melancholie Knight,* ed. by E. V. Utterson (London: Beldornie Press, 1841).

——— *More Knaves Yet? The Knaves of Spades and Diamonds,* ed. by E. V. Utterson (London: Beldornie Press, 1841).

——— *The Night-Raven,* ed. by E. V. Utterson (London: Beldornie Press, 1841).

Shakespeare, William, *Plays and Poems,* ed. by E. Malone and J. Boswell, 21 vols (London: Rivington, 1821).

The Solempnities and Triumphes doon and made at the Spousells and Marriage of the King's Daughter the Ladye Marye to the Prynce of Castile, Archduke of Austrige, ed. by John Dent (London: Roxburghe Club: 1818).

Works About the Oxburghe Club

Barker, Nicolas, *The Publications of the Roxburghe Club, 1814–1962: An Essay by Nicolas Barker, with a Bibliographical Table* (Cambridge: Printed for presentation to members of the Roxburghe Club, 1964).

——— *The Roxburghe Club: A Bicentenary History* (London: The Roxburghe Club, 2012).

Bigham, Clive, *The Roxburghe Club: Its History and its Members, 1812–1927* (Oxford: Oxford University Press, 1928).

Hitchman, Francis, 'Mr Dibdin and the Roxburghe Club', *Eighteenth Century Studies: Essays* (London: Low, Marston, Searle and Rivington, 1881), 272–302.

Maidment, James, *Roxburghe Revels and Other Relative Papers* (Edinburgh: Private circulation, 1837).

Roxburghe Club, *List of Members 1812–1991, List of Books 1814–1990* (Leeds: Roxburghe Club, Smith Settle, 1991).
'The Roxburghe Revels', *Athenaeum* (4 January 1834), 1–6.
'The Roxburghe Revels', *Athenaeum* (11 January 1834), 28–30.
'The Roxburghe Revels', *Athenaeum* (25 January 1834), 60–64.

Letters

A. C., *Gentleman's Magazine* (October 1813), 338–39.
Evans, E., 'To the Editor of the Monthly Magazine', *Monthly Magazine, or British Register* (September 1816), 115–18.
J. K., *Gentleman's Magazine* (December 1813), 544.
J. M., *Gentleman's Magazine* (September 1813), 211–12.
John Bull, Letter printed in *Morning Herald* (25 September 1818), cutting contained in The Roxburghe Revels MS (Roxburghe Club Archives).
'Mr Evans on the Pretensions of the Bibliomaniacs', *Monthly Magazine* 42 (1816), 115–18.
Staunch Bibliomaniac, A, *Gentleman's Magazine* (October 1813), 339.
Templarius, *Gentleman's Magazine* (July 1813), 3–4.

Printing, Printers, Book Collectors and Libraries

Beloe, William, *Anecdotes of Literature and Scarce Books* (London: Rivington, 1807).
'The Book-Hunter's Club', *Blackwood's Edinburgh Magazine* 90 (October 1861), 440–62.
Burton, John Hill, *The Book-Hunter* (Edinburgh: Blackwood, 1862).
——— *The Book-Hunter etc*, ed. by Richard Grant White (New York: Sheldon, 1863).
Carew, W., *Book Collector* (London: Grant, 1904).
Clarke, William, *Repertorium Bibliographicum; or, Some Account of the Most Celebrated British Libraries* (London: Clarke, 1819).
De Ricci, Seymour, *English Collectors of Books 1530–1930* (Bloomington: Indiana University Press, 1960).
Edwards, Edward, *Libraries and Founders of Libraries* (London: Trübner, 1864)
——— *Memories of Libraries* (London: Trübner, 1859).
Fitzgerald, Percy Hetherington, *The Book Fancier* (London: Low, Marston, Searle and Rivington, 1887).
Fletcher, William Younger, *English Book Collectors* (London: Kegan Paul, Trench, Trübner, 1902).
Hazlitt, W. Carew, *Book Collector* (London: Grant, 1904).
Johnson, J., *Typographia: or the Printer's Instructor*, 3 vols (London: Longman, 1824).
Lang, David, *Adversaria: Notices Illustrative of Some of the Earlier Works Printed for the Bannatyne Club* (Edinburgh: Bannatyne, 1867).
Lerer, Seth, 'Caxton in the Nineteenth Century', in *Caxton's Trace*, ed. by William Kuskin (Notre Dame, IN: University of Notre Dame, 2006), pp. 325–70.
Martin, John, *A Bibliographical Catalogue of Books Privately Printed* (London: J & A Arch, 1834).
'Of Libraries, Both Public and Private, Foreign and Domestic', *The European Magazine, and London Review* 69 (1816), 203.
Ransom, Will, *Private Presses and Their Books* (New York: Bowker, 1929).
Roberts, William, *The Book-Hunter in London* (Chicago: McClurg, 1895).

Timmins, Samuel, *Lord Spencer's Library: A Sketch of a Visit to Althorp, Northamptonshire* (Northampton: Taylor, 1870).

Antiquarian Culture and the Bibliomania

Beresford, James, *Bibliosophia* (London: Miller, 1810).
'The Bibliomania', *Satirist or Monthly Meteor* 11 (August 1812).
Braswell-Means, Laurel, 'The Influence of Romantic Antiquarianism upon Medieval English Studies', *University of Ottawa Quarterly* 52 (1982), 273–85.
Ferriar, John, *The Bibliomania, an Epistle to Richard Heber, Esq.* (London: Cadell and Davies, 1809).
Jensen, Kristian, *Revolution and the Antiquarian Book* (Cambridge: Cambridge University Press, 2011).
Lynch, Deirdre, '"Wedded to Books": Bibliomania and the Romantic Essayists', *Praxis*, Romantic Circles, University of Maryland, www.rc.umd.edu/praxis/libraries/lynch/lynch.html.
McKitterick, David, *Old Books, New Technologies* (Cambridge: Cambridge University Press, 2013).
Manning, Susan, 'Antiquarianism, Balladry and the Rehabilitation of Romance', in *The Cambridge History of English Romantic Literature*, ed. by James Chandler (Cambridge: Cambridge University Press, 2009), 45–70.
Murray, Padmini Ray, 'The Diversity of Print: Antiquarianism', in *The Edinburgh History of the Book in Scotland*, ed. by Bill Bell (Edinburgh: Edinburgh University Press, 2007).
'Sale of the Library of Joseph Haslewood, Esq. F. S. A.', *Gentleman's Magazine* 1 (London: 1834), 286–88.
Vincent, Leon H., *The Bibliotaph and Other People* (Boston and New York: Houghton, Mifflin, 1899).
Woolf, D. R., 'The Dawn of the Artifact: The Antiquarian Impulse in England, 1500–1730', *Medievalism in England*, ed. by Leslie J. Workman and Kathleen Verduin, Studies in Medievalism (Cambridge: Boydell and Brewer, 1996), pp. 5–44.

Nineteenth-Century History and Biography

Beeson, Trevor, *The Canons: Cathedral Close Encounters* (London: Clowes, 2006).
Campbell, Thomas, 'The Philosophy of Clubs', *New Monthly Magazine* 22 (January 1828), 261–73.
Chambers, Robert, *A Biographical Dictionary of Eminent Scotsmen* (Glasgow: Blackie, 1835).
Christie, Ian R., *British 'Non-Elite' MPS, 1715–1820* (Oxford: Oxford University Press, 1995).
Cole, G. D. H., *The Life of William Cobbett* (Abingdon: Routledge, 1924).
Coleridge, Arthur Duke, *Eton in the Forties by an Old Colleger* (London: Bentley, 1896).
Conser Jr, Walter H., *Church and Confession* (Macon, GA: Mercer University Press, 1984).
Hunt, Leigh, *The Autobiography of Leigh Hunt* (London: Smith and Elder, 1870).
Jones, W. Powell, 'Three Unpublished Letters of Scott to Dibdin', *Huntington Library Quarterly* 4 (July 1940), 477–84.
Kippis, Andrew, and William Godwin, *The New Annual Register or General Repository of History, Politics and Literature for the Year 1800* (London: Robinson, 1801).
Lockhart, John Gibson, 'Autobiography of Sir Egerton Brydges', *Quarterly Review* 51 (June 1834), 342–65.

McWilliam, Rohan, *Popular Politics in Nineteenth-Century England* (London: Routledge, 1998).
Melville, Lewis [Pseud.], *Some Eccentrics and a Woman* (London: Secker, 1911).
Mitchell, Austin, *The Whigs in Opposition* (Oxford: Clarendon Press, 1967).
Monkland, G., *Monkland's Literature and Literati of Bath: An Essay, read at the Literary Club, November 13, 1852* (Bath: Peach, London: Parker, 1854).
Moore, Thomas, *Memoirs, Journal and Correspondence of Thomas Moore*, ed. by John Russell (London: Longman, Brown, Green, and Longmans, 1853).
Rees, Dr Thomas, and John Britton, *Reminiscences of Literary London, from 1779 to 1853* (London: Suckling and Galloway, 1896 rep. New York and London: Garland Publishing, 1974).
Rudwick, M. J. S., 'The Foundation of the Geological Society of London: Its Scheme for Co-operative Research and its Struggle for Independence', *British Journal for the History of Science* 1 (1963), 325–55.
Sadleir, Michael, 'Archdeacon Francis Wrangham; A Supplement', *Library* 19 (1939), 422–61.
―――― 'Archdeacon Francis Wrangham (1769–1842) and His Books', *Library* 17 (September 1936), 129–30.
Smith, Michael S., 'Parliamentary Reform and the Electorate', in *A Companion to Nineteenth-Century Britain*, ed. by Chris Williams (Oxford: Blackwell Publishing, 2004).
Smith, Robert A., *Late Georgian and Regency England 1760–1837* (Cambridge: Cambridge University Press, 1984).
Southey, Robert, 'To Ignorance', *The Collected Letters of Robert Southey Part 1 1791–1797*, Romantic Circles, University of Maryland, http://www.rc.umd.edu/editions/southey_letters/Part_One/HTML/letterEEd.26.6.html.
Styles, John, *Memoirs of the Life of the Right Honourable George Canning* (London: Tegg, 1828).
Thackery, Francis St. John, *Memoir of Edward Craven Hawtrey* (London: George Bell & Sons, 1896).
Timbs, John, *Romance of London: Strange Stories, Scenes and Remarkable Persons of the Great Town* (London: Bentley, 1865).
Turner, Michael J., 'Political Leadership and Political Parties, 1800–46', in *A Companion to Nineteenth-Century Britain*, ed. by Chris Williams (Oxford: Blackwell Publishing, 2004).
Watkins, John, Frederick Shoberl and William Upcott, *A Biographical Dictionary of the Living Authors of Great Britain and Ireland* (London: Colburn, 1816).
Williams, Harold, *Book Clubs and Printing Societies of Great Britain and Ireland* (London: Curwen Press, 1929).

Literary Criticism and Other Commentaries

Anon., 'The Venerable Francis Wrangham', *Imperial Magazine* 1 (London: Fisher and Jackson, 1831), 203.
Anon., *The Venerable Francis Wrangham*, reprinted and extended edition of the article of the same name, first published in *Imperial Magazine*, 1831 – no publishing information is included in the volume owned by the Bodleian Library, Oxford.
Arnold, Matthew, *On Translating Homer: Three Lectures Given at Oxford* (London: Longman, Green, Longman and Roberts, 1861).
'Art 17', *British Critic and Quarterly Theological Review* 19 (London: Rivington, 1802), 83–84.
'Arundines Cami', *Quarterly Review* 69 (March 1842), 248.

Austern, Linda Phyllis, 'Thomas Ravenscroft: Musical Chronicler of an Elizabethan Theater Company', *Journal of the American Musicological Society* 38 (1985), 238–63.
Axon, William E. A., 'Dr. Hawtrey's 'Nugae', *Notes and Queries* (4 October 1902), 261–63.
Bate, Dudley, H., *Henry and Emma, a New Poetical Interlude: Altered from Prior's Nut Brown Maid, with additions and a new air and chorus*, http://quod.lib.umich.edu/e/ecco/004846791 0001 000?view=toc, [accessed 17 January 2015].
Bullough, Geoffrey, *Narrative and Dramatic Sources of Shakespeare*, 8 vols (London: Routledge and Kegan Paul, 1957–1976), iv (1962), *Later English History Plays King John, Henry IV, Henry V, Henry VIII*.
Coldiron, A. E. B., *Canon, Period, and the Poetry of Charles of Orleans* (Ann Arbor: University of Michigan Press, 2000).
Collier, John Payne, *The Poetical Decameron* (Edinburgh: Constable, 1820).
—— 'Reprints of Early English Poetry', *Notes and Queries* (1856), 6–7.
—— 'Review of Typographical Antiquities of Great Britain', *The Critical Review: or Annals of Literature* 4 (London: Simpkin and Marshall, 1816), 245–54.
—— *The Works of William Shakespeare* (London: Whittaker, 1844).
Croft, Sir Thomas, 'Early English Poetry', *Retrospective Review* 2 (1827), 147–56.
Dilke, Charles Wentworth, *Old English Plays: Being a Selection from the Early Dramatic Writers* (London: Whittingham and Rowland, 1814).
Disraeli, Isaac, *Curiosities of Literature* (London: Routledge, Warnes and Routledge, 1859).
Forshaw, Cliff, ' "Cease Cease to bawle, thou wasp-stung Satyrist:" Writers, Printers and the Bishops' Ban of 1599', *Entertext* 3, no. 1, pp. 101–31, http://www.brunel.ac uk/__data/assets/pdf_file/0005/111020/Cliff-Forshaw,-Cease-Cease-to-bawle,-thou-wasp-stung-Satyrist-Writers,-Printers-and-the-Bishops-Ban-of-1599.pdf, [accessed 13 February 2015].
Frost, Judith, 'Review of Butler, Lawrence, *The Yorkshire Church Notes of Sir Stephen Glynne (1825–1874)*', *Medieval Review* (November 2008), 24.
Golding, Brian, 'The Hermit and the Hunter', in *The Cloister and the World: Essays in Honour of Barbara Harvey*, ed. by John Blair and Brian Golding (Oxford: Clarendon Press, 1996), 95–117.
Goodrich, Norma Lorre, *Charles of Orleans: A Study of Themes in His French and in His English Poetry* (Geneva: Library Droz, 1967).
Habermas, Jürgen, *The Structural Transformation of the Public Sphere: An Inquiry into a Category of Bourgeois Society* (Cambridge, MA: MIT Press, 1991).
Happé, Peter, and Wim N. M. Hüsken, 'Skelton's Magnyfycence', *Interludes and Early Modern Society: Studies in Gender, Power and Theatricality* (Amsterdam: Rodopi, 2007).
Jesse, Edward, 'Dame Juliana Berners and her "Boke of Venerie" ', *Once a Week: An Illustrated Miscellany* (London: Bradbury Evans, 1867), 388–89.
Johns, Adrian, 'Changes in the World of Publishing', in *The Cambridge History of English Romantic Literature*, ed. by James Chandler (Cambridge: Cambridge University Press, 2009), 377–402.
Matthews, David, *The Making of Middle English* (Minneapolis: University of Minnesota Press, 1999).
Moore, Jane, and John Strachan, *Key Concepts in Romantic Literature* (London: Palgrave Macmillan, 2010).
Norton, Rictor, 'Lovely Lad and Shame-Faced Catamite', *The Homosexual Pastoral Tradition*, http://rictornorton.co.uk/pastor05.htm, [accessed 20 June 2008]

Otners, Harold M., *The Shakespeare Folio Handbook and Census* (Westport, CT: Greenwood Press, 1990).
Palmer, D. J., *The Rise of English Studies* (London: Oxford University Press, 1965).
Paterson, James, *The Contemporaries of Burns: and the More Recent Poets of Ayrshire* (Edinburgh: Paton, 1840).
Pearsall, Derek, 'Frederick James Furnivall', in *Medieval Scholarship: Biographical Studies on the Formation of a Discipline*, ed. by Helen Damico and Joseph B. Zavadil (London: Routledge, 1998), 125–38.
Phillips, Helen, 'Aesthetic and Commercial Aspects of Framing Devices Fifteenth and Sixteenth Century Printers' Frames; Bradshaw, Roos and Copland', *Poetica* 43 (1995), 37–65.
Prescott, Sarah, ' "What Foes More Dangerous Than Too Strong Allies?": Anglo-Welsh Relations in Eighteenth-Century London', *Huntington Library Quarterly* 69 (December 2006), 535–54.
'Richard Brathwaite', *Saturday Review of Politics, Literature, Science and Art* 47 (25 January 1879), 122.
Russell, Gillian, and Clara Tuite, *Romantic Sociability: Social Networks and Literary Culture in Britain* (Cambridge: Cambridge University Press, 2002)
Sessions, W. A., *Henry Howard the Poet, Earl of Surrey* (Oxford: Oxford University Press, 1999).
Sherbo, Arthur, *Shakespeare's Midwives: Some Neglected Shakespeareans* (Newark; London; Cranbury: University of Delaware Press, 1992).
Simmel, Georg, and Everett C. Hughes, *American Journal of Sociology* 55, no. 3 (November 1949), pp. 254–61.
Smith, Robert Howie, *The Poetical Works of Sir Alexander Boswell* (Glasgow: Ogle, 1871).
Sonntag, Manuela, *William Shakespeare: Subject of the Crown?* (Morrisville: Lulu Enterprises, 2010).
Utz, Richard, *Chaucer and the Discourse of German Philology* (Sydney: University of Sydney Press, 2002).
Warton, Thomas, *History of English Poetry* (London: Ward, Lock and Tyler, 1781).
Williams, Glanmor, 'Language, Literacy and Nationality in Wales', in *Religion, Language and Nationality in Wales: Historical Essays*, ed. by Glanmor Williams (Cardiff: University of Wales Press, 1979), pp. 127–47.

Modern Editions

Anon., *The Dialogues of Creatures Moralysed: A Critical Edition*. ed. by Gregory C. Kratzmann and Elizabeth Gee (Leiden: Brill, 1988).
Anon., *The Metrical Life of St. Robert of Knaresborough*, ed. by Joyce Bazire (London: Early English Text Society, OS 228, 1953).
Anon., *The New Notborune Mayd Vpon the Passion of Cryste: The Nutbrown Maid Converted [with text]*, ed. by Emily A. Ransom (Oxford: John Wiley, 2015).
Anon., *The Vision and Creed of Piers Ploughman*, ed. by Thomas Wright (London: Reeves and Turner, 1887).
Four Romances of England: King Horn, Havelok the Dane, Bevis of Hampton, Athelston, ed. by Graham Drake, Eve Salisbury and Ronald B. Herzman, TEAMS (Kalamazoo, MI: Medieval Institute Publications, 1997).
Howard, Henry, Earl of Surrey, Poems, ed. by Emrys Jones (Oxford, Clarendon Press, 1964).

Surrey, Henry Earle of, *Certaine Bokes of Virgiles Aenaeis, turned into English Meter* London: Tottel, 1557).
Virgilius Maro, Publius, *Certaine Bokes of Virgiles Aenaeis, turned into English Meter*, trans. by Henry Howard, Earl of Surrey (London: Tottel, 1557).
Wey, William, *The Itineraries of William Wey*, ed. by Francis Davey (London: Oxford University Press, 2010).

Miscellaneous Texts

Harman, Thomas, *A Caveat or Warning for Common Cursetors Vulgarly Called Vagabonds* (London: 1814).
Lewis, M. G., 'The Grim White Woman', *Tales of Wonder* (London: Bulmer, 1801), 101–12.
Ritson, Joseph, *Gammer Gurton's Garland* (London, Triphook, 1810).

INDEX

Abbotsford Club 152
Ackermann, Rudolph 90
Aeneid 138
Althorp, Viscount 9
  political career 49–50
Ancient English Romance of Havelok the Dane, The. See *Havelok the Dane*
Ancient English Romance of William and the Werwolf 137
Antiquarian Society
  as depicted by Cruikshank 102
Athenaeum Magazine 21, 22, 30
Atticus. *See* Heber, Richard
Auchinleck Press 95–6

Balades and other Poems 141
Bannatyne Club 16, 151
Barnfield, Richard 96, 141
Beldornie Press 20, 79, 91, 96–9, 141
Bensley, Thomas 92
Bentham, William 7, 146
Beresford, James
  Bibliosophia 125
Berners, Dame Juliana 106
bibliomania 75, 77, 78, 83, 121, 154, 157
  satire 15
  social and media attitudes towards 11, 15, 16, 17, 18–19
Bishop's Ban 139
Blandford, Marquess of 7, 9, 13
Bolland, William 6, 7, 9, 16, 138
  as an author 111–12
  collection 75, 78
  Miracles 111
  portrait 11
  St. Paul at Athens 111

The Campaign, to his Royal Highness the Duke of York 112
The Epiphany 111
book clubs
  prototype 150
books
  antiquarian, attitudes towards 17–18, 19
  as artifacts 130
  black-letter, antipathy towards 125
  Elizabethan 28
  unique or rare copies 131
booksellers
  advertising 42
Boswell, James 9, 13, 96
  as an editor and author 116–17
  collection 67
  Malone-Boswell *Shakespeare* 116
Boswell, Sir Alexander 11, 13
  as an author 117–19
  Auchinleck Press 91
  Clan-Alpin's Vow 117
  collection 67
  death following a duel 53
  Jennie's Bawbee, The Old Chieftain to his Sons 118
  Jenny Dang the Weaver 118
  Skeldon Haughs 96, 117
  political career 53
  Spirit of Tintoc 117
  The Tyrant's Fall 96
  The Woo' Creel or the Bill O'Bashan 117
  tribute to James Boswell 118
Brathwaite, Richard 107
Breton, Nicholas 94
British Bibliographer 106, 109
Browne, William 94

Brydges, Sir Samuel Egerton 7, 83
  as an author and editor 109–10
  collection 76–7
  Lee Priory Press. *See* Lee Priory Press
  political career 51
Buckingham, James Silk 23, 26
Butler, George 97
Butler, Venerable Archdeacon Samuel 62
  book collection 84
  career at the Royal Free Grammar
    School at Shrewsbury 62
  collector of forgeries 84

Caltha Poetarum or, The Bumble Bee 92, 139
Campbell, John Frederick, Earl of
    Cawdor 137
Carr, Rev. William Holwell 9, 60, 133
catholic emancipation 48, 51, 52, 56,
    58, 125
Cavendish, William George Spencer,
    6th Duke of Devonshire. *See*
    Devonshire, Duke of
Caxton, William 73, 80, 92
  memorial to 11–12
Censura Literaria 114
*Ceremonial at the Marriage of Mary Queen of
    Scotts with the Dauphin of France* 146
*Certaine Bokes of Virgiles Aenaeis, turned into
    English Meter* 132
Chaucer 165
Chester Mysteries 92, 113
Clive, Edward, Viscount 14
  political career 52
Clive, Hon. R. H. 52
Cobbett, William 47
Cock Lorell's Boat 145
collections
  British public 155, 156
Collier, John Payne 20
  criticism of Dibdin 20
  forgeries 81
culture, antiquarian
  anti-Catholic sentiment 125
Cymreigyddion 8n. 7

Daiphantus, or the Passions of Love 134
Dent, John 7, 90
  collection 69–70
  dog tax 55
  political career 54
Devonshire, 6th Duke of 9, 80, 135
  as an author 111
  collection 80–1
  Handbook of Chatsworth and Hardwick 111
  political career 50
Diana 127
Dibdin, Rev. Thomas Frognall 1, 6, 7, 22
  as an author 102–5
  attacks on his social class 43
  bibliographer 39, 158–9
  Bibliographical Decameron 96, 102
  Bibliomania 16, 102
  clerical career 60
  collection 77
  criticism of 20, 37, 41, 44
  defence of black-letter devotees 132
  financial difficulties 38, 42
  lectures at the Royal Institution 132–3
  Library Companion 41, 159
  on snobbery 39
  promotion of early British literature 132–3
  published sermons 104–5
  Reminiscences of a literary life 30
  Reminiscences of a Literary Life 102
  Thomas More's *Utopia* 102
Dilke, Charles Wentworth 22
*Disputation between John Knox and the Abbot of
    Crossraguel, The* 96
Dodd, Rev. James William 9, 62
  as an author and editor 112
  Ballads of Archery, Sonnets &c 113
  career at Westminster School 62–3
  Southey's 'To Ignorance' 62
Dolarny's Primerose 133
Drury, Rev. Henry 62, 145
  as an author 110
  career at Harrow 62
  collection 67

Early English Text Society 152–3
Egerton Brydges, Sir Samuel 18, 40n. 10
*Elegiacal Poem on the Death of Thomas Lord
    Grey, An* 129
*Encomion of Lady Pecunia, or The Praise of
    Money* 96
Evans, R.H, 5, 27, 78

Ferriar, John 15
  Bibliomania 15
First Three Books of Ovid De Tristibus 130
Freeling, George 7, 133, 146, 147
Freeling, Sir Francis 7, 33, 47, 133
  collection 79
Funeralles of King Edward the Sixt, The 129

Gaufridi Arthurii Monemuthensis Archidiaconi 144
Georgian sociability 20–1, 149, 159
Gibbon, Edward 74
Glynne, Sir Stephen Richard 162
  Notes on the Churches of Cheshire 120
  Notes on the Churches of Kent 120
  Notes on the Churches of Lancashire 120
  posthumous works 119–21
  Yorkshire Church Notes of Sir Stephen Glynne 120
Goldingham, Henry 127
Gower, John 141
Greene, Robert 94
Grenville, Hon and Rev. George Neville 59, 144
Guiscard and Sigismund 135

Hagthorpe Revived 145
Haslewood, Joseph 7, 13, 21, 90
  attacks on his social class 25–7, 32, 38, 43, 44
  as an author and editor 106–9
  collection 66–7
  journal. See *Roxburghe Revels, The*
  literary collaborations with Egerton Brydges 109
  reputation 24–5, 26–7, 28, 30, 31, 32, 33, 43, 106
Havelok the Dane 13, 136–7
Hawtrey, Rev. Edward Craven 60
  career at Eton 60–2
  collection 67–8
  Il Trifoglio, ovvero Scherzi Metrici d'un Inglese 119
  religious tolerance 60–1
  as a translator and author 119
  Two Translations from Homer 119
Heber, Rev. Thomas Cuthbert 7, 11
Heber, Richard 7, 13, 15

  collection 70–2
  political career 51
  sale of collection 3
  scandal and exile 72
Hibbert, George 81, 115
  collection 81–2
  political career 57
Ho Ro Mo Nighean Donn Bhoidhach
  Ho Ro My Nutbrown Maiden 129
Hood, Eugenius pseud. *See* Haslewood, Joseph
Hortensius. *See* Bolland, William
Howard, George, Viscount Morpeth. *See* Morpeth, Viscount
Howard, Henry, Earl of Surrey 138
  inventor of blank verse 138
Hunt, John 59
Hunt, Leigh 59, 75

Informacōn for Pylgrymes unto the Holy Londe 146
Iona Club 152
Isted, George 7
  as an author 111
Istoria Novellamente Ritrovata di due Nobili Amanti 133

Jenson, Kristian 40
Johnson, John 92, 161
  Typographia or the Printer's Instructor 92
Jolliffe, James 97
Judicium, a Pageant 126
  Towneley manuscript 126

Kelmscott Press 161
Kemble, John Philip
  English drama collection 80

La Contenance de la Table 147
La Rotta de Francciosi a Terroana novamente facta. La Rotta de Scocesi 146
Lang, Robert 7, 66
  collection 66
  political career 57
Le Morte Arthur 144
Lee Priory Press 92–5

Leveson-Gower, George Grenville 7
  political career 52
libraries
  Abbotsford 84
  Auchinleck 67
  Damper, Dr, Bishop of Ely 80
  ecclesiastical collections 74–5
  Heathcote 69
  individualism of 65
  inherited 67, 73, 76, 80
  John Rylands 73
  Lincoln cathedral 74
  linguistics 68, 69, 72
  practical value of aesthetics 65
  scholarly 67, 72
  Sledmere 76
  Spencer 73
Literature, English
  as a developing academic
    subject 169–71
  widening the canon 136
literature, national 163–5
Littledale, Edward 9
Littledale, Mr. Justice Joseph 9
  politics 57
Lloyd, John Arthur
  collection 82
Lydall, J. N. 97
Lyvys of Seyntes, The 127

Madden, Sir Frederic 13, 107,
    136, 137
*Magnyfycence
  an Interlude* 126–7
Maitland Club 152
Major, John 77
Manuscripts 69, 76, 82
Markland, James Heywood 9, 113
  as an author 113–15
  *A Few Plain Reasons for Adhering to the
    Church* 57
  political career 57
  religious activities 57
Marlborough, Duke of. *See* Blandford,
    Marquess of
Masterman Sykes, Sir Mark 7
  political career 54

*Metrical Life of Saint Robert of Knaresborough,
  The* 127, 128
Middleton, Thomas 99
Morpeth, Viscount 9
  political career 50–1
Morte Artus 144
Morte d'Arthur 144

New Notborune Mayd, The 128
*Newes from Scotland, declaring the Damnable Life
  of Doctor Fian* 133, 147

Palmer, G. E. 97
Parker Society 152
Percy Society 152
Phelps, John Delafield 7, 145
Plays
  Elizabethan 134
  Jacobean 134
  Mystery, Morality and Allegorical 113,
    126, 127
*Poems written in English, by Charles, Duke of
  Orleans* 142
*Poems, Chiefly in the Scottish
  Dialect* 164
poetry
  Elizabethan 106, 107, 129
  fifteenth-century 147
  Tudor 131
Ponton, Thomas 9
Powis, Earl of. *See*
  Clive, Edward, Viscount 14
printing
  history of 81
Printing Press
  private 87
printing techniques
  facsimiles 90
  lithographic reproduction 90
  traditional 91
Private Press Movement 161
*Proceedings in the Court Martial held upon John,
  Master of Sinclair* 146
*Proper new Interlude of the World and the
  Child, otherwise called Mundus et
  Infans, A* 126
Pynson, Richard 90

INDEX

Quillinan, Edward 94

Raleigh, Walter 94
Ramsay, George 96
Renouard, Philippe 156
romanticism 168–9
Rowlands, Samuel 97
Roxburghe
  sale 5, 75
Roxburghe Club
  aristocratic 7, 35
  black ball 9
  clerics 38, 47, 58, 82
  criticism of 19, 20–1, 28–30, 143
  demographic of 35, 40
  elitism 39
  interest in typography 88, 89–90
  issues of class 36–7, 38, 39, 41, 45
  lawyers 57
  links with the Arts and Crafts
    movement 99–100
  members of Parliament 47
  a platform for the exchange of ideas 63–4
  political affiliations 48
  schoolmasters 60
  subscription 3
  toasts 8, 37
  widening the public debate 159–60
Roxburghe Club Editions
  methods of editing 161–3
  parallels with modern digital
    facsimiles 88–9
  system of publication 11, 13, 158
  texts of pre-Reformation Catholic
    provenance 125–30
Roxburghe Garland, A 92, 147
Roxburghe Revels and Other Relative Papers 30
Roxburghe Revels, The 6, 21–2
  an act of revenge 23–4
Roxburghe, John Ker, 3rd Duke of 5

Scott, Sir Walter 13, 32, 105–6, 146
  collection 84
  on dining with the club 32–3
  political views 54
*Selections from the Works of Thomas
  Ravenscroft* 134

Sempronius. *See* Wilbraham, Roger
Shakespeare Society 152
Shakespeare, William
  first edition of Hamlet 80
  influences, context and sources 106, 126,
    132, 133–5
  Malone-Boswell *Shakespeare* 116
  Romeo and Juliet, source of 133
Six Bookes of Metamorphoseos 131
Skelton, John 126
slavery, abolition 55, 56, 70
Smeaton, Joseph & George 90
*Solempnities and Triumphes doon and made at
  the Spousells and Marriage of the King's
  Daughter* 90
Sotheby, Samuel
  Principia Typographia 74
Southey, Robert 74
Spalding Club 152
Spencer, George John, 2nd Earl 7,
    14, 40, 49
  book collection 75
  collection 73–4
  political career 49
Spencer, John Charles, Viscount Althorp.
  See Althorp, Viscount
Stanzaic Morte Arthure 144
Sutherland, James 'Jamie' 96
Sykes, Sir Mark Masterman
  collection 76

Taylor, George Watson 142
  as an author 115–16
  Croppies Lie Down 56
  Cross Bath Guide 115
  England Preserved 56
  political career 56
  The Old Hag in a Red Cloak, a Romance 115
  The Profligate 115
texts
  controversial or censored 37, 97, 99,
    139, 141
  inaccuracies 98–9
  of pre-Reformation Catholic
    provenance 138
  promotion of early English texts 165–7
  rare or unique 158

Texts, Middle English 166
The Chorle and the Birde 145
The Complaint of a Lover's Life 145
The Glutton's Feaver 145
The Hors, the Shepe, and the Ghoos 145
The Life of St Ursula 135
The Love of Wales to their Soveraigne Prince 52
The Owl and the Nightingale 162
Tory 48
   conservatism 52
Towneley, Peregrine Edward 9, 48
two interludes: Jack Jugler and Thersytes 94, 107, 127

Utterson, Edward Vernon 20, 144
   Beldornie Press. *See* Beldornie Press
   collection 80
   politics 58
Utterson, Sarah Elizabeth 96

Valdarfer, Christophorus
   Boccaccio 5, 7, 37
Valdarfer, Cristofer pseud. *See* Haslewood, Joseph

Warwick, John 92
Wey, William 146

Wheatley, Benjamin 75
Whig 48
   anti-radicalism 49, 51
   familial ties 48, 49, 50
Wilbraham, Roger 7, 134
   An Attempt at a Glossary of some Words used in Cheshire 112
   as an author 112
   collection 69
   political career 51
Wrangham, Venerable Archdeacon Francis 13, 18
   A Sermon on the Translation of the Scriptures into the Oriental Languages 121
   Advantages of Diffused Knowledge, a Sermon 121
   as an author and translator 121–2
   collection 82–3
   Earnest Contention for the True Faith 121
   Sertum Cantabrigiense 121
   Poems, The Sufferings of the Primitive Martyrs 121
   radical politics 58–9, 122
   Reform: A Farce modernised from Aristophanes 122
   Sonnets from Petrarch 121

www.ingramcontent.com/pod-product-compliance
Lightning Source LLC
Chambersburg PA
CBHW021826300426
44114CB00009BA/341